CURRENT ISSUES IN INTERNATIONAL TRADE

Current Issues in International Trade

Second Edition

Edited by

David Greenaway
Professor of Economics
University of Nottingham

Published by
MACMILLAN PRESS LTD
Houndmills, Basingstoke, Hampshire RG21 6XS
and London
Companies and representatives
throughout the world

A catalogue record for this book is available
from the British Library.

ISBN 0–333–57748–5 hardcover
ISBN 0–333–57749–3 paperback

First published in the United States of America 1996 by
ST. MARTIN'S PRESS, INC.,
Scholarly and Reference Division,
175 Fifth Avenue,
New York, N.Y. 10010

ISBN 0–312–12594–1

Library of Congress Cataloging-in-Publication Data
Current issues in international trade / edited by David Greenaway. —
2nd ed.
p.   cm.
Includes bibliographical references and indexes.
ISBN 0–312–12594–1
1. Commercial policy.   2. International economic relations.
I. Greenaway, David.
HF1411.C83   1996
382'.3—dc20   95–5638
                                                      CIP

Selection and editorial matter © David Greenaway 1985, 1996
Individual chapters © Ali M. El-Agraa, Bruno S. Frey and Hannelore Weck-Hannemann,
Carl Hamilton and G. V. Reed, Henryk Kierzkowski, Chris Milner, J. Peter Neary, Ian
Steedman and J. S. Metcalfe, Klaus Stegemann, P. K. M. Tharakan and G. Calfat 1996

First edition 1985
Second edition 1996

10   9   8   7   6   5   4   3   2   1
05   04   03   02   01   00   99   98   97   96

Printed and bound in Great Britain by
Antony Rowe Ltd, Chippenham, Wiltshire

Contents

Contents

List of Figures

List of Tables

Preface

The *Current Issues* series now extends to 11 volumes, more or less covering the entire undergraduate syllabus. The pilot for the series was *Current Issues in International Trade*, published in 1985. The success of this book as a supplement to a core text on International Trade courses encouraged Macmillan to press on to a full series and encouraged me to take on the job of editing it. The series has now come full circle and we have decided to integrate *Current Issues in International Trade* into it: hence this second edition.

This edition preserves the essential objective of the first edition, namely a set of essays which are accessible to final-year students and which provide some insight to 'current issues'. The coverage in terms of topics is much the same as the first edition. Some chapters are almost identical, since the literature has not moved on significantly. This is true, for instance, of those dealing with adjustment in the open economy and capital goods and trade. In other cases, however, substantial revision was required to take account of recent developments. This is especially true of those chapters with a significant empirical content: for example, the chapters dealing with empirical analyses of trade flows and the political economy of protection.

I hope very much that instructors and students find this a useful collection of essays. I am grateful to the contributors for their cooperation in putting the volume together and hope that they too are happy with the final product.

University of Nottingham   DAVID GREENAWAY

Notes on the Contributors

G. Calfat is Research Officer at the University of Antwerp.

Ali M. El-Agraa is Professor of Economics at Fukuoka University, Japan.

Bruno S. Frey is Professor of Economics at the University of Zurich.

David Greenaway is Professor of Economics at the University of Nottingham.

Carl Hamilton is Deputy Director at the Institute for International Economic Studies, Stockholm.

Henryk Kierzkowski is Professor of Economics at the Graduate Institute of International Studies, Geneva.

J. S. Metcalfe is Professor of Economics at the University of Manchester.

Chris Milner is Professor of International Economics at the University of Nottingham.

J. Peter Neary is Professor of Economics at University College, Dublin.

G. V. Reed is Senior Lecturer in Economics at the University of Nottingham.

Ian Steedman is Professor of Economics at Manchester Metropolitan University.

Klaus Stegemann is Professor of Economics at Queens University, Ontario.

P. K. M. Tharakan is Professor of Economics at the University of Antwerp.

Hannelore Weck-Hannemann is Research Officer at the University of Zurich.

1 Models of International Trade in Differentiated Goods

HENRYK KIERZKOWSKI

1.1 INTRODUCTION

It takes only casual observation to realise that a great deal of international trade is carried out among the industrialised countries. As reported by the World Bank in its 1994 World Development Report, 63 per cent of all exports from the developed countries in 1981 had as their destination markets of industrialised countries. A little research would further reveal that the bulk of this trade is within, rather than between, industries. The UK exports and at the same time imports cars from Germany, France, Italy, the USA and other industrial countries. This is an example of intra-industry trade. Refrigerators, television sets, radios – you name it – are also traded back and forth. While intra-industry trade is predominantly observed among high-income countries,[1] it also shows up and is perhaps of increasing importance in the trade relations of developing countries.[2]

The questions of how to measure intra-industry trade, what kind of regularities manifest themselves over time and across countries, and other empirical issues are discussed by Tharakan and Calfat in Chapter 4 of this book. The purpose of this chapter is to discuss recent models of intra-industry trade in both differentiated and identical products.

The first question that springs to mind is why does one need new trade models explaining a particular phenomenon? One would expect that international trade theory, as the oldest branch of economics, would have a model general enough and sufficiently robust to be capable of explaining the new phenomenon. Yet the spate of literature that has recently been produced on the subjects of intra-industry trade, product differentiation and monopolistic competition stands in sharp contrast to the traditional models of international trade. There had been a feeling that the Ricardian and Heckscher–Ohlin models cannot explain intra-industry trade and hence new theoretical departures had to be made. The basis of this dissatisfaction was the fact that the traditional framework needed some structural differences, be they factor endowments or technology, to generate trade; the more pronounced these differences were, the more trade would be expected to occur. Yet in reality, as has already been pointed out, intra-industry trade is intensive between countries which have few structural differences.

This new and exciting field is surveyed in the following way: in the next section one particular family of new trade models is described. The model presented there goes to an extreme: it shows that two absolutely identical countries may engage in international trade. Section 1.3 shows various models of trade in differentiated products under monopolistic competition. Without question, these models have captured the centre stage in current research and they offer a number of new insights. The penultimate section models product differentiation under perfect competition and re-examines supposed failures of traditional trade theory, while the final section briefly tries to put the new field in some perspective.

1.2   INTRA-INDUSTRY TRADE UNDER DUOPOLY

The first group of models that we are about to review links trade flows with industrial structure and shows that the latter can be an independent source of the former, regardless of factor endowments, technology and other influences which play the key role in traditional models. In the extreme case, two completely identical countries of the same size, with the same taste patterns and access to technology, may still engage in trade provided that perfect competition is absent from the markets.

To fix the main idea let us first consider an isolated economy in which the entire supply of a particular commodity is produced by a monopolist. Profit maximisation requires that marginal revenue be equated with marginal cost, $MR = MC$. Now suppose that the domestic market consists of two sub-markets, 1 and 2, and that they are really *segmented*; that is to say, were there price differentials, no commodity arbitrage would take place. In this case the first-order condition for profit maximisation is the standard condition for a price discriminating monopolist:

$$MC = P_1 (1 - 1/e_1) = P_2 (1 - 1/e_2) \qquad (1.1)$$

where e_1 and e_2 stand for the price elasticities of demand in the two sub-markets, and P_1 and P_2 are respective prices. As long as the two elasticities differ, price discrimination will take place. The monopolist will set a higher price in the market with smaller e, and charge a lower price (or 'dump' the product, to use the language of international trade theory) in the market with relatively elastic demand.

The basic model of price discrimination and market segmentation has been applied with startling results to open economies by Brander (1981), Brander and Krugman (1983), Brander and Spencer (1984), and Neven and Phlips (1984). The results are startling because they show that even in the world of a single homogeneous product, two-way trade can occur. The very same commodity may be exported by, say, England to France, while it is also imported from France by England. This extreme is possible even though transportation of the good between the two countries is costly. We now turn to a simple variant of the basic model, following closely Brander and Krugman (1983).

Instead of a closed economy with two separate markets, consider a world consisting of two countries with single markets. There is only one firm in each market. The domestic (foreign) firm may produce for the local as well as the foreign market. Denote output produced by producer i for the market j by X_{ij}. The total supply in the home market (1.1) thus equals $X_{11} + X_{21}$ and the aggregate quantity in the foreign market amounts to $X_{12} + X_{22}$. For the sake of simplicity the demand functions are assumed linear and identical in the two countries; they are represented in inverted form as follows:

$$P_1 = a - b (X_{11} + X_{21}) \qquad (1.2)$$

$$P_2 = a - b (X_{12} + X_{22}) \qquad (1.3)$$

The total cost functions are also assumed to be linear and they have a fixed cost element, F, and constant marginal cost c.

While delivery of the good to the local market requires no transportation costs, these costs have to be incurred when the producers export abroad. It turns out to be very useful indeed to specify transportation costs in terms of the iceberg model: when X_{12} quantity of the good is exported by the domestic firm, some of it melts away before arriving in the foreign market, so ultimately only $g\,X_{12}$ $(0 \leq g \leq 1)$ reaches the final destination.

Profit functions of the two firms can now be specified:

$$\pi_1 = [a - b\,(X_{11} + X_{21})\,]\,X_{11} + [a - b\,(X_{12} + X_{22})\,]$$
$$X_{12} - c\,(X_{11} + 1/g\,X_{12}) - F \tag{1.4}$$

$$\pi_2 = [a - b\,(X_{11} + X_{21})\,]\,X_{21} + [a - b\,(X_{12} + X_{22})\,]$$
$$X_{22} - c\,(X_{22} + 1/g\,X_{21}) - F \tag{1.5}$$

In establishing their optimal output the two firms are assumed to behave according to the Cournot model: each producer believes that his actions will not cause his competitor to alter production. Thus in deciding on X_{11} and X_{12}, the domestic firm treats X_{21} and X_{22} as parameters (as does the foreign firm). The first-order conditions for profit maximisation can then be stated as follows:

$$\frac{\partial \pi_1}{\partial X_{11}} = -2bX_{11} - bX_{21} + a - c = 0 \tag{1.6}$$

$$\frac{\partial \pi_2}{\partial X_{12}} = -2bX_{12} - bX_{22} + a - c/g = 0 \tag{1.7}$$

$$\frac{\partial \pi_2}{\partial X_{21}} = -2bX_{21} - bX_{11} + a - c/g = 0 \tag{1.8}$$

$$\frac{\partial \pi_2}{\partial X_{22}} = -2bX_{22} - bX_{12} + a - c = 0 \tag{1.9}$$

It can be immediately observed that equations (1.6) and (1.8) can be separated from equations (1.7) and (1.9) and independently solved for X_{11} and X_{12}. What will emerge are equilibrium quantities of the good sold by the domestic and foreign firm in the home market. Equation (1.6) constitutes the Cournot reaction for firm 1 and is represented by locus $X_1 X_1$ in Figure 1.1. The reaction function[3] of the foreign firm given by equation (1.8) is depicted by the locus $X_2 X_2$. It can be readily demonstrated that the domestic firm's reaction function must be steeper (its slope being -2.0) than the slope of the foreign firm's ($-1/2$). The point of intersection, E, depicts equilibrium in the home market.

It turns out that the domestic firm will capture a larger part of the domestic market in the presence of positive transportation costs. This can be seen by inspection of the equations (1.6) and (1.8). If it costs

Henryk Kierzkowski 5

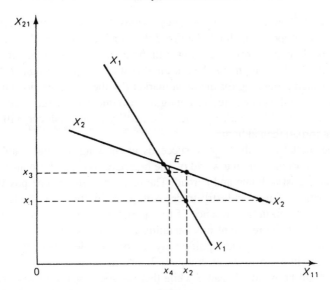

FIGURE 1.1   Cournot reaction functions

nothing to move the good across the border, i.e, $g = 1.0$, the two reaction functions would be symmetrical and hence X_{11} would have to be equal to X_{12} and the equilibrium point E would have to lie on the 45° line from the origin. Note that as transportation becomes more expensive and g tends toward zero, the X_{22} curve shifts inwards. As a result the equilibrium point moves along the X_1X_1 locus towards the X_{11} axis. The domestic firm captures an increasingly large part of the home market and in the limit no foreign good is imported. This limit is defined by the intersection of the horizontal axis and the home reaction function.

The equilibrium depicted in Figure 1.1 is stable; any departure from it will trigger off an adjustment by which the system will move back to E. Suppose that the foreign firm was producing quantity x_1 for export. The domestic firm would then elect to produce x_2 for its own market believing that its competitor would continue producing x_1. Alas, that would not happen; the response of the foreign firm to domestic production of x_2 would be x_3. With foreign production for export of x_3, the domestic firm would choose to produce x_4. The Cournot game goes on until the system settles at E.

The solution for the foreign market is symmetrical, given our assumption of identical cost functions, and therefore it need not be discussed. Relating the model to our previous discussion of the discriminating monopolist, it should be noted that for each local producer, the perceived marginal revenue is lower in the domestic than in the foreign market. On the other hand, the marginal cost of exported production is higher than producing for the local market (by the transportation cost). Each firm will equate perceived marginal revenue with marginal cost in both markets. The mark-up price charged by each producer will be lower abroad than at home.

The model described above succeeds in showing that international trade can occur even in a world of one homogeneous good produced at the same cost at home and abroad. The result constitutes one possible explanation of intra-industry trade. Note that this two-way trade can take place even in the presence of transportation costs. One is tempted to think that the resultant cross-hauling must be socially wasteful: it involves moving goods pointlessly across borders and uses up resources in the process of doing so. If one had this intuitive feeling, one would be wrong, because while there is social waste of resources stemming from transportation costs that must be incurred, there is also social gain resulting from increased competition. Duopoly introduces fewer distortions than monopoly. The final effect, therefore, cannot be clearly evaluated in welfare terms, but then welfare considerations are not the subject of this chapter.

It is always important to know how restrictive the assumptions of a particular model are. It turns out that the model under discussion is quite robust. Constant marginal costs are not crucial to the results, and neither do they have to be the same in both countries.[4] However, the results become more cumbersome with non-constant marginal costs, because all four profit-maximising conditions, equations (1.6)–(1.9), Brander (1981) and Krugman (1984) discuss extensions of the basic model in this direction, with extremely interesting implications for commercial policy. With increasing returns to scale, the marginal cost of production gets smaller as the firm produces more. Now consider that a country imposes a tariff on imports to protect the domestic market. The local firm profits from protection and captures a larger share of the home market. But in addition, by producing more for the domestic market it is able to reduce the marginal cost, and hence it becomes more competitive abroad. Protection may, then, serve as an instrument of export promotion through the realisation of economies of scale.

Do reaction functions always slope downward, as in Figure 1.1, with linear demand curves and constant marginal costs? In a more general world, one cannot be sure. The second-order conditions are spelled out by Brander and Krugman (1983): it is necessary that a firm's marginal revenue becomes smaller when the competitor increases its output.

While the Cournot model is often used in the analysis of non-competitive markets, it is not the only model explaining the behaviour of duopolists. There is no reason to think that output is the relevant decision variable; in fact it would be more realistic to assume that in non-competitive markets firms make decisions based on their expectations about prices rather than quantities. Eaton and Grossman (1983) show that using alternative assumptions with regard to the decision variable alters results and also gives different welfare conclusions.[5]

1.3 PRODUCT DIFFERENTIATION WITH IMPERFECT COMPETITION

While it is helpful, and indeed ingenious, to explain intra-industry trade in a one-good model, casual observation suggests that the empirical phenomenon to be illuminated involves more than across-the-border dumping of the same product. Intra-industry trade is trade in similar but not identical products. British cars are not the same as French or German cars. In fact, automobile producers go to a great deal of trouble, and spend a lot of money, to produce cars somewhat different from those of their competitors. So what is needed is an explanation of trade in differentiated products, which naturally involves the modelling of demand for differentiated products. Why do British consumers buy shoes produced in Italy, France and Spain in addition to shoes provided by British shoe manufacturers?[6] One possible explanation is that the consumer likes variety.

Neo-Chamberlinian monopolistic competition

Fundamental work on demand for variety was done by Dixit and Stiglitz (1977) in the context of a closed economy organised along the lines of the Chamberlinian model of imperfect competition. The Dixit–Stiglitz model was then applied to the open economy by Krugman in a series of articles (Krugman, 1979, 1980, 1982), as well as by Dixit and Norman (1980). In following these authors, the essential elements of their approach will be brought out with the simplest possible model.

It is assumed that all consumers are alike and that their taste patterns can be represented by the following utility function:

$$U = \sum_i v(c_i) \qquad v' > 0, \, v'' < 0 \tag{1.10}$$

where c_i denotes consumption of the ith good by the representative consumer. The goods entering the above utility function are produced by one differentiated-product industry: there is no need to bring in an outside homogeneous good at this stage. The discussion refers initially to a closed economy.

Equation (1.10) has the property that the level of utility increases as the number of goods consumed by an individual goes up, *ceteris paribus*. To see this point, let us represent equation (1.10) in a more specialised form:

$$U = \sum_i c_i^\theta \qquad 0 < \theta < 1 \tag{1.10a}$$

Suppose now that initially n goods were consumed, that their prices were the same and equal to one, and that the representative consumer had a money income of I. It follows that he must have consumed the same quantity of each good, $\bar{c}$ (in fact, $\bar{c} = I/n$). Given the initial conditions, the level of utility reached by our individual was:

$$U(n) = n \, \bar{c}^\theta \tag{1.11}$$

Now let us assume that the same consumer with the same income and prices is offered nk goods to consume. Through straightforward substitution, the difference in the utility levels associated with the two bundles can be shown as

$$U(nk) - U(n) = n \, \bar{c}^\theta \, (k^{1-\theta} - 1) \tag{1.12}$$

If variety is greater in the second situation, $k > 1$ and the expression above must be positive. By consuming less of every good (I/nk instead of I/n) but *more* goods, the level of utility attained goes up even though one's income is the same and prices are unchanged. This is how variety makes you better off. It is only simple logic to conclude that every individual would wish to have an infinite number of goods available on the market and would actually consume quantities of them all, however, small (as dictated by his budget constraint). Alas this is not to happen in the Dixit–Stiglitz–Krugman model.

Turning to the supply side of the model, assume that only one factor, labour, is required, and production functions are the same for all goods.

They can be represented in terms of the number of labour units, l_i, required to produce x_i quantity of good i:

$$l_i = \alpha + \beta x_i \quad \alpha, \beta > 0 \tag{1.13}$$

Given that the coefficient α is assumed to be greater than zero, there are economies of scale in production. With increasing returns to scale (l_i/x_i goes down as x_i increases) there will only be one producer of a particular good, and there will be as many producers as the number of products supplied to the market. Every producer will try to exploit his monopoly power over a segment of the market, and that means equating marginal revenue with marginal cost. Given the utility function (2.12) and the production function (1.13), the profit-maximising condition becomes:

$$P_i (x_i) (1 - 1/e_i) = \beta w \tag{1.14}$$

where e is the elasticity of demand facing the individual firm, and w stands for the wage rate.

If new firms can be set up, no profits can be made in equilibrium even though every producer tries hard to achieve this goal, as equation (1.14) testifies. This is a property of Chamberlin's model of monopolistic competition. Total costs of production of good i have to be equal to total revenue or, to put it differently, price equals average cost.

$$P_i x_i = (\alpha + \beta x_i) w \tag{1.15}$$

If total revenue exceeded total costs, new firms would enter the industry attracted by the existence of pure profits. If the inequality sign were reversed, sales could not cover production costs and some firms would go out of business. The Chamberlinian zero profit condition can be further simplified by setting $w = 1.0$ and noting that in the closed economy $x_i = Lc_i$, where L represents the total labour force.

$$P = \frac{\alpha}{Lc} + \beta \tag{1.16}$$

The subscript i has disappeared because, as should be obvious by now, the solutions for P, x and c will take the same values for all is.

The equilibrium conditions (1.14) and (1.16) can be conveniently presented in Figure 1.2 as in Krugman (1979) The PP schedule depicts equation (1.14); it is upward-sloping because it is assumed that the elasticity of demand facing an individual producer gets smaller as his output expands.[7] The ZZ curve in Figure 1.2 shows equation (1.16).

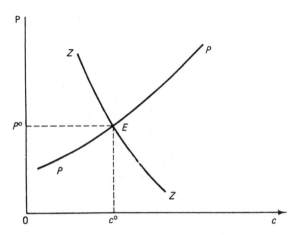

FIGURE 1.2   Equilibrium in the Krugman model

The intersection of the two schedules determines the equilibrium price (in terms of w), $P°$; and the level of per caption consumption of every good, $c°$. The level of output of every firm, $x°$, can be obtained by multiplying $c°$ by L. The number of products in the economy is still left undetermined. But this can be easily taken care of by relying on the full employment condition, stating that:

$$L = n(\alpha + \beta x°) \tag{1.17}$$

The only unknown in this equation is n, the degree of product variety.[8]

We are now in a position to show how this model can be applied to open economies and used to explain intra-industry trade. Suppose that in addition to the home country which we have been discussing, there also exists a foreign country absolutely identical in every respect. The foreign country produces the same number of products, the local prices there are the same, and foreign firms generate the same output. No country has a comparative advantage in any sub-set of goods and yet there is a basis for trade: demand for variety. If consumers get twice as many products as they used to, they surely must be better off. In the case of the specific utility function (1.10a), the gains from trade for each country are given by equation (1.12); it suffices to set $k = 2$. Of course, in the new equilibrium, products produced at home will differ from those produced abroad whatever the pre-trade selection of goods. This outcome is guaranteed by the fact that, with economies of scale, there is room for only one producer of a particular good.

The basic model could be extended in several directions: countries of different size can be handled with no problem whatever. Additional factors of production can be introduced as well. In addition to the differentiated-product industry (or industries), an industry producing a homogeneous good can be readily incorporated into the analysis, thus giving the model a more general equilibrium format. The last extension is particularly worthwhile because it allows us to analyse and compare inter- and intra-industry trade.

Models stemming from the Dixit–Stiglitz framework point out the possibility of inadequate measurement of gains from trade. In the standard framework, gains from trade result from improvements in the terms of trade and subsequent specialisation. In the Dixit–Stiglitz framework there are two separate sources of gain: the gains from specialisation which in fact have been suppressed in the Krugman model, and gains from greater variety. This is good news because some empirical studies have suggested that the first type of welfare gains may not be very sizeable. In one famous article, Harry Johnson attempted to give an estimate of British gains from joining the European Economic Community (EEC). He established that the gain to Britain would be worth just about 1 per cent of its gross national product (GNP). Perhaps the increased variety caused by international trade offers more substantial benefits, but it all depends if and how much people love variety.

Neo-Hotelling monopolistic competition

In the Dixit–Stiglitz–Krugman approach every single consumer wishes to buy all available differentiated products, and so does the society as a whole being an aggregation of individuals. And it is the *aggregate* demand for goods of varying specification that is the *raison d'être* of the differentiated product industry. But does one need a love of variety at the micro level to generate a macro demand for diversity? The answer is unambiguously no. Every individual may desire only one type of differentiated product, but provided that individuals' tastes and preferences are different, a demand for variety of products will emerge at the aggregate level.

It was up to Kelvin Lancaster (1979) to develop this basic insight into a comprehensive theory of consumer demand. Lancaster's recent work on product variety derives naturally from his previous work on the characteristics approach to consumer theory, and has its intellectual predecessor in Hotelling. The framework requires thinking of consumers as viewing goods as collections of characteristics. Thus a car represents a bundle of characteristics such as speed, comfort, colour, size, and so on. In general,

> these characteristics are objective, and the relationship between a good and the characteristics it possesses is a technical one, determined by the design of the good or by 'nature' if the good is not synthesized. Individuals are interested in goods not for their own sake but because of the characteristics they possess, so that the demand for goods is derived and indirect, and depends on preferences with respect to characteristics and on the technical properties that determine how characteristics are embodied in different goods. Differences in individual reactions to the same good are seen as expressing different preferences with respect to the collection of characteristics possessed by that good and not different perceptions as to properties of the good. (Lancaster, 1979, p. 17)

The approach rules out advertising: the consumer knows the truth and cannot be fooled, and does not need any additional information to make a rational decision.

Every individual has a preferred 'model' of the differentiated product given exogenously. Does this mean that he will not consider buying a good slightly different from his ideal product under any circumstances? It depends how one specifies the utility function for an individual consumer, but it would seem desirable to allow for at least the possibility of substitution between the ideal model and products which do not possess all characteristics of the most preferred good in the proportions desired. Suppose that you wish to buy a sweater and colour is the only characteristics that distinguishes different 'models'.[9] Now, the colour you like best is navy blue and a sweater in this colour costs £40. However, there are also light blue sweaters available at only half the price. (Alternatively, consider that you can have two less-than- perfect sweaters instead of one). Most lovers of navy-blue sweaters would at least take a moment to consider the alternative. In order to formalise this situation, Lancaster introduces the concept of a compensating function. Let us measure the characteristic (colour) by distance along the horizontal axis in Figure 1.3.[10] The spectrum of goods available is defined on an interval ranging from 0 to 1. (0 may be thought of as white and 1 as some different specification.) The steeper this curve is, the more it takes to keep the consumer indifferent as regards alternative

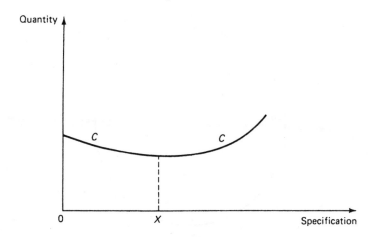

FIGURE 1.3   **A consumer's compensating function**

models. It seems reasonable to argue that the compensating function should be symmetrical, i.e., if one deviates a distance g to the left of $\tilde{X}$ the same compensation should be required as would be if one deviated the same distance g to the right of $\tilde{X}$. Of course, the larger is the distance g, the more compensation would be needed. In Figure 1.3, the curve CC cuts the vertical axis and, by the symmetric argument, it must also take on the same value for a specification corresponding to 1, if $\tilde{X}$ is halfway between 0 and 1. In general, however, CC may shoot up towards infinity for certain specifications. If you really hate white sweaters, you might not even want them if they were free.

With the basic notions of the Hotelling–Lancaster model spelled out, international trade can be brought into the picture. This task was recently accomplished by Lancaster (1980) and Helpman (1981). Their work has a much more general equilibrium character than any of the models previously discussed. In fact, they take the Heckscher–Ohlin model into the world of monopolistic competition. Thus there are two sector; one produces a homogeneous good, the other is a differentiated product industry. Both labour and capital are indispensable factors of production but, while the homogeneous good is produced under constant returns to scale, there are economies of scale to be achieved in the differentiated product industry. It is also assumed that every model of the non-homogeneous good is produced with the same increasing-returns-to-scale production function. There are no barriers to entry and hence profits must be driven to zero in equilibrium.

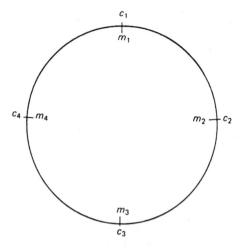

FIGURE 1.4   **Alternative specifications of a horizontally differentiated commodity**

Under increasing-returns-to-scale technology, only a limited number of differentiated products can be supplied to the market even though an infinitely large number of products is demanded. Suppose that just before trade were to take place, the situation in the home country was as depicted in Figure 1.4. Unlike in the previous figure, we now use a circle specification of the tastes for the differentiated products.[11] The consumers are uniformly distributed along the circumference of the circle, each point representing an ideal model for some individuals. What is the total number of consumers? Suppose now that four models were produced in autarchy: m_1, m_2, m_3 and m_4. (The number of models produced depends on factor endowments, technology and demand in a very complex way.) The consumers with ideal models c_1, c_2, c_3 and c_4 were very lucky indeed: they got exactly what they liked best. Others were less lucky, having to pay the same price for models that did not correspond to their preferred specifications. Where do they buy their products? It is clear that consumers located at or close to m_1 will buy this model if m_2 is available at the same price (remember the compensating function?). But as one moves away from m_1 towards m_2, there must be a point where certain consumers will prefer the latter model. Given the symmetry of costs and the distribution of consumers, the switching point will be halfway between m_1 and m_2.[12] The n consumers at the switching point will be indifferent regarding m_1 and m_2. The analysis carries over to the rest of the taste spectrum.

Suppose now that free trade can take place between the home country and an identical foreign country. There are also four foreign firms but, instead of producing models m_1, m_2, m_3 and m_4, they happen, by pure luck, to produce four models, one of which is halfway between m_1 and m_2, one between m_2 and m_3, and so on. Let us assume that the number of producers under free trade is equal to the sum of the producers under autarchy, that each will continue to generate the same output and charge the same price. It can be quickly seen that free trade would be beneficial under these circumstances for some (especially 'marginal') consumers and harmful to none.[13] Some consumers could get models much closer to their ideal specification. Trade in this situation would be entirely of the intra-industry character. And this, in a nutshell, is how the Lancaster–Helpman model works.

We have given a highly simplified presentation of the Lancaster–Helpman model. Unfortunately it is not possible to do it full justice without getting into heavy mathematics. But it is certainly worthwhile at least listing their main results as regards intra- and inter-industry trade. As our example has just shown, when two countries are like twins, trade will nevertheless take place and it will be entirely intra-industry trade. Suppose now that the factor endowments differ between countries and that the differentiated product industry is relatively capital-intensive. As Helpman and Lancaster have shown, intra- and inter-industry trade will coexist in this case. Both countries will be exporting and importing the differentiated good; however, the country with the higher overall capital: labour ratio will end up as a net exporter of the products in question, while the other country will be a net importer. It follows immediately that in order to balance trade, the relatively capital-poor country will be a net exporter of the homogeneous good. (There is no crosshauling of the standard good in this model.) As the difference in the capital: labour ratio grows more pronounced between the two countries, the share of intra-industry trade in overall trade will decline. The model thus accords well with the observed empirical regularities.

1.4 VERTICAL PRODUCT DIFFERENTIATION

The models of intra-industry trade and product differentiation presented in the preceding sections relied heavily, or even hung entirely, on the existence of imperfect competition. It would therefore not be surprising if the reader were to form the opinion that imperfect competition in one form or another is a necessary ingredient in any attempt to explain the phenomena discussed here. This view carries with it an indictment of traditional trade theory. In fact Paul Krugman has put it very forcefully:

> Most students of international trade have long had at least a sneaking suspicion that conventional models of comparative advantage do not give an adequate account of world trade. This is especially true of trade in manufactured goods. Both at the macro level of aggregate trade flows and at the micro level of market structure and technology, it is hard to reconcile what we see in manufactures trade with the assumptions of standard trade theory. In particular, much of the world's trade in manufactures is trade between industrial countries with similar relative factor endowments: furthermore, much of the trade between other countries involves two-way exchange of goods produced with similar factor proportions ... Where is the source of comparative advantage? (Krugman, 1983, p. 343).

The question to be addressed in this section is whether imperfect competition is really a necessary condition for product differentiation and intra-industry trade, or, to put it differently, can one rescue the traditional models and refute the criticism levelled against them?

Instead of horizontal product differentiation á *la* Lancaster–Helpman-cum-Hotelling, consider vertical differentiation.[14] Goods represent different qualities. Previously we thought of differentiated products as being in many respects identical: the same production technology was used to manufacture them and they cost the same amount. Of course, they also had to have some objective difference like colour, and this difference meant a lot to consumers. But different products represented different 'value' to different consumers. Some preferred yellow Vokswagens to green Volkswagens, for others it was the other way around, and yet others were indifferent regarding the two choices. It is clear that in the case of horizontal differentiation society as a whole could not, if it had to, agree on a consistent ranking of goods. Yet there are situations where everybody would agree that a particular model is superior to any other. A Rolls-Royce is generally considered the best car there is.

The immediate task is to model vertical product differentiation. Suppose there is only one product, x, and it comes in different qualities, s. The utility function of a consumer takes the following form:

$$U = u\,(x,\,s) \tag{1.18}$$

It will be assumed that *all* consumers have the same utility function. We can now look at some properties of equation (1.18). This is done in Figure 1.5. In this one-commodity world, the representative consumer spends all his income on rental accommodation, so x represents the size of a flat measured in square feet. Apartments are available in different locations and the distance along the horizontal axis measures their quality, s. Think of point A as, say, Acton, B as Hammersmith, and C as Knightsbridge. When the individual has a rather limited income he will rent a smallish flat in location A, and the initial equilibrium is represented by point V. As his income increases he will move to location B and also get a larger flat. Thus both 'goods' are normal. If he becomes rich he will move to a really large place at C.

The example used in Figure 1.5 can clearly illustrate different approaches to product differentiation. In the Dixit–Stiglitz–Krugman framework every individual would like to have flats at A, B and C (they would have to be very small indeed if one's income was very limited). In the Lancaster–Helpman approach some individuals would prefer location A, for some B would be the ideal place, and others would want to be at C. In the Falvey–Kierzkowski model all individuals would

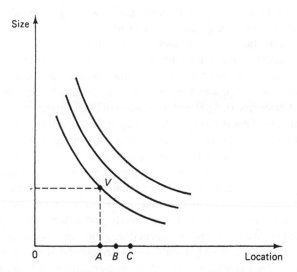

FIGURE 1.5   A model of vertical product differentiation

rather live in Knightsbridge but few could afford it. Some could not even afford to live in Hammersmith and would therefore have to settle for Acton. It should be clear that in order to generate aggregate demand for various differentiated products individuals must have different incomes.[15]

The application of the basic idea of vertical product differentiation to international trade is rather straightforward. First, generalise the utility functions to include a homogeneous product, y, as well.

$$U = u\,(x,\,s,\,y) \tag{1.19}$$

Of course, x and y must be traded goods. The next step involves specifying technology in production. The homogeneous good is produced with a Ricardian production function requiring only labour. Production of the differentiated good requires both labour and capital: It is assumed that all models of the differentiated product require inputs of one unit of labour, and varying amounts of capital. The higher the quality of the product the more capital will have to be used, in addition to the unit labour input. With *perfect competition* prices of the two goods are equal to their unit costs of production:

$$P_y = a_{LY}\,w \tag{1.20}$$

$$P(s) = w + s\,r \tag{1.21}$$

The first of the above equations is straightforward. The second says that the price of product of quality s (s can vary from, say, 1 to 100) will be the sum of the labour cost, w, and capital cost, $s\,r$.

Now suppose that there are two countries with different factor endowments. Also assume that the home country has more efficient technology in the production of y, i.e., a_{LY} is smaller at home than abroad. Under free trade P_y will be equalised between the two countries and hence the domestic wage rate will be higher than the foreign wage. Given relatively high labour costs, the home country cannot be very competitive in low quality products where the cost of production is dominated by w. However, as the quality improves it is the capital cost that begins to dominate. It stands to reason, then, that the home country will concentrate on production and export on the upper part of the quality spectrum, importing lower quality goods for consumers with low income. We have thus succeeded in generating intra- and inter-industry trade in a model containing Ricardian and Heckscher–Ohlin features without relying on monopolistic competition. Of course, one could introduce monopolistic competition but it does not seem necessary for the purpose at hand.

1.5 CONCLUDING COMMENTS

In this chapter various approaches to the explanation of trade in differentiated goods have been outlined. The models discussed are capable of explaining the two-way international exchange of vertically and horizontally differentiated goods. Furthermore, we have reviewed models that are oligopolistic in structure, as well as several that can be described as monopolistically competitive. Many of these models provide basis to trade other than initial differences in factor endowments although, as we saw in the case of vertical product differentiation, differential factor endowments may have a role to play. Despite the fact that a great many issues remain to be settled, it is undoubtedly the case that the growing literature on imperfect competition and international trade has provided us with a number of very important insights into the emergence of international trade.

2 Capital Goods and the Pure Theory of Trade

IAN STEEDMAN and J. S. METCALFE

2.1 INTRODUCTION

Although the pure theory of trade has become a large and highly specialised branch of economics, the thoughtful student will be aware that, in principle, it constitutes no more than an application of the general theory of value, distribution and resource allocation. It follows at once, of course, both that each possible approach to general economic theory has its corresponding theory of trade and that any changes or developments in general theory must have implications for the theory of international trade. The purpose of this chapter is to introduce the student to the trade theory implications of certain debates over value, distribution and capital goods which flourished in the 1960s, following the publication of Piero Sraffa's *Production of Commodities by Means of Commodities* (1960).

It need hardly be said that capital goods – that is, produced inputs, whether they be long lived or short lived – are of the very greatest importance in all modern economies. And it is no less true that international trade flows, far from consisting solely of consumption commodities, contain a large and growing volume of producer goods. Any adequate theory of trade and resource allocation must, then, be able to deal, in a clear and coherent manner, with the important role of produced inputs, and it is therefore to be expected that 'capital theory', broadly interpreted, should have significant implications for trade theory. While the reader will be assumed, throughout this chapter, to

20

have a basic knowledge of pure trade theory in both its Ricardian and Heckscher–Ohlin–Samuelson (H–O–S) forms, it would perhaps be rash to suppose an equal familiarity with capital theory. We therefore devote the next section to a brief and simplified introduction to those elements of capital theory which will be immediately relevant to our subsequent discussions of trade theory.

2.2 SOME CAPITAL THEORY

Consider a highly stylised closed economy in which there is just one constant-returns-to-scale process for making a homogeneous commodity, 'corn', by means of homogeneous labour and a 'machine'. Furthermore, assume that there exists one constant-returns-to-scale process for making the machine, again using inputs of homogeneous labour and the same kind of machine. Let α and β be the inputs of machines and of labour to make one unit of corn, while a and b are the corresponding inputs to make one machine. If a machine is completely worn out in one production period (whether it be used in making corn or in making machines), if p is the price of a machine in terms of corn, if r is the rate of interest, and if w is the real wage rate, in terms of corn, which is paid at the end of the period, then under competitive conditions,

$$p = (1+r)\, ap + bw \tag{2.1}$$

$$1 = (1 + r)\, \alpha p + \beta w \tag{2.2}$$

Equation (2.1) states that the gross revenue obtained by selling one machine, p, is just sufficient to replace the value of used-up machines, ap, and pay both the wages bill, bw, and interest on the value of the used-up machines, rap. Equation (2.2) makes the analogous statement for the corn industry. From (2.1) and (2.2),

$$p = \frac{b}{\beta + (\alpha b - a\beta)(1 + r)} \tag{2.3}$$

$$w = \frac{1 - a(1 + r)}{\beta + (\alpha b - a\beta)(1 + r)} \tag{2.4}$$

Suppose first that $\alpha b = a\beta$ or $(\alpha/\beta) = (a/b)$; the number of machines per worker is the same in both industries. Then (2.3) and (2.4) become simply

$$p = (b/\beta) \tag{2.3a}$$

$$w = \beta^{-1} [1 - a (1+ r)] \tag{2.4b}$$

When $(\alpha/\beta) = (a/b)$, the price ratio p is *independent* of r, and w is a decreasing *linear* function of r. It is equally clear from (2.3) and (2.4), however, that when $(\alpha/\beta) \neq (a/b)$ – when the machine/labour ratio differs as between the two industries – p will vary as r varies and w will be a non-linear function of r; Figure 2.1 illustrates the three possible cases.[1]

For the moment, the feature of Figure 2.1 that is to be noted is that, except in the fluke case $(\alpha/\beta) = (a/b)$, the relative commodity price, p, is *not* determined by technical conditions alone, even in the single technique economy considered so far. The value of p depends both on technical conditions (α, β, a, b) and on the values of r, w.

Suppose now that our simple economy produces a *net* output consisting solely of corn. (Machines are, of course, being produced but only in such a quantity as just to replace those used up in production.) Let y be the net corn output per worker and k be the *value*, in terms of corn, of

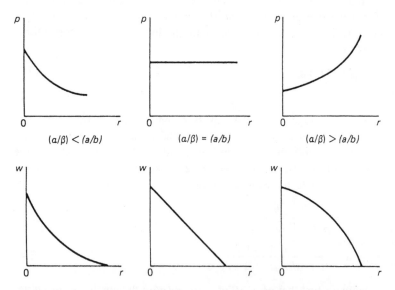

FIGURE 2.1   Relative commodity prices and the wage rental frontier

the number of machines per worker in the economy as a whole. It is then a national accounting identity that

$$y \equiv w + rk \tag{2.5}$$

(income $\equiv$ wages + interest), or provided that $r \neq 0$,

$$k \equiv \frac{y - w}{r} \tag{2.6}$$

Figure 2.2 reproduces part of Figure 2.1, for the case $(\alpha/\beta) > (a/b)$. When $r = 0$, the whole net product goes to wages and thus y is identical to the maximum possible wage rate, as shown in Figure 2.2. Suppose that $r = r^*$ and $w = w^*$, as shown. From (2.6), k is then identical to the tangent of the angle ø; the division of the net product between wages and interest, defined by (2.5), can thus be read off on the vertical axis of Figure 2.2. More important, however, is that as r^* increases (and w^* thus decreases), we see that k increases. For a given technique, the capital:labour ratio is *not* defined by technical conditions alone but varies with r, w. Why is this, when the number of machines per worker is, by assumption, unchanged? It is because k is not the *number* of machines per worker but the corn *value* of those machines and, as shown in Figure 2.1, when $(\alpha/\beta) > (a/b)$, the corn value of each machine rises as r increases (w decreases). The reader is now asked to draw the equivalent diagrams to Figure 2.2 for the cases $(\alpha/\beta) < a/b$ and $(\alpha/\beta) = (a/b)$ and to check that, in the former case, k is inversely

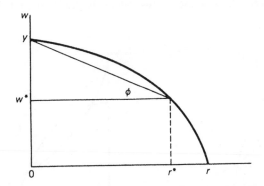

FIGURE 2.2   The division of the net product between wages and interest

related to r while, in the latter case, k is independent of r. Only in the fluke case $(\alpha/\beta) = (a/b)$ is the value of capital per worker, k, an index of technical conditions alone; in general it depends also on r, w.

Suppose now that there is a second kind of machine, which can be used, by homogeneous labour, to make either corn or machines of this second kind. Everything said above could (but need not) be repeated with respect to this second technique for the production of corn. In particular, there will again be a relation such as (2.4), relating w to r. In Figure 2.3(a), the w/r curves for two different techniques – to be called T_1 and T_2 – are superimposed. It can be shown that competitive cost-minimising pressures will force the economy always to be on the 'north-east' boundary of Figure 2.3(a), so that at 'low' values of r technique T_1 will be used but at 'high' values of r technique T_2 will be used. As r is notionally *increased* across the value at which the change of technique is made, from T_1 to T_2, the value of k *falls*, as the reader should check using the argument of Figure 2.2. We find, in other words, the conventional inverse relation between capital-intensity and the rate of interest. Now consider Figure 2.3(b), in which the w/r curves for T_1 and T_2 intersect twice. (It can be seen from equation (2.4) that two – but not more than two – intersections are possible.) Technique T_1 is used at both 'low' and 'high' values of r, with T_2 being used in between. Hence there is *not* a monotonic relationship between the interest rate and the choice of technique, contrary to what is often supposed. Moreover, the argument of Figure 2.2, when applied at the second change of technique, from T_2 to T_1, shows that here capital-intensity, k is *positively* related to the interest rate. (The reader should check this.)

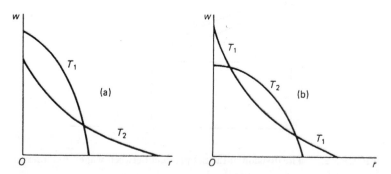

FIGURE 2.3   Choice of technique and the interest rate

It has thus been shown that, in a competitive, contant-returns-to-scale economy using produced inputs, (a) relative prices depend on the rate of interest, even for a given technique; (b) capital-intensity depends on the rate of interest, even for a given technique; (c) the choice of technique need not be monotonically related to the rate of interest; and (d) capital-intensity, in a multi-technique economy, need not be inversely related to the rate of interest. Each of these findings continues to be valid in far more general models of production than the simple corn/machine model used here for expositional purposes. (See, e.g., the *QJE* Symposium, 1966, or Pasinetti, 1977.) Rather than generalise the above arguments here, we turn briefly to two extensions which will be useful in our discussion of trade theory.

We now introduce a positive rate of steady growth, $g > 0$. For a given technique of the corn/machine kind, let c be corn output per employed worker and m be machine output per employed worker. In steady growth,

$$m = (1 + g)(am + \alpha c) \tag{2.7}$$

$$1 = bm + \beta c \tag{2.8}$$

Equation (2.7) states that the output of machines, m, is just sufficient to replace those used up in production ($am + \alpha c$) and to expand the stock at rate g; equation (2.8) ensures that m and c are indeed quantities per unit of employment. From (2.7) and (2.8),

$$c = \frac{1 - a(1 + g)}{\beta + (\alpha b - a\beta)(1 + g)} \tag{2.9}$$

Comparison of (2.9) with (2.4) shows at once that the c/g relation is identical to the w/r relation so that it has, in effect, been discussed already. Net output now contains both corn and extra machines (net investment in physical terms), so that (2.5) and (2.6) must be generalised to

$$y \equiv w + rk \equiv c + gk \tag{2.5a}$$

and

$$k \equiv \frac{c - w}{r - g} \tag{2.6a}$$

provided $r \neq g$. (The reader should quickly work out how Figure 2.2 needs to be modified when $0 < g < r$.)

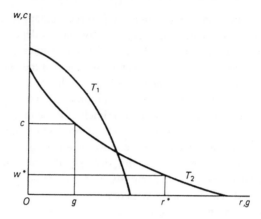

FIGURE 2.4   Choice of technique, consumption and growth

Consider now Figure 2.4, in which, at an interest rate r^*, competition will lead to the use of technique T_2. If the growth rate is g, consumption per worker will be c, which is less than is technically possible at growth rate g, since maximisation of consumption per worker at that growth rate would require the use of technique T_1. Only if $g = r$, the so-called Golden Rule case, is it ensured that the competitive choice of technique will be optimal with respect to the consumption/growth trade off.

We may now consider the final point to be made in this section. Suppose that production is carried out using inputs of homogeneous land, as well as homogeneous labour and produced inputs. It is a standard piece of economic analysis that, as land becomes more expensive relative to labour, the choice of technique will change from a more land-intensive to a less land-intensive technique. Let there be a given, positive rate of interest on the value of capital (the produced inputs). For reasons closely related to the results given above, it is no longer the case that a rising rent: wage ratio must necessarily be associated with a falling land: labour ratio; quite the opposite relationship may hold. There is not space to demonstrate this result here (see Metcalfe and Steedman, 1972, and Montet, 1979) but an important corollary must be noted: this is that, in the presence of a positive rate of interest, an *increase* in the relative price of the more land-intensive commodity may be associated with a *decrease* in the output of that commodity (and an increase in the output of the labour-intensive commodity). In other words, there may be a 'perverse' supply response.

In brief, then, capital theory discussions have alerted us (or re-alerted us, for in 1901 Wicksell (1967) was well aware of some of these complications) to the distribution-relative nature of relative commodity prices; to the fact that capital-intensity depends on distribution as well as on technical conditions; to the possibility that both capital-intensities and land:labour ratios may respond in 'unexpected' ways to changes in interest, wage and rent rates; to the fact that supply responses can differ from those traditionally supposed; and to the possibility that competitive technique choice need not be optimal with respect to the *c/g* trade-off. We can now, at last, turn to the implications of these findings for the pure theory of trade.

2.3 'TEXTBOOK' RICARDIAN THEORY

The reader will no doubt be thoroughly familiar with the textbook version of Ricardian trade theory, in which wages are the only kind of income, labour is homogeneous, and – as a result of these two assumptions – the autarchy price ratios in an economy are exactly proportional to the quantities of labour required to produce the various commodities. Yet when we turn to Ricardo's famous Chapter VII, 'On Foreign Trade' (1951, first published 1821), we see at once that Ricardo supposes there to be a *positive* rate of profit and, indeed, shows how the opening of trade can increase that rate. To this extent, then, 'textbook' Ricardian trade theory is a travesty of Ricardo's trade theory. (And any student who has not read the latter in the original is urged to do so at once.) Any attempt to excuse this vulgarisation of Ricardo would probably appeal to the fact – and it is a fact – that in his Chapter VII Ricardo, whilst acknowledging the presence of both wages and profits, took no account of the influence of distribution on autarchy-relative prices; he simply identified these latter with relative labour quantities. Yet a large part of Ricardo's Chapter I, 'On Value', is concerned precisely with the fact that, as was seen in our previous section, relative commodity prices depend in part on distribution and not on technical conditions of production alone. The apparent inconsistency is explained by Ricardo's readiness to assume that relative labour costs provide a 'good enough approximation' to relative prices, even though he fully acknowledged that prices really depend on distribution. This explanation, though, is not a justification of Ricardo's procedure in Chapter VII, for he gave quite inadequate grounds for his claim about the 'good enough approximation'. It follows that we should examine carefully what happens to Ricardo's propositions concerning foreign trade when full recognition is given to the distribution-relative nature of autarchy prices.

Consider then a two-country, two-consumption commodity model in which in each country, the autarchy price ratio of the two consumption commodities *depends on* the ruling r, w under autarchy. Such a dependence could arise from the use of (non-tradable) machine in making the consumption commodities, as in the model of the previous section; or from the fact that the consumption commodities are *also* capital goods, being used in the production of one another; or from the fact that wages are paid in advance and that the production period over which they have to be advanced differs as between the two consumption commodities. There are many different models which capture the dependence of relative prices on r, w, all of them providing examples of what Samuelson (1975) has called 'time-phased Ricardian systems'. Now if, in either economy, the autarchy rate of interest should happen to be zero, the autarchy price ratio of the two consumption commodities will indeed equal the ratio of their total (direct and indirect) labour costs. This must be true when the only form of income payment is that of wages paid to homogeneous labour. But if, as will generally be the case, the autarchy interest rate is not zero and fluke technical conditions do not obtain, that autarchy price ration will *not* equal the corresponding labour cost ratio.

Let free trade be opened between our two economies, labour and money capital being internationally immobile. Will the direction of trade be determined by a comparison of the two countries' autarchy price ratios or by a comparison of their labour cost ratios? By the former, of course; competition works via wages, interest rates and prices. Each country will export that commodity for which it has the lower relative autarchy *price*. It may or may not export that commodity for which it has the lower relative *labour* cost and certainly the pattern of trade is not determined by technical conditions alone but depends also on the autarchy (r, w) in each country, simply because autarchy-relative prices so depend. Notice the corollary that two economies with the *same* technical conditions, for producing commodities by means of homogeneous labour and produced commodities, could enter into free trade if their autarchy (r,w) would be different. It is not the case that 'Ricardian' trade models must necessarily suppose different technical conditions in each country, even if it is the case both that Ricardo did make such an assumption and that it is eminently sensible to do so.

Consider now a single, small economy of the kind considered above, which faces given terms of trade for trade in the two consumption commodities. Its pattern of trade will depend on how the given terms of trade compare with its *autarchy price ratio*. But whether its fully specialised, free trade consumption bundle lies outside its autarchy consumption possibility frontier will depend on that pattern of trade and on how the terms of trade compare with the economy's *labour cost ratio*. Since this latter ratio is not equal, in general, to the autarchy price ratio, it is *not* ensured that the with-trade bundle will lie outside the autarchy frontier. Consider Figure 2.5, in which c_1 and c_2 are quantities of the first and second consumption commodities per unit of employment. C_2C_1 is the autarchy consumption possibility frontier, whose absolute slope is of course equal to the labour cost ratio for the two consumption commodities. P_2P_1 is a line whose absolute slope is equal to the economy's autarchy price ratio, and T_2T_1 a line with slope equal to the given terms of trade. Since T_2T_1 is less steep than P_2P_1, the economy will be driven to specialise in commodity 2, but since T_2T_1 is steeper than C_2C_1, the economy's free trade consumption bundle, T, which must of course lie on T_2T_1, will be *below* the autarchy frontier C_2C_1 (unless at C_2 itself). It will be clear that this result would not obtain if T_2T_1 were either steeper than P_2P_1 (with specialisation at C_1) or less steep than C_2C_1 (with specialisation at C_2). But the fact remains that Ricardo was

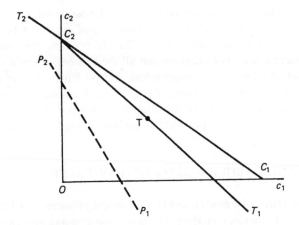

FIGURE 2.5 Consumption possibility frontiers

able to be 'sure' about the gain from trade only because he illegitimately supposed C_2C_1 and P_2P_1 to have the same slope. This argument can be extended to a steadily growing economy, to show that if $g = r$ (the Golden Rule case) then the with-trade bundle must lie outside the achievable autarchy frontier, but that if $g < r$ then it may or may not do so (as in Figure 2.5, which simply provides a special case of this result, with $0 = g < r$). Since the adoption of a particular specialisation can, from a formal point of view, be thought of as a particular choice of technique, the present argument is just an application, to the trade context, of the capital theory result concerning competitive choice of technique and its possible non-optimality in terms of consumption and growth. It is important to notice that this result, concerning, the possible (not certain) 'loss from trade', belongs to the class of 'comparative dynamics' results; it is best thought of as providing a *comparison* between a small closed economy and an (otherwise identical) small open economy. It is not a result about the effects on a given economy of the process of opening up to trade, full account being taken of what happens during the transition from the autarchic state to the free trading state. But the same is true, it must be noted, of the textbook demonstrations of the gain from trade, in a 'Ricardian' framework, with which the reader is familiar.

While 'factor price equalisation' is most often discussed within the H–O–S framework, it is of interest to consider whether free trade in all commodities will bring about real wage rate and interest rate equalisation in the type of model considered in this section. If all the freely trading economies have the same available choice of techniques, in a constant-returns-to-scale and homogeneous labour world, then it is certainly true that, if they all have the same rate of interest, they will all have the same set of relative prices. But the converse does *not* hold, when there is a choice of technique; all the economies could face the same set of relative commodity prices and yet have different interest rates and real wage rates. Hence free trade in all commodities does not entail wage and interest rate equalisation, even when all the economies have the same technical possibilities and are incompletely specialised.

2.4   LAND, LABOUR AND POSITIVE INTEREST

We now turn to the much loved H–O–S model of international trade, in which two countries produce the same two commodities, using the same two primary inputs (which are in fixed supply) and having the same, constant-returns-to-scale technology. The primary inputs are qualitatively the same in both countries, fully mobile within each economy but completely immobile between them. There are no factor-intensity reversals, there is completely free trade, and all consumers, in both countries, share a common homothetic preference map (so that consumption proportions depend only on the commodity price ratio, being quite independent of income distribution). If the two primary inputs are homogeneous land and homogeneous labour, and if there are no produced inputs (capital goods) of any kind, then it is easy to establish the H–O–S theorem on the pattern of trade (in both its price and quantity forms), the factor price equalisation theorem, the Stolper–Samuelson theorem and the Rybczynski theorem, all of which are assumed to be well known to the reader.

Suppose now that, retaining all the other assumptions, we allow the two consumption commodities also to be capital goods, being necessary inputs to the various productive processes. What difference does this introduction of produced inputs make to the standard theorems? None whatever! It is now more appropriate to think of land/labour intensities in production in terms of *total* (direct and indirect) uses of land and labour but, since the intensity ranking of commodities in these total terms is necessarily the same as that in direct terms, this introduces no really significant difference from the model without produced inputs. Thus far, then, produced inputs make no difference. But the position changes as soon as we allow not only for the presence of such produced inputs but also for a given, *positive* rate of interest on the value of those inputs (circulating capital goods). The presence of a positive interest rate does not alter the fact that the relative price of the land-intensive commodity will be a monotonically increasing function of the rent:wage ratio. But, as pointed out earlier, it does mean that an increase in the rent:wage ratio is not necessarily associated with a fall in the land:labour ratio; it then follows that, if land and labour are always fully employed, an increase in the relative price of the land-intensive commodity may be associated with a *fall* in its net output. In Figure 2.6, which relates to a single economy, y_i is the net product of i, p_i is the price of i, SS is the full employment 'relative supply curve' and DD is the 'relative demand curve' derived from the common homothetic preference map; the diagram illustrates the case of a 'perverse' supply response. It will be seen at once that such a supply response immediately gives rise to the possibility of multiple equilibria, the 'first' and 'third' equalibria both being stable.

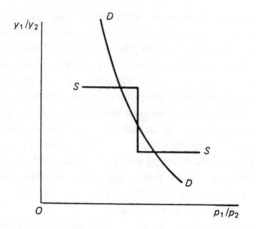

FIGURE 2.6   Multiple equilibria

Let two economies, A and B, have the same positive rate of interest; let A be relatively better endowed with land and let commodity 1 be the land-intensive commodity. Figure 2.7 extends Figure 2.6 to this case, $S^i S^i$ being the full employment relative supply curve for economy i. Suppose that point A represents A's autarchy equilibrium, while point B represents B's. At every $p_1 p_2$ lying *between* the autarchy price ratios,

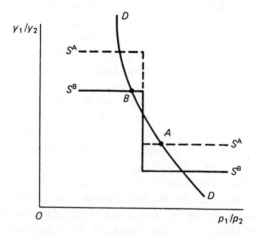

FIGURE 2.7   Multiple equilibria and the H–O–S price theorem

$S^A S^A$ and $S^B S^B$ both lie on the same side of DD; hence on such price ratio can be an equilibrium terms of trade. The terms of trade lie *outside* the autarchy price range. Whether the international equilibrium is found to the left of B or to the right of A, economy A (which is well endowed with land) will be exporting commodity 1 (which is the land-intensive commodity). Thus the H–O–S quantity theorem holds good. Yet the H–O–S price theorem, which is sometimes thought rather trivial, is actually *false* here. Since A has the higher autarchy (p_1/p_2), it has the higher autarchy rent:wage ratio, so that A is exporting the commodity which uses intensively A's relatively *expensive* factor under autarchy! Notice also that if international equilibrium is found to the left of B, p_1/p_2 will have fallen, with trade, in economy A and thus the wage:rent ratio will have *risen*; in fact trade will have *benefited* A's relatively scarce factor (labour), contrary to the usual H–O–S prediction.

If A and B have the *same* positive interest rate, as above, they have the same relationship between $p_1 p_2$ and the rent:wage ratio; it is thus not surprising that free trade will equalise rents and wages (with incomplete specialisation) and that the Stolper–Samuelson theorem also holds good. If A and B have *different* positive interest rates, however, almost everything collapses. The exception is the Rybczynski theorem, and it is important for the student to understand why. All 'capital theoretic' problems for H–O–S theory reduce in the end to the fact that relative commodity prices vary with the rate of interest, but relative prices are fixed *by assumption* in the Rybczynski theorem, so that that theorem must be immune to such problems.

In the land and labour model, then, the presence of produced inputs makes no difference *per se*. But a positive rate of interest on their value does make a difference to some (but not all) H–O–S theorems, if it is the same in both countries, while a difference in interest rates undermines all the standard H–O–S results, other than the Rybczynski theorem.

2.5 LABOUR AND CAPITAL

In the typical textbook presentation of H–O–S theory, the two 'factors' in given supply are not labour and land, as above, but labour and 'capital'. (Notice, though, that Samuelson, 1948 and 1949, was careful to stipulate labour and land). Yet that typical presentation suggests no immediate connection between the two produced commodities and the physical composition of the capital stock, despite the fact that 'capital goods' are, by definition, produced means of production! Indeed, one interpretation of most textbook theory is that 'capital' is simply a misnomer for land, the problems of capital theory being evaded by a simple misuse of terms. Alternatively (and more favourably) the 'given capital supply' can be interpreted to mean that the total *value* of capital goods must always be equal to – or, at least, not greater than – an exogenously given value. An immediate difficulty with this interpretation is that, since relative autarchy prices differ between the two economies, the very *ranking* of the two countries' capital:labour endowment ratios may depend on which standard of value capital is given in terms of! And what does it *mean* economically to suppose that total capital value is given in terms of one standard and yet, necessarily, is *not* given in terms of all other possible standards (since relative commodity prices are to be determined endogenously)?[2] Even if we ignore these questions – which there is no justification for doing – we know from capital theory that value capital:labour ratios need not be related inversely or, indeed, even monotonically to the rate of interest. This, of course, immediately suggests that some of the H–O–S theorems may be at risk. Moreover, it can be shown that in a model with many produced inputs, the price ratio between any two particular commodities need not be monotonically related to the rate of interest, *even when* one of the two commodities is always more value capital-intensive than the other. But if neither the capital:labour ratios nor the relative commodity prices need be monotonically related to the rate of interest – even in the absence of factor-intensity reversals – then it will at once be clear, to any student who really understands H–O–S theory, that its theorems (other than the Rybczynski theorem) cannot be logically valid when one of the two factors is a 'given value of capital'. This stems fundamentally from the simple fact stated by Wicksell in 1921:

> Whereas labour and land are measured each in terms of its own *technical* unit ... capital ... is reckoned, in common parlance, as a sum of *exchange value* – whether in money or as an average of products. In other words, each particular capital-good is measured by a unit extraneous to itself. [This] is a theoretical anomaly which disturbs the correspondence which would otherwise exist between all the factors of production. (Wicksell, 1967, p. 149)

To illustrate the above negative conclusions, we may use an example in which there are two consumption commodities (two kinds of 'corn'), each producible by means of many alternative types of machine, just as in our earlier section on capital theory. The consumption commodities are tradable but the machines are not. Full numerical details of this example can be found in Metcalfe and Steedman (1973); here we confine ourselves to the diagrammatic presentation of Figure 2.8, in which k_i is the value capital:labour ratio involved, directly and indirectly, in the production of the ith consumption commodity, expressed in terms of the first consumption commodity. It will be seen on the right of Figure 2.8 that neither k_1 nor k_2 is monotonically related to r, but that $k_1 > k_2$ at all r on the left we see that, the absence of factor-intensity reversal notwithstanding, the price ratio (p_1/p_2) is not monotonically related to r. It follows at once that the 'factor price' equalisation theorem, the Stolper–Samuelson theorem and the price form of the H–O–S theorem on the pattern of trade are *not* of general logical validity. But if the pattern of trade theorem is not valid in its price form, then it will not be valid in its quantity form either, even if it is the case (which it may not be) that the economy with the higher capital:labour endowment ratio has the lower autarchy interest rate.

When produced inputs are introduced into H–O–S theory in the form that one of the two 'factors' is taken to be a given total value of capital that theory simply disintegrates.

It is perhaps fair to warn the student of an apparent denial of the above negative conclusion by Ethier (1979), who states that 'The central message ... is simple. The four basic theorems of the modern theory of international trade ... are insensitive to the nature of capital'

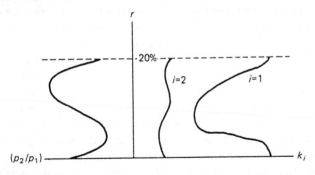

FIGURE 2.8 **Alternative interest rates, capital intensity and the product price ratio**

(p. 236). In fact Ethier's paper constitutes a striking confirmation of our negative conclusion, because in order to maintain the *appearance* that capital has no influence on H–O–S trade theorems, Ethier finds himself compelled to *replace* the familiar theorems, which predict trade outcomes on the basis of exogenous data, by entirely different theorems, which merely describe trade outcomes in terms of trade equilibrium prices, etc.

2.6   GROWTH, INTERNATIONAL INVESTMENT AND TRANSITIONS

To focus on the role of capital goods in trade and in trade theory is, implicitly, to direct attention also to such matters as growth (capital accumulation), international investment and transitions between steady growth paths. While it will not be possible to enter into an adequate discussion of these extensive issues here, it would perhaps be strange to conclude without at least sketching out their connections with our preceding discussion; once those connections are seen, the interested student will be able to pursue matters further.

Since the typical trading economy uses many produced inputs (some traded and some not), accumulates capital goods, and experiences (often embodied) technical change, along both quantitative and qualitative dimensions, the ideal theory of trade would be able to handle all these closely related issues in a manner which was both informative and simple. Needless to say, such an ideal theory is not available; international trade theory in these respects can, in the long run, be no more advanced than the general theory of accumulation and technical progress. Our preceding discussion can, however, serve to warn us that growth models in which there is a single, physical capital good can almost certainly not be readily generalised to the many capital goods case and are thus of *very* limited interest. It is also useful to note, as a simple matter of fact, that while the number of countries in the world is of the order of 200, the number of distinct commodities – when defined at the level of detail relevant to careful value theory – runs into millions. This both tells us that incomplete specialisation must be the rule and directs our attention to economic growth models in which the number of commodities can be arbitrarily large; the Von Neumann model deserves to be used more extensively by trade theorists than it has been, its very abstract nature notwithstanding.

When thinking of capital accumulation, the international economist will naturally pay considerable attention to the role of international investment. Here it is most important to recognise that, although they are often connected in practice, there is a perfectly clear – indeed a sharp – distinction between international investment as a flow of finance on the one hand, and trade in physical capital goods on the other. This is obvious enough perhaps when stated explicitly, but it is to be noted that the idea of a 'factor' capital, conceived of as a sum of value, in fact makes it dangerously easy to confuse financial flows with capital goods flows. That the danger is a real one is illustrated beautifully by Batra (1973, p. 323) who, in his chapter on international investment, tells us that 'By international mobility of capital is meant the physical movement of the capital goods in response to different rentals of capital in the two countries. The capital owners in either country can take part of the given stock of 'capital' in their own country and move it bodily to the other country! This example, like our earlier discussion, suggests strongly that the student would do well to avoid the concept of a 'quantity of capital' altogether, referring only to stocks and flows of specified capital goods on the one hand, and to international flows of finance on the other. Such a practice would not only make it easier to avoid capital theory traps but would also facilitate thought about the badly needed integration of pure trade theory with international monetary economics.

We conclude this section with a brief comment on 'transitions'. Consider first a closed economy whose homogeneous land and homogeneous labour are allocated between strawberry production and raspberry production. No produced inputs are used, not even strawberry and raspberry plants! (Which reminds us, incidentally, of just *how* strained is any picture of direct production of consumption commodities by primary inputs). If free trade should suddenly become possible, at terms of trade different from the autarchy price ratio, there is no difficulty at all in re-allocating the land and labour to the newly desired output pattern. The 'transition' from the autarchy steady state to the with-trade steady state is problem free and can be achieved instantaneously. By contrast, consider now the analogous 'transition' for an economy which does use produced inputs. Except by a complete fluke, the economy's industries will use the various produced inputs in different proportions from one another and it will now *not* be possible to change instantaneously to the free trade pattern of output. Since the production of the produced inputs takes time, there will have to be a 'transitional' period, during which the physical composition of the economy's aggregate capital stock is adjusted to the new output pattern. Just how long this period will be depends, of course, on how different the input requirements are as between industries, on whether or not some previously used capital goods simply have to be scrapped, on how many of the capital goods are tradable and how many non-tradable, etc. Changing the pattern of net output is a far more complicated process in an economy using produced inputs. This issue is avoided in textbook discussions of the gain from trade *and* in the 'comparative dynamics' results given earlier in this chapter; yet it can hardly be denied that the issue is important in many trade policy applications and in many day-to-day debates about trade protection, industries which are under increased international competitive pressure, and so on. It is therefore important that the transitional implications of the presence of produced inputs should be studied further. (At the same time, it may be pointed out, it is far less clear that transitional complications need be considered in hypothetical gain-from-trade *comparisons* between the actual trading world and a hypothetical autarchic world.)

Although this section has merely touched on three large problem areas in trade theory, it is hoped that enough has been said to stimulate the student to think further about growth, international investment and transitions, all of which are intimately related to the role of produced inputs.

2.7   CONCLUSION

Sufficient reason has perhaps been given above to justify the rather general conclusion that the student who finds trade theorists referring to 'capital' should immediately be 'on guard'. The presence of produced inputs, with a positive rate of interest on their value, does make a considerable difference to the logical coherence of H–O–S theory, as has been seen above in some detail. Moreover, 'textbook' 'capital' at all, ought to make such reference and, if it did, would discover that here again the presence of a positive interest rate makes it far harder to reach any clear-cut, logically valid theorems. To give full recognition to the role of produced inputs certainly makes trade theory more difficult; but can that be a good reason for ignoring them, when that theory is intended to aid our understanding of a world in which produced inputs are, in fact, centrally important?

3 Theory and Policy of Adjustment in an Open Economy

J. PETER NEARY

3.1 INTRODUCTION

Almost all discussions of economic policy are concerned with issues of adjustment, and this is especially true in matters relating to international trade. Whether it is the effects of changes in world prices, increased foreign competition or a currency realignment, policy-makers and the general public want to know how the economy will move towards its new equilibrium and not just what that equilibrium will look like. Economists, whose job it is to answer such questions, must dip into their theoretical tool-kit and attempt as best they can to apply the most relevant theoretical framework to the problem at hand. Typically, the most difficult part of this task is not to elucidate the properties of a particular model, but to choose in the first place which model is appropriate to a given problem.

In this chapter, we will illustrate the range of theoretical tools which may be used to examine how an open economy adjusts from one equilibrium to another. We emphasise in particular that very different models may be relevant, depending on the time period under consideration. Thus, the next section deals with the very short run, during which only one factor, labour, is mobile between sectors. The following section looks at the medium run, in which both capital and labour are mobile. We then go on to consider the long run, when all factors are

39

mobile and the rate of capital accumulation is endogenous. These sections consider how the economy is likely to adjust in the absence of government intervention, whereas the penultimate section discusses the rationale for such intervention and the forms it is likely to take in practice. Finally, we make some concluding remarks.

3.2   SHORT-RUN ADJUSTMENT: LABOUR MARKET DISEQUILIBRIUM

We begin by considering what is probably the simplest example of adjustment to an exogenous shock. We deal with the case of a competitive, small, open economy which produces and consumes two goods facing given world prices, and we ask what will be the consequences of a fall in the relative price of imports. To highlight the main issues we wish to stress, we abstract from a great many real-world features, including government activity, non-competitive behaviour and the interaction of real and monetary phenomena.

Figure 3.1 shows how the effects of this change are typically portrayed. Curve *PP* is a production possibilities curve showing the maximum amounts of the two goods that can be produced, given the economy's technology and factor endowments, while the curves *II* and *I'I'* are social indifference curves.[1] Before the change, the economy produces at point *A* and consumes at point *G*, with the value of good *Y* exported matching the value of good *X* imported. The exogenous fall in the world relative price of its exportable, *Y*, worsens the economy's terms of trade. Production of *Y* is discouraged and the production point shifts from *A* to *B*, while consumption of *Y* relative to *X* is encouraged as consumption shifts from *G* to *H* on the lower social indifference curve *I'I'*.

This illustration is familiar from introductory textbooks, but in fact it ignores a whole host of issues. We can perhaps concede that adjustment of demand patterns to changed circumstances is relatively rapid, although even this is a major simplification. Habits die hard, especially if the level of current consumption is related to the existing stock of durable goods (as was the case with developed countries' oil imports in the 1970s, for example). An even more serious simplification of reality is the assumption that the pattern of production adjusts instantaneously. In fact, the movement from *A* to *B* conceals a great deal of what is going on in the economy. To examine this further we must go behind

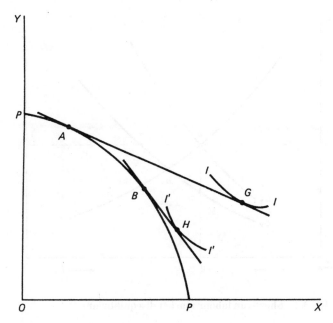

FIGURE 3.1   Adjustment to a deterioration in the terms of trade

the production possibilities curve and make more specific assumptions about the structure of production and the organisation of factor markets.

Figure 3.2 illustrates one set of assumptions about the underpinnings of Figure 3.1 which is both simple to understand and reasonably plausible as a description of short-run equilibrium. Known as the *specific-factors model*, this assumes that each sector uses a single factor, labour, in common with other sectors. In addition, each sector uses a range of other factors specific to it, which may include plant and equipment, non-traded natural resources and entrepreneurial and managerial skills. The law of diminishing returns implies that as more of the variable factor is applied to the specific factor, its marginal product falls, and this is illustrated in the diagram. The curve labelled L_X (drawn with respect to the origin O_X) shows the value marginal product of labour and hence (under competitive assumptions) the demand for labour in sector X. The same applies to the curve labelled L_Y (which is drawn with respect to the origin O_Y). It should be clear that point a represents the unique competitive equilibrium in this economy. Only at this point

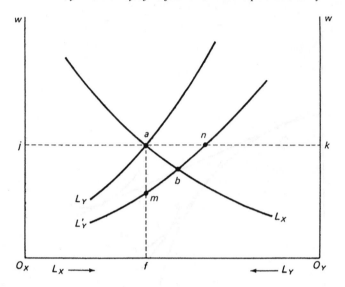

FIGURE 3.2   Short-run labour market disequilibrium

is the aggregate demand for labour in the economy, $O_X t$ from sector X plus $O_Y f$ from sector Y, equal to the fixed total supply, $O_X O_Y$. Hence, $O_X j$ measures the competitive market-clearing wage rate in the initial equilibrium.

Consider now the effects of a fall in the relative price of Y. Without loss of generality, we choose good X as numerative, which implies that price changes do not affect the location of the L_X curve and that the vertical axis measures the wage rate in terms of good X. The reduction in the price of good X therefore leads to an equiproportionate down-ward shift in that sector's labour demand schedule from L_Y to L'_Y. Evidently, the new equilibrium is at point b (which corresponds to point B in Figure 3.1): the restoration of labour market equilibrium requires a fall in the wage rate in terms of X, leading sector X to expand its output and employment and sector Y to contract.

The question we must now consider is how the economy will actually move from the initial equilibrium represented by points A and a to the new equilibrium represented by points B and b. Two extreme cases may be distinguished. In the first, the labour markets in the two sectors are temporarily segmented (i.e., even when wage differences exist, arbitrage between the two sectors will not occur), but the wage rates within each adjust freely to ensure full employment. In this case, sector X is insulated from the shock in the very short run, whereas the wage in sector Y falls by the full amount of the price change from *fa* to *fm*. Over time, the resulting disparity in wages between sectors induces migration from the sector Y labour market to that in sector X. Hence, the production points in the two sectors move along the L_X and L_Y schedules until the new equilibrium at b is attained. The second extreme case is where the two sectors draw on a common labour market, with no barriers to intersectoral labour mobility even in the very short run, but the common wage rate is downwardly sticky. Assuming for simplicity that it is pegged in terms of X, the wage remains equal to O_Xj in the short run. Once again, sector X is temporarily insulated from the change and its production point remains at a. By contrast, entrepreneurs in sector Y are no longer able to pay the same wage and instead reduce their employment from *ak* to *nk*. The resulting unemployment of *an* tends to reduce the wage rate over time and both sectors move down their labour demand schedules towards b. Naturally, the process of adjustment in an actual economy is likely to combine elements of both these extreme mechanisms, with both sectors exhibiting a combination of unemployment and sluggish wage change throughout the adjustment period.

The two alternative paths of adjustment in this model may be illustrated in a different fashion. In Figure 3.3, the vertical axis measures the wage in terms of good X, just as in Figure 3.2, whereas the horizontal axis measures the price of good Y (relative to the numeraire good, X, of course). The curve LL shows those combinations of w and p which equate demand and supply of labour. In obvious notion, the equation of this curve is:

$$L^X(w) + L^Y(w/p) = L \tag{3.1}$$

This curve must be upward-sloping, since, starting from a point of labour-market equilibrium, a higher wage rate alone generates unemployment (U), while an increase in p with unchanged w generates excess demand for labour (*EDL*). Furthermore, it must be less steeply sloped than a ray from the origin, as shown, reflecting the fact that an increase in p requires a less than proportionate increase in w if labour market equilibrium is to be maintained.[2]

The two alternative adjustment paths introduced in Figure 3.2 may now be illustrated in Figure 3.3 as well. (Once again, corresponding

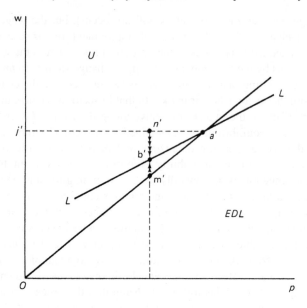

FIGURE 3.3   Short-run labour market disequilibrium in wage-price space

points in the two diagrams have been given matching labels, to facilitate comparison between the two.) With initial equilibrium at a', the fall in p implies a new equilibrium at point b'. Under the first adjustment mechanism introduced above, sectors X and Y move to points n' and m' in the short run[3] and then converge towards b', as shown by the arrows while, under the second adjustment mechanism, the new short-run equilibrium for both sectors is represented by point n', and unemployment gradually drives down the economy-wide wage rate.

Figure 3.3 tells the same story as Figure 3.2 but has the advantage that it is more easily adapted to the case where goods prices are endogenous. Even the smallest open economy typically produces some goods which are differentiated from goods produced abroad, so that their prices are at least in part influenced by home conditions, as well as some non-traded goods or services, whose prices are exclusively determined by the interaction of domestic supply and demand. (Indeed, an additional aspect of the adjustment process, which we do not consider here, is that the degree to which the prices of different goods are domestically determined may itself vary with the time horizon under consideration.) To examine how domestic price determination affects the adjustment process, it is convenient to concentrate on an extreme case where the economy produces and consumes a single traded and a single non-traded good. Assume that the good previously labelled X is the traded good, a composite commodity aggregating both imported and exported goods, and that that labelled Y is now non-traded. The price ratio, p, is therefore the relative price of non-traded to traded goods, sometimes referred to as the *real exchange rate*. A rise in p – a 'real appreciation' – encourages a move of production towards non-traded relative to traded goods and an opposite move in consumption. Because of this pivotal role of the real exchange rate in measuring the incentives to switch production and expenditure between the two sectors, it is often viewed as a generalised measure of the 'competitiveness' of the home economy.

The determination of equilibrium in this model is illustrated in Figure 3.4. The schedule LL is the same as in Figure 3.3; the new feature of this diagram is that p is no longer exogenous but must adjust to equate domestic supply and demand of non-traded goods. The curve NN is the locus of (w, p) combinations which ensure this, and its equation is:

$$X^N (w/p) = c^N [p, z (p)]$$ (3.2)

where z denotes real national income in terms of traded goods. This curve must be upward-sloping. A rise in p alone gives rise to excess supply of the non-traded good, while an increase in w is needed to discourage its production and restore equilibrium. In addition, this schedule must be more steeply sloped than a ray from the origin as shown: an equiproportionate increase w and p leaves production of the non-traded good unchanged but reduces demand for it, so giving rise to excess supply.[4] The last feature of the diagram worthy of comment is that the arrows indicate the direction of movement when the economy is out of equilibrium. Thus, the vertical arrows reflect the assumption that the wage rate falls when the labour market is in a state of unemployment (at points above LL) and conversely when it is in a state of excess demand for labour; while the horizontal arrows show that p is bid up by excess demand for the non-traded good (i.e., at points to the left of the curve NN) and bid down by excess supply. It is clear that the equilibrium at a' is globally stable under these assumed adjustment mechanisms.[5]

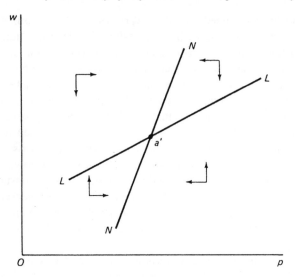

FIGURE 3.4   Simultaneous adjustment of wages and prices

Now, consider the effect of an exogenous shock to the equilibrium depicted in Figure 3.4. For concreteness, we focus on a particular shock, an increase in computerisation in the traded goods sector, which is assumed to take the form of labour-saving technological progress. (Readers should attempt to work out the implications of different shocks for themselves.) Since this shock represents real growth in the economy, it increase the demand for the non-traded good at any given wage and price; since supply is not directly affected, the region of excess demand for the non-traded good in the diagram expands and so the *NN* locus shifts rightwards, as shown in Figure 3.5. The second effect of the shock is to reduce the economy-wide demand for labour at any given *w* and *p*, so shifting the *LL* curve downwards to *L'L'* as shown. Once again, the transition from the initial equilibrium *a'* to the new equilibrium *b'* may take many forms, and the diagram illustrates one of these: the real exchange rate is assumed to adjust rapidly to eliminate incipient disequilibrium in the non-traded good market, while the wage rate is assumed to be downwardly sticky (in terms of traded goods) but equalised at all times across the two sectors. Under these assumptions the shock we have considered generates an example of real exchange rate 'overshooting': *p* first rises by more than its equilib-

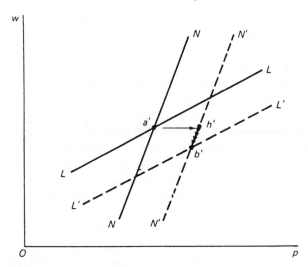

FIGURE 3.5   Real exchange rate overshooting as a result of computerisation in the traded goods sector

rium change, as excess demand for the non-traded good drives the short-run equilibrium from a' to h'. Over time, the resulting unemployment leads to a gradual downwards drift in the wage and the economy gradually converges along the $N'N'$ schedule towards the new full equilibrium point, b'. It may be checked that many other configurations for the time path of p and w are possible, depending on the nature of the exogenous shock and on the combination of adjustment mechanisms assumed.

To sum up, we have concentrated in this section on different patterns of adjustment in the labour market, both with and without endogenous changes in relative goods prices. This focus has drawn attention to a number of important phenomena which are likely to manifest themselves in any real-world adjustment process. Nevertheless, we have obviously ignored or glossed over a number of important aspects of short-run adjustment, especially monetary considerations and the disequilibrium feedbacks from one market to another. In addition, we have adopted a strictly short-run framework by assuming that only labour is mobile between sectors and that the aggregate supplies of all factors are fixed. In the next two sections, we attempt to relax these assumptions.

3.3   MEDIUM-RUN ADJUSTMENT: RESOURCE REALLOCATION

The key feature to which the last section has drawn attention is that adjustment does not simply happen: in a competitive economy it takes place because any exogenous shock changes the *incentives* facing factor owners and entrepreneurs to adjust. However, it is not only suppliers of labour services who face such incentives: capital owners face them too, and in this section we consider a simple model that attempts to capture this additional feature of the adjustment process. The model in question is the one most commonly found in international trade textbooks: the two-sector, two-factor version of the Heckscher–Ohlin model. The additional feature assumed here is that only one of the factors, labour, is assumed to be mobile in the short run, whereas the other, capital, adjusts slowly over time. The short-run equilibrium of this model is therefore identical to the specific-factors model of the last section, and so the initial equilibrium can be depicted in the upper panel of Figure 3.6, this panel being identical to Figure 3.2. (Note that for simplicity we return now to the case where both goods are traded at exogenously given prices, and we also ignore the transitional labour market disequilibrium issues considered in the last section.) The lower panel of Figure 3.6 is an Edgeworth–Bowley box, whose dimensions correspond to the country's factor endowments. By measuring labour along the horizontal axis of the box, it can be placed directly below the upper panel, allowing us to trace both the short-run and long-run consequences of any exogenous shock. Point *a* in the upper panel corresponds to point *A* in the lower, and the latter lies on the contract curve, indicating that the initial equilibrium is one in which both labour and capital are allocated in such a way that they receive the same return in each sector. Note finally that the contract curve lies above the diagonal of the box, reflecting the arbitrary assumption that *X* is the relatively capital-intensive sector.

Consider now a fall in the relative price of good *Y*. As in Figure 3.2, the new short-run equilibrium is represented by point *b* in the upper panel of Figure 3.5. As already noted, we ignore the alternative process discussed in the last section by which labour is bid away from sector *Y* to sector *X*, even though in practice adjustments in the labour and capital markets are likely to occur simultaneously.[6] Assuming therefore that the move from *a* to *b* is instantaneous, this corresponds to a move in the lower panel from *A* to *B*. The allocation of capital between the

49

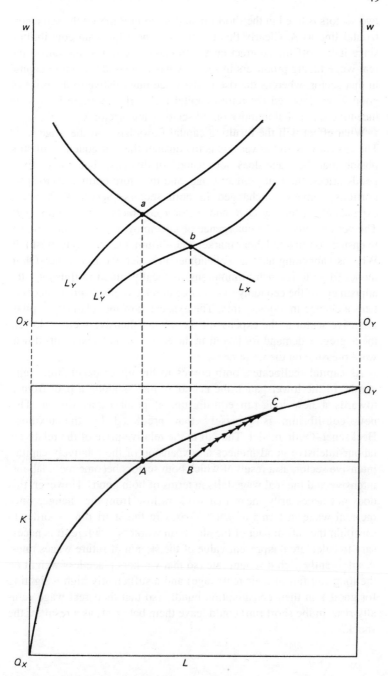

FIGURE 3.6 Intersectoral capital reallocation

two sectors is fixed in the short run and so point *B* lies on the same horizontal line as *A*. Clearly this cannot be a new long-run equilibrium, since it lies off the contract curve. In economic terms, the fall in the real wage facing producers in sector *X* has increased the return capital in that sector, whereas the rise in the wage rate relative to the price of good *Y* has lowered the return capital there. Hence, there is now an incentive for capital to move out of sector *Y* into sector *X*.

What effect will the resulting capital flows have on the wage rate? The easiest way to answer this is to consider the consequences of supposing that the wage does not change. In this case, because of fixed goods prices, the real product wage, and therefore optimal factor proportions, remains unchanged in both sectors. Sector *X* therefore expands along the ray Q_XB, and sector *Y* contracts along the ray Q_YB. The net outcome is the emergence of unemployment of labour and so, to ensure continuing labour market equilibrium, the wage rate must fall. What is happening here is a phenomenon which the Heckscher–Ohlin model (despite its many limitations) is ideally suited to illustrate: the adjustment of the economy to a change in relative goods prices necessitates a change in industry mix. The expansion of the relatively capital-intensive sector at the expense of the labour-intensive sector *Y* lowers the aggregate demand for labour in the economy and hence puts downward pressure on the wage rate.

As capital reallocates, both curves in the upper panel shift rightwards. In the lower panel, the economy moves along a path from *B* towards a new long-run equilibrium at point *C*, as shown. This new equilibrium is precisely that predicted by the textbook Heckscher–Ohlin model. The fall in the relative price of the relatively labour-intensive good induces an expansion of the relatively capital-intensive sector, as a result of which both sectors become more labour-intensive and the real wage falls in terms of both goods. However, this does not necessarily mean that workers lose from the change, since the real wage in terms of good *Y rises* in the short run. In order to ascertain the full impact of the shock on workers' welfare, it is necessary to calculate the present value of the stream of future wages rates. A sufficiently high discount rate (so that workers place less weight on the long-run fall in their real wage) and a sufficiently high weighting for good *Y* in their consumption bundle (so that their real wage actually rises in the short run) could leave them better off as a result of the shock.

3.4 LONGER-RUN ADJUSTMENT: CHANGES IN INDUSTRIAL STRUCTURE

The analysis of the last section allowed for complete adjustment of factor markets but continued to assume that the aggregate supplies of both labour and capital were fixed. This makes it inappropriate for the study of long-run adjustment. However, attempts by economists to model formally the process of long-run growth have not met with great success. One of the least plausible features of the many models of economic growth developed in the 1960s is their view of long-run equilibrium as a steady process whereby the economy reproduces itself with no change in economic structure. By contrast, in the real world the processes of growth and structural change appear to be intimately connected, with each phase of growth dominated by a number of 'leading sectors' coexisting with stagnant or declining ones. Fortunately, the small open economy assumption allows us to construct an interesting model where this phenomenon can be illustrated.

The model to be considered is based on R. W. Jones (1974). It assumes that the economy has two factors of production, labour and capital, and has access to technology for producing any number of a variety of goods that are traded with the rest of the world at fixed prices. In a competitive equilibrium, such an economy will in fact produce at most two goods,[7] possibly exporting both in exchange for imports of all the other commodities it consumes.

To fix these ideas, assume that there are at most three goods which the economy could profitably produce. The relationship between the domestic wage:rental ratio (w/r) and the degree of capital intensity in the production of each of these goods (k) is shown by the three dashed curves labelled X_1, X_2 and X_3 in Figure 3.7. (For simplicity, we assume that there are no factor-intensity reversals: at all factor price ratios, the ranking of sectors by factor intensity is the same, with sector 1 the least capital-intensive and sector 3 the most.) Which of the three goods will actually be produced by this economy depends on world prices and on its factor endowments. For any given aggregate factor endowment ratio, world prices determine an optimal pattern of specialisation and the locus of such patterns is shown by the solid line *abcdef* in Figure 3.7.[8] Thus, if the economy's capital:labour ratio is less than k^B, only the labour-intensive commodity X_1 can be profitably produced; for endowment ratios between k^B and k^C it pays to diversify and produce both X_1

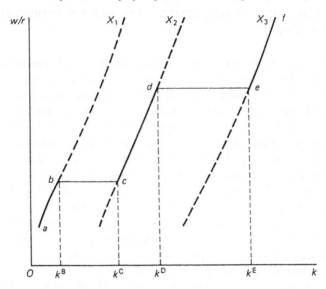

FIGURE 3.7   Equilibrium production patterns for a small country in a three-commodity world

and X_2, and so on: specialisation in X_2 along cd, both X_2 and X_3 produced along de and specialisation in X_3 for capital:labour ratios greater than k^E.

Figure 3.7 shows the alternative production patterns corresponding to different factor endowment ratios. To close the model it is necessary to examine how this ratio is determined, and this is illustrated in Figure 3.8. Essentially, this is the same diagram as that used to illustrate the Solow–Swan one-sector growth model, familiar from almost every intermediate macroeconomics textbook, with the solid curve showing the value of national output per head (y) attainable with different capital:labour ratios. The new feature of the diagram is that the assumption of fixed world commodity prices allows us to aggregate the different goods produced by the economy into a single composite output. Thus the solid curve is actually the outer envelope of the production functions for the three sectors. It is expressed in intensive form giving national output per head (y) as a function of capital input per head (k). The different segments of the solid curve correspond exactly to the same alternating phases of specialisation and diversification illustrated

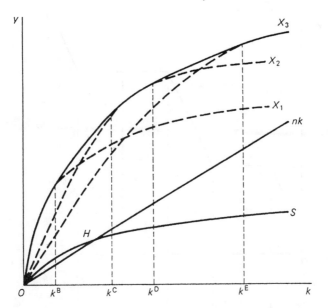

FIGURE 3.8 Determination of steady-state capital-labour ratio

in Figure 3.7, as the labelling of the borderline capital:labour ratios makes clear.

Just as in the standard Solow–Swann model, the location of the steady-state equilibrium is determined by the interaction of savings behaviour and population growth. The latter is assumed to take place at an exogenous rate. For simplicity we assume that savings are a constant proportion of aggregate income. This gives rise to a supply of savings schedule labelled s in the diagram, which is a downwards displacement of the solid national output schedule. Steady-state equilibrium occurs at point H when this savings schedule intersects the line labelled nk, where n is the rate of population growth. At this point the supply of savings that is forthcoming leads to a rate of growth in the capital shock which is just sufficient to provide employment for the new entrants to the labour force with no change in the aggregate capital:labour ratio.

Now, to illustrate the workings of the model, we consider Figure 3.9, which brings together the salient features of the two preceding diagrams. The initial steady-state equilibrium is at the capital:labour ratio k^H, where the economy produces both X_1 and X_2. Consider now a

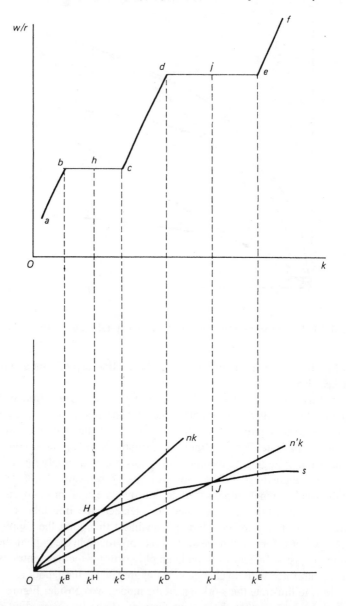

FIGURE 3.9   Effect on industrial structure of a fall in population growth rate from *n* to *n'*

disturbance to this equilibrium. To keep the diagram simple, we assume a once-for-all fall in the population growth rate from n to n'. This implies that at the initial capital:labour ratio k^H the economy is accumulating capital faster than the labour force is growing. Hence the capital:labour ratio must rise over time. If markets operate smoothly and competitively, both X_1 and X_2 continue to be produced for a period until the aggregate capital:labour ratio rises above k^C and sector 1 is competed out of existence. A phase of specialisation in X_2 is then followed by production of both X_2 and X_3 until the new steady-state equilibrium with a capital:labour ratio of k^J is attained. Of course, in practice the short-run and medium-run phenomena considered earlier are likely to play a role. Even without government intervention sector 1 is likely to remain in operation after the capital:labour ratio rises above k^C. Indeed, it is quite likely that all three goods will be produced simultaneously for a period, until pressures towards specialisation assert themselves.

3.5   POLICIES TOWARDS THE ADJUSTMENT PROCESS

The passing reference to government activity at the end of the last section raises a number of issues that have been ignored until now. In discussing government policies towards the adjustment process, much needless confusion (and much unjustified criticism of the relevance of economic advice) is generated by the failure to distinguish two separate strands of argument: on the one hand, what should be done by a government seeking to maximise the welfare of its citizens (however that welfare is defined), and, on the other hand, what actions are most likely to emerge from the interplay of different lobbies and interest groups both inside and outside the government machine. The answers to these two questions bring us into the realm of welfare economics and political economy respectively, and space precludes a detailed discussion of either. (Further discussion of many of these issues may be found in other chapters of this volume, in particular Chapters 6 and 8.) However, some basic points may be made here.

Consider first the normative question of what optimal intervention towards the adjustment process should be. The essential principles of optimal intervention are no different from those that apply in static cases. Provided markets are competitive and free of 'distortions', the resulting equilibrium will be Pareto-efficient. If, in addition, the government respects individual preferences as manifested in market behaviour, and lump-sum taxes and transfers are available to redistribute income as desired, then no interference with the market mechanism is warranted. A rationale for intervention is introduced once departures from this idealised state of affairs are admitted, whether in the form of market distortions (such as externalities, non-competitive behaviour or increasing returns to scale), paternalism (e.g., the pursuit of 'non-economic objectives' which individuals, left to themselves, would not seek), or the unavailability of lump-sum taxes and transfers.

This catalogue is so all-embracing that it might be thought to justify intervention in almost all circumstances. However, even if this is the case, recent work on the theory of optimal policy has added the important qualification that departures from the textbook ideal do not of themselves justify intervention of any kind but only of whatever form is the most efficient to combat the specific market failure in question. The general principle is that intervention will be more efficacious the closer it is to the source of the distortion. One immediate implication of this principle is that many arguments for intervention are not justifications for protection in the conventional sense of restrictions to trade, but rather justifications for subsidies or taxes targeted to particular industries or markets.

In considering optimal intervention towards dynamic adjustment in the economy, new features arise in the case of each of the justifications for intervention discussed above. For example, various kinds of distortion are often alleged to be especially significant in a dynamic context. One of these, that of wage stickiness which gives rise to transitional unemployment, has already been mentioned. Another is the alleged 'irreversibility' problem, often used to justify the prohibition of 'dumping' by foreign producers: because of imperfect capital markets or other market failures it may not be possible for domestic producers to ride out a temporary disruption to their markets without assistance. As for the requirement of a coincidence of preferences between the state and private individuals, in a dynamic context this has the additional implication that the private and social rates of discount must be equal. Thus intervention is often defended on the grounds that the present generation pays inadequate attention to the interest of future generations. Intervention would also be justified if individual participants, though sharing the state's valuation of future events, had imperfect information or irrational expectations concerning them. Finally issues of distribution are especially acute in the context of adjustment, since almost all changes are likely to lead to short-run losses for some groups, and attempts to protect their incomes by distortionary means are likely to slow up the adjustment process itself.

This last point leads naturally to a move from considerations of optimal intervention to those of political economy, for it is often the case that workers about to be displaced from declining industries are relatively well paid and are not necessarily the most deserving targets for special assistance. Nevertheless, they are likely to have a strong claim on such assistance because their plight is geographically concentrated and therefore highly visible. Compensatory payments made to such groups are likely to be easy to justify on political grounds; by contrast, there are fewer votes to be won from the losses to consumers who are prevented from enjoying cheaper imports or to prospective employees *not* hired by the new firms that would have set up if no intervention had been undertaken in the first place.

In general, inter-party competition in democratic political systems may be expected to give rise to a number of undesirable tendencies in the context of granting adjustment to declining industries. One just mentioned is a likely bias towards action of a visible kind rather than inaction where the resulting benefits are likely to remain intangible for the immediate future, or opaque, or are widely diffused. A second is a tendency towards protecting the existing incomes of different groups at the expense of improving the potential income of all.[9] Third, there is a tendency to exaggerate the importance of non-economic considerations in deciding whether assistance should be provided: strategic importance is often used to justify continued support for loss-making oil refineries, national airlines, agricultural protection, etc. Finally, a feature which is by no means peculiar to democratic systems is the tendency for bureaucracies to pursue their own self-interest. This leads to, among other features, a tendency for agencies and assistance programmes to outlive the circumstances which justified their establishment in the first place.

In the light of these points, it might be though remarkable that liberal trading arrangements have survived at all. The fact that they have reflects to a large extent a widespread awareness of the need to establish 'rules of the game' which limit the ability of all participating countries to resort to protectionist measures under the guise of adjustment assistance. In this context, the General Agreement on Tariffs and Trade (GATT) has been very successful in limiting the degree of intervention in recent years. The economist may regret that his or her role has thereby been diminished and that of the arbitrator and trade lawyer enhanced. Nevertheless, it cannot be denied that the willingness of governments voluntarily to restrict their own freedom to limit trade has been a major stimulus to worldwide economic growth in the post-war era.

3.6 CONCLUSION

This chapter has merely scratched the surface of the issues that arise in discussing the question of adjustment in an open economy. For the most part we have concentrated on illustrating the implications for adjustment of a number of different models. However, it is important not to be misled by the mode of analysis adopted. In considering each model we have started from an initial equilibrium which is assumed to be disturbed by an exogenous shock, the consequences of which are traced out until they become negligible and a new equilibrium is reached. By contrast, in the real world, the economy is constantly being buffeted by new shocks, before the consequences of earlier ones have had time to work themselves out. Moreover, as we have stressed at a number of points, the mechanisms highlighted by each individual model will almost always coexist in the real world. Thus, the transitional unemployment discussed in the section on short-run adjustment will typically coincide with the intersectoral resource flows considered in the following section, and these in turn will be difficult to distinguish from changes in the aggregate capital shock with the consequences outlined in the section on longer-run adjustment. The simultaneity of these adjustments makes it impossible simply to apply naively any one of the models we have presented to a given situation. Rather, it suggests that, in trying to understand any real-world sequence of events, the lessons of each of the models should be kept in mind.

4 Empirical Analyses of International Trade Flows

P. K. M. THARAKAN and G. CALFAT

4.1 INTRODUCTION

Empirical analysis of international trade flows has grown rapidly since the publication of the Leontief paradox (Leontief, 1953) and the confirmation of the existence of intra-industry trade (Verdoorn, 1960). More recently, the remarkable progress achieved in modelling crucial imperfect competition variables, such as economies of scale and preference diversity in a general equilibrium framework, has triggered the proliferation of other insight-yielding empirical exercises.

An exhaustive survey of all the above-mentioned developments is of course beyond the scope of this short chapter. By necessity we have to be selective. The objective of the present chapter is to illustrate the direction of the advancements registered and highlight the major issues that have been raised. First we review the empirical contributions in inter-industry trade analysis. Subsequently intra-industry studies, including the calibration studies of strategic trade policy models, are considered. In reviewing the empirical studies we also very briefly mention some of the basic theoretical issues which at times provided the framework for the empirical exercises and on other occasions developed out of the analysis of empirical findings themselves.

4.2   EMPIRICAL ANALYSIS OF INTER-INDUSTRY TRADE FLOWS: SOME IMPORTANT ISSUES

At the very core of the neo-classical factor proportions theory – which itself is an outgrowth of the Ricardian theory of comparative advantage – is the proposition that trade between countries will be determined mainly by the concordance of the pattern of the factor endowment of trading countries with the factor intensities of the production processes of the commodities traded. Thus, pre-trade commodity price relationships will reflect differences in initial factor endowments through factor price ratios. In turn, this will determine the composition of exports and imports, once trade is opened up.

The proponents of the H–O–S theory see it as both positive and normative. Within its first capacity it can be predictive in the sense that it will be able, if a highly restrictive set of assumptions is held valid,[1] to indicate the commodity composition of trade between countries with different types of factor endowments. Under such conditions – and perhaps even without the fulfilment of some of them – the theory can explain what actually takes place. More significantly, the theory is held to be normative in the sense that the predicted pattern of production and trade would be consistent (under a rigorously defined set of welfare criteria) with the optimal national and international allocation of resources.

Empirical studies deal with the positive, or 'revealed', pattern of trade flows and product characteristics, but what is thus observed in reality is almost always 'distorted' by conditions that are different from those assumed by the H–O–S theorem. Hence, even paradoxical findings such as those reached by Leontief need not refute the normative aspects of the theory. However, the jolt was strong enough and the lack of normative properties in *some* of the assumptions of the H–O–S theory was clear enough to induce further theoretical and empirical investigations.

Human capital endowments

One of the directions taken by such investigations was to stress the fact that physical capital is only one form of produced means of production and that the other, and equally important, form is skill, which requires acts of investment in much the same way as the accumulation of physical assets. According to this line of reasoning, the concordance between the endowment of human capital and the human capital intensity of the production process is an important determinant of the commodity composition of trade. Leontief himself favoured such an explanation as a way out of his 'paradox'. He re-estimated his model (Leontief, 1956) using the 1951 trade pattern of the USA and disaggregating the total labour force into different occupational classes with differing skill intensities. His results showed that US exports embody considerably more labour skill than US imports, but the paradox with respect to physical capital remained. Since then this extended version of the factor proportions theory has provided the framework for a large amount of empirical work, aimed not only at overturning the Leontief paradox, but also at ascertaining an optimal inter-industry mix in the international division of labour. The main earlier, empirical contributions in this area came from R. E. Baldwin (1971), Bharadwaj and Bhagwati (1967), Branson (1971, 1973), Fels (1972), Keesing (1965, 1968), Roskamp and McMeekin (1968) and Waehrer (1968).

Various methods have been used to construct an index of skill or human capital intensity. It has been measured on the basis of the importance of different occupational groups in the production of exports and imports. Again, costs of human capital have been calculated based on the sum of the direct costs of education and training plus forgone earnings. Further, assuming that human capital is reflected in earned income, wage differentials of skilled labour relative to unskilled labour have been calculated to capitalise such differentials at some appropriate discount rate. All these measures have their limitations, yet, on the basis of the results of the empirical studies mentioned above, it is now widely believed that the concordance between the endowment of human capital and the human capital intensity of the production process is an important determinant of the commodity composition of trade. This is believed to have significant policy implications for the industrial division of labour,[2] particularly between the high-income and the developing countries (Fels, 1972).

Natural resources

The two-factor assumption of the H–O–S theorem is of course a simplification, and some economists have raised the question of whether the omission of natural resources from Leontief's calculations could explain the paradox. Vanek (1959) defined natural resources as products of extractive industries such as agriculture, forestry and mining, and investigated the importance of such products in US trade during the period 1870–1955. He found that over that period the USA had become a net importer of the services of natural resources. He also found a strong positive correlation between capital and natural resource requirements. This led him to conclude that while capital is actually relatively abundant in the USA, relatively less of its productive services are exported that would be needed for replacing imports because the *scarce* natural resource factor can enter productive processes only in conjunction with *large* amounts of capital. Diab (1956) also argued that the resource-based, non-manufacturing group would account for a large part of the high capital content of American imports. An almost standard device, which researchers now use and which implicitly recognises the problem posed by the omission of natural resources from the theoretical framework, is to work with a sample containing only manufactured products, presumably with low natural resource content.

Similarity of production functions

In a conceptually powerful attack on the similarity-of-production-functions assumption of the H–O–S theorem, Minhas (1963) argued that with different elasticities of substitution between labour and capital, it is inevitable that at some critical values of factor price ratios, industries will change their *relative* factor intensities. If these 'critical values' fell within the observable range of relative prices of labour and capital, then commodities could not be unambiguously ranked according to their factor intensities and the H–O–S model would break down. Minhas claimed that such *factor intensity reversals* do take place. Using elasticities of substitution obtained through constant elasticity of substitution (CES) production functions,and taking the range of relative factor price ratios given by those prevailing in India and the USA, he demonstrated such reversals for five pairs of industries. His comparison of factor intensity *rankings* between the USA and Japan yielded a rank correlation coefficient of 0.73 when only direct capital and labour requirements were taken into account, but it fell to 0.33 when both direct and indirect factor requirements were taken together

Although Minhas's findings opened up an important area of research, subsequent investigations by Hufbauer (1970), Lary (1968), Leontief (1964) and others suggested that factor intensity reversals may not be widely prevalent if we exclude natural-resource-intensive industries from the sample and take into account only direct factor intensities. Because most of the empirical analyses deal with manufacturing industries, and since intermediate and final product industries are locationally separable, researchers have in general tended to accept the refutation of the thesis on Minhas. This is also implied in the use, in much of the econometric work on the commodity composition of trade, of factor intensities observed in one country (usually the USA) as a proxy for factor intensities in al countries. Whether such an assumption of 'non-reversals' can be extended to all product characteristics is an open question.

Technology gap trade

In a major extension of our knowledge of the determinants of comparative advantage, Posner (1961) advanced the technological gap theory which stresses those elements that provide a firm or country with a comparative advantage due to product innovation rather than lower costs. A somewhat similar, and yet conceptually distinct, explanation was offered by Vernon (1966) in his 'product life cycle' theory, which postulates exporting and investment abroad as separate stages in the same dynamic process by which firms with a monopolistic advantage – acquired mainly due to product innovation – expand to foreign markets in order to conserve their leadership.

The introduction of technology as a separate independent variable in explaining the commodity composition of trade poses a number of conceptual and empirical problems. Part of the difficulty is that technology is a dynamic phenomenon, and hence difficult to quantify and inappropriate to introduce in static empirical tests. It is also closely related to some of the other explanatory variables which are believed to be important, namely human capital, product differentiation and economies of scale. Further, technological knowledge is not, at least in market economies, a free good. If it were, there would not be any incentive for private firms to invest in its creation. Innovations and their commercial use are protected by patents and copyrights which institutionalise, at least temporarily, 'imperfect competition'. Thus in this set of theories, a certain form of imperfect competition becomes a necessary condition for the creation of comparative advantage.

A number of studies have included a technology variable in tests designed to verify the determinants of the commodity composition of trade. We shall mention only a few of them here. In a study by Gruber and Vernon (1970), technology-intensive industries were considered as those in which the number of engineers and scientists amounted to 6 per cent of total industry employment. Only in the case of US exports did the technology intensity variable yield an unambiguously significant result. Hirsch (1974) attempted to study the neo-factor proportions and neo-technology accounts of international trade. Not surprisingly, he found that the country *endowment* measures for physical and human capital, as well as the technology factors, were inter-correlated with each other, and with per capitum income. He ranked industries according to their correlation between export performance and average value-added per employee (representing capital and skill endowments), and compared these rankings with rankings based on neo-technology and neo-factor proportions variables. This exercise yielded some interesting insights, particularly about the choice of industries suitable for different phases of economic development,[3] but the apparent close correlation between the variables used makes a clear distinction between the determinants difficult.

Aquino (1981) investigated the shifts over time of comparative advantage in manufactures from technology-rich towards technology-poor countries within the framework of the orthodox version of the product life cycle model. The method used by Aquino was to try to explain the Balassa index of 'revealed comparative advantage'[4] of particular countries in given products for chosen years, first by the technology endowment and home market size of the countries concerned, and second by these two variables plus physical capital endowment. Although Aquino measured the technology endowments for fifteen out of the twenty-six countries in his sample on the basis of past expenditures on research and development activities, number of innovations per capitum, and total wage cost per working hour, he found that a crude measure – such as gross domestic product (GDP) per capitum – empirically performed just as well as a proxy for technology endowment. The variations in the sign and level of significance shown by the technology coefficients across industries and over the period of time considered are interpreted by the author as evidence of the extension, pace and timing of the shifts of comparative advantage in each class of products towards countries with lower technology endowment. However, given the strong correlation between the independent variables, doubts can be expressed about the possibility of the correct interpretation of the results.

Multi-country, multi-industry studies

In a study that is justly considered as a watershed in the empirical testing of trade theories, Hufbauer (1970) used a cross-section, multi-country, multi-industry approach and sought to determine which set of models best explains actual international trade patterns. He computed rank correlation between national attributes such as GDP per capitum, shares of manufacturing in GDP and of skilled employees in the labour force, and commodity attributes such as skill and capital intensities, scale economies and other characteristics. For most variables he found the correlations to be positive, which led him to suggest that actual trade patterns are explained by an amalgam of theories.

Subsequent research in this field has, by and large, leaned towards multiple regression analysis. As we have already noted, the strong intercorrelation between the explanatory variables poses a problem in this respect. Another difficulty is that some of the theories represented by the variables are static in nature, while others are dynamic.

Using a comparative cross-section regression analysis, Leamer (1974) sought to explain the commodity imports and the ratio of imports to exports for twelve Atlantic-area countries for the year 1958. In the first variant of the model, Leamer used development variables such as GNP and population in the exporting and importing countries, resistance variables such as tariff levels and distance to markets, and a number of national attributes representing the H–O–S, neo-factor proportions and neo-technology theories. One of his findings was that GNP and population variables offered the best predictions of the import: GNP ratio, and the distance and tariff variables the next best predictions. But when the ratio of imports to exports was used as the dependent variable, the group of factor endowment performed better than the trade-resistance and development variables.

A number of economists have attempted to derive policy implications from empirical analyses of the type mentioned above. We have already mentioned Hirsch's (1974) contribution in this context. Herman (1975) suggested a scheme of optional export composition for eleven groups of countries classified according to their physical and human endowments and taking into account industry characteristics. Balassa (1979a) went one step further and investigated the changing pattern of comparative advantage in manufactured goods. Out of thirty-six countries included in Balassa's sample, eighteen were classified as developed and eighteen as developing. For each country, regression equations were estimated relating their 'revealed' comparative advantage in 184 manufactured product categories to the relative capital intensity defined using both a stock and a flow measure. Next, he tested the hypothesis that the inter-country differences in the coefficients obtained in the above exercise can be explained by differences in country characteristics. This was done by regressing the coefficients estimated for the individual countries on variables representing their physical and human capital endowments. This is the empirical basis for Balassa's *stages* approach to comparative advantage, according to which the structure of exports changes with the accumulation of physical and human capital.

Some of the studies published in late 1970s and early 1980s shed further light on the Leontief paradox and, more significantly, suggested better ways of comparing the factor requirements of trade when more than two commodities, factors and countries are involve. The theoretical basis of these contributions was an earlier paper of Vanek (1968), in which he tried to develop a theorem for rigorously analysing the factor content structure of trade when trading partners are endowed with more than two factors of production. An important element of his contribution was to show that under certain assumptions, the factor content of a country's trade can be inferred from a chain of factor endowment rankings. In an article published a decade later, Harkness (1978) carried out regression analysis using US data to show how net commodity exports can be predicted from the knowledge of the intensity of the use of factors in producing such commodities. He also argued that a ranking of the coefficients on each factor intensity in the regression equation will duplicate a ranking of the corresponding relative factor abundances. But the claim of Harkness that such an approach can be seen as a test of the H–O–S theorem was disputed by Leamer and Bowen (1981), who pointed out that the H–O–S theory, which assumes constancy of the factor intensities across countries, implies relationships among commodity outputs and factor inputs for all countries. This constancy cannot be tested with reference to data from a single country alone.

In another contribution, Leamer (1980) interpreted Vanek's (1968) generalisation of the H–O–S theorem to more than two goods and two factors to argue that the Leontief paradox rests on a simple conceptual misunderstanding According to Leamer, if the capital per person embodied in exports is less than the capital per person embodied in import, then the proposition that the country is poorly endowed in capital relative to labour is true only if the net exports of labour services is of the oposite sign to the net exports of capital services. When both are positive, as in the case of Leontief's study, the proper comparison, according to Leamer, is between capital per person embodied in *net* exports and capital per person embodied in *consumption*. Stern and Maskus (1981) adapted their methodology to take into account Leamer's strictures and found that although the Leontief paradox held for the year 1958, it was reversed by the year 1972, probably because of the decline in the relative importance of imports of natural resource-intensive goods.

In the same article, Stern and Maskus also used regression methods to analyse changes in the determinants of the structure of US foreign trade over the period 1958–76. They started out with a model in which physical capital, human capital and unskilled labour were the main explanatory variables. Subsequently they introduced more refined measures of human capital, together with some technological variables. The first version of the model (using three direct factor inputs) provided·a reasonable interpretation of US trade in manufactures, but physical capital yielded a negative sign. Following an approach used by Harkness and Kyle (1975), Stern and Maskus then tried probit[5] analysis for each year for the sample and this time the physical capital yielded a positive sign, although it was never statistically significant. The technological variables they used in further variations of their original model showed a positive correlation with net exports. Similar findings concerning physical capital (as well as for human capital) for the USA were also obtained by Branson and Monoyios (1977).

A subsequent study, by Bowen, Leamer and Sveikauskas (1987), is base on the idea that an appropriate test of the Heckscher–Ohlin theory requires independent measures of trade flows, factor input requirements and factor endowments. They use data for a sample of twenty-seven countries and twelve factors of production embodied in those countries' net exports, calculated by using the US matrix of total input requirements for 1967. The authors claim to perform a valid test of the Heckscher-Ohlin-Vanek (H–O–V) hypothesis of an exact relationship between factors of production embodied in a country's exports and imports and excess factor supplies. This means that, having calculated the factor service embodied in a country's exports and imports, one might find that a country is, for example, a net exporter of the factor of production with which is relatively abundantly endowed. The empirical results do not confirm the predictions of the theory. When comparing the ratios of net factor exports and the abundance ratios for each factor, the sign match is higher than 70 per cent only in the case of four out of the twelve factors. Their results suggest that the effects of endowments as presented in the strong version of the Heckscher–Ohlin theory may not be considered as the most important trade determinant.[6]

After having cast doubt on the usefulness of factor abundance measures infered from regression studies carried out over the past thirty years, Bowen and Sveikauskas (1989) launched a rescue operation to reconcile the two different approaches that have attempted to test the Heckscher–Ohlin theory: (a) those which used the inter-industry regression methodology to infer factor abundance and (b) the studies dealing with the relation between factors embodied in trade and measures of factor endowment.

After undertaking inter-industry regressions for thirty-five countries and the 'rest of the world', they compared the sign of the significant regression coefficients with revealed factor abundance as measured by the countries' net trade in factor services. The results indicated that the sign of the regression coefficients obtained by approach (a) can be taken as reliable indicators of revealed factor abundance.

The chain of comparative advantage

As we have seen in the analysis so far, empirical testing has dealt with the commodity version and the factor content version of the H–O–S theorem, and has sought to extend it beyond the two-factor, two-good, two-country model. Substantial progress has been made both at the theoretical and empirical levels in the work concerning the factor content version of the theorem. As far as the commodity version of the theory is concerned, a number of difficulties remain, particularly in generalising it. Nevertheless, theoretical work (see Deardorff, 1980, 1982) indicated that considerable headway is being made. In concluding this section with inter-industry trade flows we shall briefly note empirical work that has been carried out on one particular aspect of the generalised commodity version of the H–O–S theorem. This investigation deals with the so-called 'chain of comparative advantage'. Writings of R. E. Baldwin (1979), Deardorff (1979), Krueger (1977) and Yungho You (1979) suggest that although the H–O–S theorem must hold valid in constructing some ranking of commodities to predict the pattern of trade between any two countries, in a world of unequal factor prices it need not hold in this 'ordering sense' for a country's trade under conditions of factor price non-equalisatfon. Stated otherwise, the pattern of a country's multilateral trade is likely to be inconsistent with the rankings constructed according to the H–O–S proposition, although, interestingly, it will hold between any pair of countries.[7] R. E. Baldwin's (1979) analysis of thirty countries yielded some partial evidence as to the validity of this proposition. C. Hamilton and Svensson (1984) have investigated the proposition that when trade flows are broken down regionally, the basket of exports from a capital-abundant country to a labour-abundant one could be expected to be more capital-intensive than the basket of imports from the labour-abundant country. Analising eleven industrialised countries, Hamilton and Svensson found considerable empirical support for this particular formulation of the H–O–S theorem. A clear exception was Latin America, the trade flows of which appeared to be more capital abundant than that of most industrialised countries.

4.3 INTRA-INDUSTRY TRADE AND STRATEGIC TRADE POLICY MODELS: EMPIRICAL CONTRIBUTIONS

The empirical phenomenon that a country may export and import varieties of the same basic product, exhibiting similar factor requirements, motivated trade theorists to search for alternative models of trade. Through the marriage of international economics with industrial organisation this search ended up in two main groups of models: intra-industry trade models and models of strategic trade policy. Intra-industry trade models provide an explanation for the simultaneous export and import of fairly similar goods. In these model countries' markets are characterised by imperfect competition involving differentiated products and increasing returns to scale. The opening of trade results in greater product variety, rationalisation effects and increased competition with a consequent reduction in costs and prices. Also within the framework of models that attribute trade to imperfect competition we find the 'strategic trade policy models'. The basic argument of the model initially developed by Brander and Spencer (1983) is that in many industries where economies of scale are large enough and act as a barrier to entry, firms can earn above-normal profits. If this argument is correct, government targeting policies could be developed to shift profits in favour of domestic firms, hence raising national welfare at the expense of other nations.

For obvious reasons, the empirical analysis of the intra-industry trade and strategic trade policy models do not share a common methodology. In general, intra-industry models have been analysed by means of econometric studies, while strategic trade policies models have been subject to empirical evaluation through calibration/counterfactual experiments.

4.4   EMPIRICAL ANALYSIS OF INTRA-INDUSTRY TRADE FLOWS: SOME IMPORTANT ISSUES

Sources of intra-industry trade

Intra-industry trade, or the simultaneous export and import of products which are very close substitutes for each other in terms of factor inputs and consumption, remained for a long time an empirical phenomenon in search of a theory. Some of the hypotheses that were advanced mainly within the framework of *inter*-industry trade analysis were later found to be more suitable for explaining *intra*-industry trade. This is particularly true of the contributions of Linder (1961) and Drèze (1960, 1961).

The crux of Linder's argument is that while factor endowments, as well as the process of product development, innovation and economies of scale, can create export potential in certain goods, this potential can be developed only if substantial domestic demand for the product exists. Once domestic commerce is developed on the basis of such demand, international trade can follow, particularly between countries that have similar (but differentiated) domestic demand patterns. If income levels are good proxies for patterns of domestic demand, it would then mean that, unlike in the case of H–O–S theorem, the international trade propensity will be the highest between countries having similar per capitum income levels.

However as Drèze's work suggested, the existence of similar income levels and product differentiation need not by themselves lead to intra-industry trade unless the interaction of such product differentiation with economies of scale is introduced into the argument. While high and similar income levels would give rise to a demand for different varieties of products in the two countries being considered, each country will be able to produce only a sub-set of products within each group of industry if economies of scale in production are to be reaped. Under such circumstances, intra-industry specialisation and trade will develop between countries with similar income levels and factor endowment patterns.

More specifically within the framework of intra-industry trade analysis, Krugman (1979) and others have stressed the crucial role of economies of scale. If an industry consists of a large number of firms all producing somewhat differentiated products and all operating on the downward-sloping parts of their average cost curves, then there will be two-way international trade within an industry, because firms in different countries will produce alternative differentiated products. What prevents firms in each country from producing a complete range of products domestically is the existence of fixed costs of production.

The above line of analysis suggests that variables such as similarity of factor endowment patterns between trading countries, the prevalence of product differentiation and economies of scale are important determinants of intra-industry trade. Further, such trade could also arise for more prosaic reasons such as transport costs and protectionist policies, seasonal variations between countries, entrepôt arrangements and cross-hauling by multinational companies (Grubel and Lloyd, 1975). But the introduction of variables such as product differentiation and economies of scale raises some important questions that have relevance to welfare and policy analysis. These have been dealt with elsewhere (see Lancaster, 1980; Greenaway, 1982).

Categorical aggregation

In addition to the late development of a theoretical base, conceptual ambiguities about the notion of an 'industry' impeded the growth of systematic, advanced, econometric work in the field of intra-industry trade. In fact there is no unanimity as to what level of international trade classification corresponds to an 'industry' and hence is most suitable for the calculation of intra-industry trade indices. In practice, the two-, three- or four-digit levels of the Standard Industrial Trade Classification (SITC) ar often used in the estimates, although a clear preference for the third digit is discernible in empirical work. SITC three-digit groups often contain products of heterogeneous characteristics (see R. E. Lipsey, 1976). However, the use of more detailed systems of classification in the estimates does not necessarily solve the problem for, as Balassa (1979b) correctly points out, a too-detailed system of disaggregation would tend to separate commodities that are good substitutes in production. The problem is complicated by the fact that there is no unique criterion that is used for the re-grouping of commodities within the classification systems used for reporting international trade data.

Economists have reacted in different ways to the apparent problem posed by categorical aggregation. Some (R. E. Lipsey, 1976; Finger, 1975) have argued that most of the observed intra-industry trade can be explained away by the level of aggregation of the data used, and that intra-industry trade is in effect nothing much more than a 'statistical artefact'. Another type of reaction (see, e.g., Lundberg and Hansson, 1985) has been to argue that the important point to verify is whether the variation of factor intensity within the levels of aggregation at which intra-industry trade is observed is less than that *between* such aggregation levels. If that is the case, the costs of industrial structural adjustment – the process by which the factors of production move from stagnant sectors to sectors with growth potential – resulting from the increases in intra-industry trade is likely to be less than those from adjustments to inter-industry trade. The implicit reasoning here is that the costs of such shifts are inverse to the degree of the homogeneity of the factor input requirements. Thirdly, econometricians testing the determinants of intra-industry trade have attempted to take into account the aggregation problem by including in their specifications a variable which captures the degree of aggregation, but the results obtained by such exercises, though not always conclusive, suggest that inter-industry variations in intra-industry trade cannot be explained away by the level of aggregation used (see Greenaway and Milner, 1983b).

Intra-industry trade and trade imbalance

Economists have used different methods to measure the level of intra-industry trade. A number of these methods have similar properties. As they have been surveyed elsewhere (see Tharakan, 1981), here we will refer only to an important controversy that has arisen concerning the necessity for correcting the intra-industry trade index for trade imbalance.

The most extensively used formula in the intra-industry trade literature is the Grubel and Lloyd (1975) measure.[8] The index obtained by their particular formula would vary between 0 and 100, with the former representing complete inter-industry trade and the latter complete intra-industry trade. But Aquino (1978) has established that such an index would be biased downwards owing to (multilateral aggregate) trade imbalances. Assuming that the imbalancing effect of the total trade surplus or deficit is equiproportional in all industries, Aquino proposed that, first, estimates of what the values of exports and imports of each commodity would have been if total exports had been equal to total imports should be carried out; using these 'corrected' values, intra-industry trade indices at various levels of aggregation could be measured.[9] But the so-called Aquino correction has drawn criticism (see Greenaway and Milner, 1981; Bergstrand, 1983) for its restrictive assumptions and implicit neglect of important developments in international trade theory such as those contributed by R. E. Baldwin (1979) and Deardorff (1979), which we have mentioned in the context of the chain of comparative advantage notion. Other authors have also proposed measures with interesting properties (see Glejser, Goossens and Vanden Eede, 1982; Bergstrand, 1983; and Greenaway and Milner, 1983b).

Econometric analysis of intra-industry trade

The econometic analysis of intra-industry trade has grown substantially in recent years. A detailed survey of the contents of such studies is impossible within the scope of this chapter. We shall attempt to illustrate some of the important findings by dividing them into two categories: those dealing with the intra-industry trade between countries with similar factor endowments patterns, and those between countries with different factor endowment patterns.

The first mentioned type of studies include, among others, those by Bergstrand (1983), Hansson and Lundberg (1989), Helpman (1987), Loertscher and Wolter (1980), Marvel and Ray (1987) and Pagoulatos and Sorensen (1975).

One of the early concerns of the researchers in this field was the relationship between trade obstacles and intra-industry trade. In their econometric work, Pagoulatos and Sorenson (1975) used data on US intra-industry trade with the rest of the world in 102 industries (at three-digit SITC) in 1965 and 1967 as the dependent variable. Among the eight exogenous variables used in their specification, four pertained to trade barriers. They were: average height of tariff barriers, the height of non-tariff barriers, the USA–EEC tariff differential, and the non-tariff barrier differential. Of these four variables, the height of non-tariff barriers and the non-tariff barriers differential did not yield significant coefficients. In order to test whether the similarity in per capitum income exerts a positive influence on intra-industry trade, a variable defined as the percentage of the total OECD–USA trade in manufactures in *total* US trade in manufactures was also used. This variable yielded the expected positive sign and was significant at the 1 per cent level. Similar significance was also shown by a variable consisting of the mean distance shipped, suggesting that intra-industry trade is higher for commodities that have small transportation costs. The variable that was used for taking into account the level of aggregation yielded a coefficient with positive sign and was significant at the 5 per cent level, suggesting that some of the observed intra-industry trade is simply the result of statistical aggregation. But the proxy used for taking into account the more than average degree of product differentiation did not give any significant results in the regressions for 1965 and 1967.

Loertscher and Wolter (1980) tried to explain differences in intra-trade intensity among countries *and* across industries simultaneously. They used a sample of bilateral trade flows among OECD (Organisation for Economic Coöperation and Development) countries. Among the determinants of intra-industry trade postulated by them, they made a distinction between 'country hypotheses' and 'industry hypotheses'. It was expected that intra-industry trade among countries would be intense if the average of their development (average per capitum income) was high, differences in their levels of development relatively small, the average of their market size small, barriers to trade low, geographical, linguistic and cultural differences small, and the trade partners belonged to the same customs union or had common borders. The industry hypotheses postulated that intra-industry trade would be intense if the potential for product differentiation was high, transaction costs low and the definition of industry comprehensive. A Grubel–Lloyd-type measure of intra-industry trade and an equivalent of the Aquino correction were tried as alternative dependent variables. Pooling of the country observations and industry observation was apparently used. Results indicated that the intra-industry trade intensity across countries was significantly and negatively correlated with differences in stage of development, differences in market size and the distance between the trading partners, although the performance of the last-mentioned variable was clearly misinterpreted. The correlation was significant and positive for the average market size and the existence of

customs union. Among the product hypothesis, the level of aggregation and proxy for product group showed positive an significant correlation. The product differentiation variable gave neither a consistent nor
significant result. The proxy for scale of production was significant and
had a negative sign. The total explanatory power of the equation was
low.

Bergstrand (1983), by extending the model of Yungho You (1979),
which we have already referred to in the context of the 'chain of comparative advantage', has shown that the presence of intra-industry trade
at the multilateral level is not surprising, but it is at bilateral level. The
reason is the inability of the generalised commodity version of the
H–O–S theorem to hold valid for a country's multilateral trade while it
remains valid at the bilateral level, and hence at the latter level the
prevalence of intra-industry trade needs an 'explanation'. Balassa
(1986) has examined the determinants of intra-industry trade in bilateral trade among thirty-eight countries including a number of developing countries. The explanatory variables included: inequality of income
levels between countries, country size, distance, trade orientation of the
countries, plus a number of dummies[10] to represent participation in
integration arrangements, common language groups and the existence
of former colonial ties. The results indicated that the common country
characteristics explained much of the variation in the extent of intra-
industry trade and the introduction of variables for economic integration, common language and colonial ties augmented the explanatory
power of the regression equation relatively little, except in explaining
intra-industry trade among developing countries.

Exploring the hypothesis that a larger share of intra-industry trade is
associated with similarities in income per capitum, Helpman (1987)
confirms the results of Loertscher and Wolter (1980). Helpman's study
uses a large data set for both manufacturing and non-manufacturing
industries for a group of fourteen developed nations. Carrying out
cross-section comparisons, over time, the author is able to confirm the
link between a larger share of intra-industry trade with a lower degree
of dispersion in per capitum income. One interesting feature of the
study is that the strong relation in the bilateral trade flows between the
share of intra-industry trade and the similarity in income per capitum
weakens towards the end of the sample period. Helpman suggests that
the influence of multinational corporations in the volume of trade might
provide an alternative explanation to this phenomenon.

In their study Hansson and Lundberg (1989) analyse inter- and intra-industry trade, using a conventional neo-classical two-factor multi-sector model for the production side with the assumption that goods are not homogeneous on the demand side, but differentiated with respect to country of origin. They show that the share of intra-industry trade will be lowest in sectors with extreme factor requirements, e.g., for industries with very high or very low capital intensity. Further, some measures of factor proportions are likely to be related to the elasticity of substitution in demand between products of different origin, thus affecting intra-industry trade. Their empirical tests are carried out using Swedish data.

The results obtained by Marvel and Ray (1987) are inconsistent with the dominant product differentiation scale economies model of intra-industry trade. They show that two-way trade flows occur where conditions are favourable to an international division of labour and demonstrate that intra-industry trade has the effect of mitigating protection. Other authors (see Tharakan and Kol, 1989) have also stressed the complementarity between the sources of intra-industry and inter-industry trade.

Empirical studies on the intra-industry trade of the developing countries remained an underresearched area for a long time, but increasing attention has been paid to this area in recent years. The nature and coverage of the main studies on intra-industry trade of (with) the developing countries can be summarised as follows. Three such studies (Laird, 1981; Lee, 1987; and Gunasekera, 1989) are general appraisals. Schumacher's (1983) study took into account the Federal Republic of Germany's intra-industry trade with the developing countries, while Tharakan (1989) analysed bilateral intra-industry trade flows of selected EC countries with certain developing countries for some manufactured products at very detailed (SITC 5 digits) level. The studies of Willmore (1972) and Balassa (1979b) dealt with economic integration and intra-industry trade in South American countries. Eight papers (Havrylyshyn and Civan, 1983; Tharakan, 1984, 1986; Balassa, 1985; Lee, 1989; Forstner and Ballance, 1990; Ray, 1991; and Fukasaku, 1992) contain econometric exercises. Note that the studies of Havrylyshyn and Civan (1983), Balassa (1985) and Forstner and Ballance (1990) cover a broader area than the intra-industry trade of the developing countries, but they also take into account the intra-industry trade of a large number of developing countries. Similarly the papers of Lee (1989) and Fukasaku (1992) cover the Pacific basin countries which include some industrialised and some newly-industrialising countries (NICS). Ray (1991) analyses the intra-industry trade of some industrialised countries and developing countries.

Generalising broadly, one could sum up the main findings of these studies as follows. Intra-industry trade of the developing countries in manufactures is far from negligible when considered at the level of aggregation (corresponding in most cases more or less to the equivalent of 3- or 4-digit SITC used in most of these studies. Intra-industry trade appears not only in the case of NICs where it is very important and growing rapidly, but also in the trade of other developing countries between themselves and between the developing countries and the industrialised world. Membership of a customs union or a regional grouping seems to influence intra-industry trade positively, particularly among the members of that group. But it is not clear whether this is because of the reduction of trade obstacles or the geographical proximity of the member countries. There is also the likelihood that trade-diverting associations do not contribute to the growth of intra-industry trade. Similarly, the generalised scheme of preferences (GSP) does not seem to contribute to intra-industry trade between the industrialised countries. Further similarity in income levels and the stage of industrialisation appear to contribute to intra-industry trade. In such cases it might be due to the preference similarity as Linder (1961) has suggested, supplemented by the interaction between product differentiation and economies of scale. The commodity composition of intra-industry trade between small industrialised countries and developing countries appears to be influenced by the interaction between product differentiation and economies of scale. But this variable does not seem to explain the intra-industry trade between the larger industrialised countries and the developing world. In general the country characteristics appear to be more consistent than the product characteristics in explaining the intra-industry trade involving the developing countries. Some studies show that vertical product differentiation (quality difference) is significant in explaining the intra-industry trade between the developing countries and industrialised countries. Since in such models the quality difference is determined by relative factor inputs, this explanation goes some way towards reconciling such intra-industry trade with the Heckscher–Ohlin theory. The finding that the intra-industry trade between the industrialised countries and developing countries is concentrated in intermediate goods using labour-intensive technique also suggests that sub-contracting might explain part of the observed intra-industry trade.

Calibration studies of strategic trade policy models

The calibration methodology is familiar from computable general equilibrium models and has an analogy in comparative statics. The basic procedure consists of specifying a partial equilibrium model capturing the imperfect competitive features of an industry. In the next step estimates of some of the parameters (demand elasticities, average price, average quantity produced, etc.) are taken from existing industry studies and econometric estimates. The other parameters are inferred by calibrating the model using a benchmark period's data base. This procedure will then produce an equilibrium that replicates the historically observed prices, quantities and market shares. Finally, the counterfactual step implies allowing for changes in the parameters (trade policy in the forms of import tariffs or export subsidies or a combination of both), and simulating the new resulting equilibrium prices and quantities. Although calibration studies have not been primarily intended to analyse the determinants of the patterns of trade (their main purpose has been to quantify welfare effects of trade policies and optimum targeting of trade and industrial policies) they do provide indications of the determinants of trade flows in industries characterised by imperfect competition.

Review of the results of calibration studies

Empirical evaluation of strategic trade policies started with the pioneering works of Venables and Smith (1986), R. Baldwin and Krugman (1988a) and Dixit (1988), all of them sharing the common methodology of calibration.[11] The approach used by these studies is based on partial equilibrium, with an emphasis on calculating the impact of trade policy changes in an industry or sub-set of industries without taking into account cross-sector and factor price effects between industries.

Existing calibration studies have concentrated on identifying sources of welfare gains in imperfect competitive settings characterised by (a) strategic trade policies in the form of rent-shifting or strategic infant industry arguments (as defined by R. Baldwin (1988) and (b) increased competition in the domestic market and increased product variety, this last application having been initiated by Smith and Venables (1988) and followed by the same authors in series of articles.

Calibration studies have been used to simulate the effects of hypothetical trade and industrial policies in several industries. There have been calibration studies done on the UK refrigerator and footwear industries by Venables and Smith (1986); the market for Airbus's A300 and Boeing's 767 by R. Baldwin and Krugman (1988a); the automobile industry by Dixit (1988), Laussel, Montet and Peguin-Feissolle (1988), Digby, Smith and Venables (1988) and Krishna, Hogan and Swagel (1989); semiconductors by R. Baldwin and Krugman (1988a); the 30–40 Seat Commuter Aircraft by R. Baldwin and Flam (1989); the Norwegian ski market and the Miami market for Caribbean cruises by Daltung, Eskeland and Norman (1987), and a set of industries by Venables and Smith (1986).

The classical work of Avinash Dixit (1988) on the US auto industry used a series of calibrated models to evaluate strategic trade policies. The US automobile market is modelled as a non-cooperative oligopoly, where cars are differentiated by nation of supply (USA or Japan) and produced by a fixed number of firms. The demand system is assumed to be linear, and the marginal costs of the firms in both countries are constant. Dixit calibrates his model with data taken from actual industries. For example, direct and cross-price elasticities of demand are taken from econometric estimates of the automobile market; the cost structure is derived from industry studies and the number of firms is derived indirectly by using Herfindahl indices. Given the first-order conditions for the typical firms, and the demand equations having already plugged into the system the missing parameters such as prices, quantities, costs, market share and elasticities for a base year, it is possible to solve for the remaining unknown parameters the conjectural variation (i.e. expectation by firms about how other firms will respond to their actions) parameters. The model specification is then completed with a US welfare function defined as the sum of consumer surplus, US firms' profits, government revenue and monopoly rents to labour. Once calibrated, the model is used to perform some policy experiments to compare the effectiveness of particular policy instruments, such as tariffs, production subsidies, or a combination of both. The results show an optimum tariff of 8–17 per cent when the tariff is the only instrument at hand. In case a subsidy to domestic production is also available, the optimal tariff is reduced. In spite of rent-shifting effects, i.e., increasing US firms' profits and causing reduction in Japanese imports,[12] in both of the cases the strategic welfare gains from the imposition of either an optimal tariff or subsidy are very small. Finally, and in contrast to total welfare gains, the redistribution effects are quite dramatic. This result could then trigger an additional incentive for interested groups in favour of an active rent-shifting policy by governments.[13]

R. Baldwin and Krugman (1988b) study the Japanese and US market of random access memory chips (RAMs) to investigate whether the alleged closure of the Japanese market enabled the industry to develop in Japan and become a net exporter.[14] In this case of a more dynamic industry, the authors assume free entry. The production of semiconductors is characterised by very steep learning curves with significant scale economies. The authors collapse this dynamic learning-by-doing into a one-shot static production function. The model is calibrated using the conjectural variation approach. The results show how strategic trade policies can strongly influence the pattern of trade specialisation. The study seems to confirm that protection has created an export-promoting effect. In an equilibrium calculated without Japanese tariffs, the Japanese industry disappears, while additional US firms enter the market.

Venables (1990b) undertakes a series of simulations to investigate the welfare implications of two trade policy instruments, an import tariff and an export subsidy. Different models of trade under imperfect competition are then applied to nine industries in the EC.[15] The simulations were undertaken for different types of competitive settings. These included price (Bertrand) and quantity (Cournot) competition, full market integration as well as an intermediate case of integrated market Cournot competition with firms playing a segmented market price game in a second stage, and oligopoly and monopolistic competition. In the cases of Bertrand and Cournot competition the markets are segmented, which means that firms' decisions are taken independently of events in other markets. With some degree of market integration, competition among firms take place in two steps. As a first step, firms choose total output, and at the second step the firms select the distribution of output between markets. The calibration of the models is somewhat different from the approach of Dixit (1988) and R. Baldwin and Krugman (1988b), who solve their model for the conjectural variation parameters. With limited information about the elasticity of substitution for different products, Venables assumes different forms of competition to solve the degree of product differentiation. According to the author, the observed data on trade and production suggests the presence of trade barriers. Using the same elasticity for each equilibrium type, the author calibrates a matrix of trade barriers compatible with firms' market share in different countries and trade flows.

In spite of changes in the functional form, calibration process and choice of industries, the results of the simulation do not differ much from other empirical studies of strategic trade policies. Venables' conclusions, which extend and enrich our understanding of the welfare implications of the use of trade policy instruments, can be summarised as follows.

1. The welfare gains derived from the use of trade policy instruments are very small. Allowing the possibility of free entry, the gains seem to be moderately larger.
2. The more concentrated the industry is, the larger the gain from a policy intervention will be. This results confirms general intuition in the sense that a tariff will improve the terms of trade of the tariff-imposing country. In addition welfare gains will be the result of distortions related with imperfect competition.
3. Although the welfare gains from strategic trade policies are very small, their quantitative effects can be very large. In the case of export subsidies especially, these quantitative effects can be particularly important. The author suggests the implementation of general equilibrium models of imperfect competition to obtain a better understanding of the effects of trade policy on factor markets.[16]
4. As in the previous studies by Venables and Smith, the choice of type of equilibrium does not seem to affect the sensitivity of the results. The results show a limited number of cases of sign reversals in welfare as a result of changes in the form of competition.

5 Strategic Trade Policy

KLAUS STEGEMANN

5.1 INTRODUCTION

The absorption of models of imperfect competition into the mainstream of international trade theory was possibly the most influential development in all of economic theory during the 1980s. Two principal strands have emerged in this new literature: one is the literature on intra-industry trade, which is surveyed by Henryk Kierzkowski in Chapter 1 above; the other major strand, to be reviewed here, has acquired the label 'strategic trade policy' for reasons that will soon become apparent.

The two types of model tend to focus on different features of imperfect competition. Models of intra-industry trade try to explain why similarly structured industrial countries trade so much with each other and why so much of their trade consists of similar products. What drives these models is product differentiation, with products (or variants) produced under conditions of increasing returns to scale; the number of producers is usually large and entry barriers are assumed to be unimportant.[1] Models of strategic trade policy, on the other hand, focus on the implications of assuming a small number of internationally competing producers, i.e., oligopoly or, typically, duopoly, with scale economies causing entry barriers that are substantial and secure. The attribute 'strategic' indicates that, in an oligopolistic model, policy-makers take into account a response by foreign firms or governments in calculating their best course of action.

Why are there policy-makers in these models, though, and what is the purpose of their strategic policy, which presumably differs from *laissez-faire* and free trade? In general terms, the objective of government intervention in models of strategic trade policy is to obtain rents or external benefits at the expense of other countries or to prevent them from doing this at our expense. Models designed to explain intra-industry trade usually imply that the production of traded goods is not associated with factor rents or external benefits, therefore the issue of whether policy-makers should promote the production of any particular product or variant of a product does not arise. Yet for models of strategic trade policy everything hinges on the assumption that rents, such as monopoly profits exist, or external benefits of production. Various models then demonstrate how government intervention could increase a country's share in these rents or benefits: 'profit shifting' or 'rent snatching' is the name of the game.

In the following sections, two of the most prominent original models of strategic trade policy are presented to convey what was new about the idea and why it has attracted so much attention. There then follows a summary of the large literature that appeared in response, including both theoretical and empirical work. The focus of this summary is the significance of strategic trade policy models for practical policy purposes.[2]

5.2 PROFIT SHIFTING BETWEEN COUNTRIES: AN EXTENSION OF STACKELBERG'S ASYMMETRIC DUOPOLY SOLUTION

Models of strategic trade policy attempt to formalise the popular notion that a government can enhance national welfare by promoting domestic development of industries that create substantial factor rents or external benefits.[3] In several pioneering articles, James Brander and Barbara Spencer demonstrated how government intervention might shift monopoly profits from a foreign producer either to the domestic treasury or to a domestic producer (Brander and Spencer, 1981, 1984, 1985; Spencer and Brander, 1983). Monopoly profits are assumed to occur for an international industry because entry to the industry is restricted. The idea of profit shifting can be explained most easily with reference to a 1985 version of the Brander–Spencer model which corresponds closely to Stackelberg's 'asymmetric' duopoly solution. Brander and Spencer (1985) assume an industry consisting of two firms making a homogeneous product. The two firms are located in two different countries and serve a common export market in a third country.

In fact, Brander and Spencer assume initially that all sales and profits are made in the third country. This assumption enables them to equate an increase in a national producer's profit (minus subsidies) with an increase in national welfare. The problem of profit shifting then is how intervention by the government of one of the producing countries can increase the profit that its domestic producer extracts from the duopolists' common export market.

Each firm in the Brander–Spencer model is assumed to use output as its strategic variable. Both are assumed to behave like Cournot duopolists, (i.e., each chooses its rate of deliveries to the common export market on the assumption that the other producer's rate of deliveries is given). In the absence of government intervention, the equilibrium in the Brander–Spencer model thus corresponds to the Cournot (Nash) solution. But as Stackelberg discovered 60 years ago, a sophisticated duopolist who anticipates the other firm's Cournot adjustment to his own output decision can do better than a Cournot duopolist. Compared to the Cournot solution, each of the suppliers can increase its profit by occupying an 'independent supply position' (now called 'Stackelberg leader' position) if its rival is content to take a Cournot duopolist's 'dependent supply position' (now called 'Stackelberg follower' position).[4] Brander and Spencer use exactly this idea for their basic model of international profit shifting, except that they cast the government of one of the producing countries in the role of a rule maker that manipulates its national firm to act as if it was the Stackelberg leader. Thus while both firms behave like Cournot duopolists all the time, one government is assumed to grant an export subsidy (which in this case is equivalent to a production subsidy) to induce its national champion to produce the volume that corresponds to the Stackelberg leader position, whereas the other government is assumed to remain inactive. The outcome is, of course, the same as for Stackelberg's asymmetric duopoly: the total volume of sales is increased by the intervention and per-unit profit falls, but because the follower 'makes room for the leader' the leading country's share of the market increases sufficiently to increase its total profit; meanwhile, the follower's profit is reduced because the follower sells a lower volume than it would without the intervention, and receives less per unit.

As acknowledged by Brander and Spencer, an 'important assumption' of their model is 'that the government understands the structure of the industry and is able to set a credible subsidy on exports in advance of the quantity decision by firms' (Brander and Spencer, 1985, p. 85).

Indeed, the assumption that a government can make a credible commitment to maintaining a leadership position while a firm cannot is the only reason why Brander and Spencer need (and can justify) government intervention in their model. Even without intervention, each duopolist would have an incentive to occupy the position of a Stackelberg leader if its rival were content to act as a follower, but moving from a Cournot equilibrium to a leadership position is not considered a 'credible choice' for either firm acting on its own. In the absence of government intervention, the two firms are assumed to be on an equal footing. Each knows that an expansion of output by either duopolist cannot be profitable if the other is determined not to retreat. An export subsidy for one firm changes the situation. Expansion of the subsidised firm's output is now regarded as a 'credible choice' by its rival because an expansion would be privately profitable even if the rival would not reduce its output. 'In essence, the government's prior action in setting a subsidy changes the domestic firm's set of credible actions' (Brander and Spencer, 1985, p. 89). This implies that the government which has acted is 'credibly committed' to its intervention; thus the foreign firm must believe that subsidisation would continue even in the event that the attempted profit shifting failed because the foreign firm refused to retreat. Brander and Spencer suggest that government intervention is credible in this sense because governments have an incentive, known to all agents, to maintain a 'reputation' for credibility (Brander and Spencer, 1985, p. 84).[5]

The essence of the Brander–Spencer model can be presented in Figure 5.1. It depicts each duopolist's reaction function, as well as two iso-profit curves for the home firm. Without government intervention, the equilibrium would be at point N, which is the familiar Cournot (Nash) equilibrium. The subsidy, by lowering the home firm's marginal cost, has the effect of shifting its reaction curve to the right. Therefore, a new Cournot (Nash) equilibrium is attained at a higher output level for the subsidised firm and a reduced output for its foreign rival. To be optimal from a national point of view, the rate of subsidisation must be such that it moves the equilibrium to point S, which is equivalent to Stackelberg's asymmetric solution that would be attained if the home firm were able to act as a leader in the absence of subsidisation. The home firm's iso-profit curve tangent to the foreign reaction curve at S represents a higher profit than the one going through N. Both represent profits net of subsidy payments. Thus the home country's income increases when the intervention causes the equilibrium to move from N to S.[6]

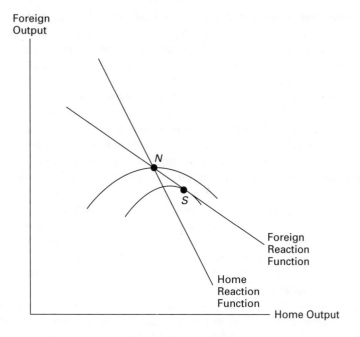

Foreign
Output

Home Output

Foreign
Reaction
Function

Home
Reaction
Function

FIGURE 5.1   Brander–Spencer profit shifting

Brander and Spencer are aware that it is not sufficient to simply show that one producing country has a unilateral incentive to capture a larger share of a profitable export market. 'Surely the two producing nations face similar incentives and there also may be some response by the importing nation' (Brander and Spencer, 1985, p. 94). They thus proceed to examine the case of a Cournot (Nash) equilibrium in subsidies in which each exporting country is assumed to choose its best subsidy level taking the subsidy level of the other country as given. Not surprisingly, Brander and Spencer arrive at the conclusion that the 'noncooperative solution is jointly suboptimal for the producing countries'; that means the total profit extracted from the export market is less than it would be with a cooperative solution (Brander and Spencer, 1985, p. 95). The jointly optimal policy would be for both producing countries to impose a tax on exports to the third country, thus shifting both duopolists' reaction curves inward. The optimum set of tax rates would be such that the duopolists are induced to move from the Cournot solution to the lower export levels of a profit-maximising cartel. Brander and Spencer assume that the producing countries are 'unable to make binding agreements of this sort' (1985, p. 96).

In sum, the Brander–Spencer model of strategic trade policy comprises all three cases that Stackelberg added to the Cournot solution: Stackelberg's asymmetric duopoly; the case of both duopolists trying to be leaders simultaneously (Bowley's Duopoly); and the case of joint monopolisation (Stackelberg, 1952, pp. 194–5). Each case can be brought about in the model by government intervention changing the 'set of credible actions' for one or both producers. Brander and Spencer emphasise the asymmetric case because they wish to demonstrate why a government might have an incentive to subsidise a home producer's profitable exports. But do they have a policy conclusion? While the first case suggests an aggressive policy, the second counsels retaliation (which might lead to mutually agreed policy abstention), and the third comes closest to orthodox theory in recommending agreed export restrictions to exploit jointly held market power. Brander admits that the policy implications of the profit-shifting model are not very robust to changes in assumptions, but believes that the basic point is more general than the specific model: 'This point is that government action can alter the strategic game played by foreign and domestic firms. In profitable markets domestic firms are made better off if foreign firms can be induced to contract (or to expand more slowly than they otherwise would)' (Brander, 1986, p. 30). Let us broaden the argument somewhat by reviewing one other prominent model of strategic trade policy before asking questions about the practical policy implications of the new theories.

5.3 RACING DOWN THE LEARNING CURVE: A STRATEGIC INFANT INDUSTRY ARGUMENT

Paul Krugman (1984) has designed a model that adds a strategic dimension to the familiar infant industry argument for government intervention. Both historically and in popular view the infant industry problem has always been perceived as a problem of international rivalry, and particularly policy rivalry between old industrial countries and aspiring ones. Alexander Hamilton, whose 1791 'Report on Manufactures' presented the reasons why he and many of his contemporaries believed that temporary protection was required to help fledgeling American manufacturing industries to get established, included the suggestion that conspiracies of foreign producers, possibly with the support of a foreign government, might have attempted to discourage the development of manufacturing in the USA. Indeed, the following passage describes very succinctly the interaction of moves and countermoves typical of strategic policy postures, and even includes the notion of credibility provided by state intervention:

> Combinations by those engaged in a particular branch of business in one country, to frustrate the first efforts to introduce it into another, by temporary sacrifices, recompensed perhaps by extraordinary indemnifications of the government of such country, are believed to have existed, and are not to be regarded as destitute of probability. The existence or assurance of aid from the government of the country, in which the business is to be introduced, may be essential to fortify adventurers against the dread of such combinations, to defeat their effects, if formed and to prevent their being formed, by demonstrating that they must in the end prove fruitless. (Hamilton, reprinted 1966, pp. 268–9).[7]

But as presented in contemporary trade texts until the early 1980s, the infant industry argument had been purged of its strategic dimension: i.e., the theoretical argument for intervention did not depend on recognised policy rivalry or on anticipated reactions by foreign rival firms.[8]

The thrust of the textbook argument has been that the case for supporting infant industries, if valid at all, is based on the existence of 'domestic distortions' in the intervening country (Corden, 1974, pp. 248–79; 1986, pp. 91–2). Three types of relevant distortion are commonly mentioned in the literature: imperfections in the capital market making it impossible (or too expensive) for potentially profitable new industries to get started; external benefits of learning-by-doing that occur when pioneering firms cannot retain the workers they train during the start-up phase; and external benefits of learning-by-doing due to knowledge diffusion, which again may be particularly significant during the infancy stage of an industry. For each type of distortion the optimum form of intervention is a domestic intervention, such as loan guarantees, training assistance or subsidies for research and development, respectively. Temporary protection of the home market would be an unnecessarily costly form of intervention, since the problem that policy-makers are trying to correct is not a 'trade distortion'. Foreign firms or foreign governments have no part to play in the traditional textbook exposition. The acting country is a small country taking world market prices as given. An intervention enabling an infant industry to slide down its learning curve gradually pushes out the country's production possibility frontier. National welfare increases because the country is able to do more with given resources. However, there are no rents to be shifted between countries and no responses are expected from foreign firms or governments. Being an extension of the traditional trade model, the traditional infant industry argument assumes a perfectly competitive world market, with numerous foreign firms that have finished learning, and a domestic industry that requires temporary assistance to catch up.

Krugman radically re-directed the focus of the analysis by making unorthodox assumptions which imply that there is an opportunity for a country to achieve a different kind of welfare gain through the strategic deployment of import restrictions. His analysis depends on two basic ingredients: international oligopoly and economies of scale. As regards oligopoly, Krugman assumes two firms, one domestic and one foreign. Each firm produces a single product which it sells in several markets, e.g., domestic and foreign, that are 'segmented' because of government policies. The products of the two firms are close substitutes, but need not be perfect substitutes. Like Brander and Spencer, Krugman assumes that both firms at all times act as Cournot duopolists. The result is 'a multi-market Cournot model' (Krugman, 1984, p. 182). As regards his second basic ingredient, Krugman distinguishes three different forms of scale economy leading to as many versions of his general model. It is only in the third version, when Krugman introduces economies of learning-by-doing, that his analysis comes close to the familiar infant industry argument, though the conclusion is the same in each version: by giving its domestic producer a privileged position in the home market, the country gives it an advantage in scale of production over a foreign rival. 'This scale advantage translates into lower marginal costs and higher market share even in unprotected markets' (Krugman, 1984, p. 181).

When one government excludes the foreign producer from a market previously open to it, the intervention causes opposite effects on the marginal cost of the two rivals. The domestic producer will sell more in its home market from which the foreign rival has been excluded and thus the domestic firm's marginal cost will fall; the foreign firm's marginal cost goes up as it produces less when excluded from the protected market.[9] But the effects do not end here because both firms are induced by opposite changes in their marginal cost to adjust sales also in unprotected markets. The domestic firm will expand its output further, while the foreign firm will retreat some more. These adjustments again have opposite effects on each firm's marginal cost, and the process continues until a new multi-market Cournot equilibrium is attained. The essential feature of the model thus is the circular causation from output to marginal cost to output; and it is this circularity that 'makes import protection an export promotion device' (Krugman, 1984, p. 185). Krugman does not provide a national welfare analysis for his model of strategic trade policy, yet, it is implied in his argument that additional exports are profitable for the domestic producer. It is, therefore, conceivable that the country's welfare increases because the additional profits on exports plus lower costs of output sold domestically outweigh the loss of consumer surplus caused by protection of the home market.

Krugman employs the same formal apparatus as Brander and Spencer, except for his assumptions concerning scale economies and market segmentation. Assume that Figure 5.1. above represented the home firm's export market. Home market protection in the Krugman model then moves out the home duopolist's reaction curve in the graph, but also shifts the foreign duopolist's reaction curve in the opposite direction (Krugman, 1984, pp. 186–7). The result is a new Cournot equilibrium where the home firm attains a higher market share in the export market for two reasons: its reduced marginal cost has made expansion attractive, and the foreign rival is willing to retreat. By symmetry, the foreign firm has two reasons to retreat: its rival's credible expansion, and its own higher marginal cost. As in the Brander–Spencer model, the strategic rationale of government intervention is that the intervention induces a profitable expansion of export sales when it would not be credible for a duopolist to attempt such an expansion on its own. Krugman does not determine the optimum level of intervention that would correspond to attaining the Stackelberg leadership position in the Brander–Spencer model; neither does he deal with the case of two (or more) countries facing similar incentives, let alone cases where countries of different size are involved.[10]

Racing down the learning curve in the Krugman model motivates government intervention only because of its strategic effect. While Krugman in one version of his model assumes 'dynamic' returns to scale that are associated also with the traditional infant industry argument, he does not depend on external benefits of learning-by-doing, or any other domestic distortion, to motivate government intervention.

Yet, much of the non-formal discussion of strategic trade policy, and of the 'technology race' in particular, has emphasised external benefits of generating knowledge as the reason for protecting or promoting certain strategic sectors. Indeed, in a subsequent paper, Krugman discounted the profit-shifting motive for strategic trade policy and suggested that 'the best bet for finding strategic sectors may be to focus on external benefits' (Krugman, 1987a, p. 221). But he then showed why only a sub-set of knowledge-generating industries might justify intervention to establish a domestic presence in those industries. In another paper, Krugman (1987b) emphasised the significance of dynamic scale economies and of the 'hysteresis' of government policy, as it is now called. The general point of such models is that trade patterns and potential gains from trade are more sensitive to policy intervention if one removes the orthodox assumptions of constant returns to scale and perfect competition. 'Particularly with dynamic increasing returns, current policy can have important permanent effects on trade because temporary learning advantages can lead to long-term comparative advantage' (Brander, 1987, p. 12).

5.4 LACK OF ROBUST POLICY IMPLICATIONS

There can be no doubt that the theory of international trade has been revitalised dramatically by at last receiving (accepting) an infusion of ideas from models that formerly were used almost exclusively for the field of domestic industrial organisation. The revitalisation has manifested itself as a rich and diversified yield of theoretical and empirical research. By design, this research came much closer than traditional international economics to dealing with problems that concern individual firms, industries, interest groups and policy-makers in the real world. However, the take-over of trade theory by imperfect competition theory would have been noticed only in seminar rooms and at academic conferences, and much less would have been written about it had the new literature not included these models of strategic trade policy with seemingly revolutionary policy implications. Avinash Dixit, who was one of the pioneers, though a sceptical one, summed it up as follows:

> Recent research contains support for almost all the vocal and popular views on trade policy that only a few years ago struggled against the economists' conventional wisdom of free trade. Now the mercantilist

arguments for restricting imports and promoting exports are being justified on grounds of 'profit shifting.' The fears that other governments could capture permanent advantage in industry after industry by giving each a small initial impetus down the learning curve now emerge as results of impeccable formal models. The claim that one's own government should be aggressive in the pursuit of such policies because other governments do the same is no longer dismissed as a non sequitur. (Dixit, 1986, p. 283)

Whether intentionally or not, the new models served a historically strong demand in the USA for intellectual underpinnings to support a shift towards a more interventionist trade policy or a more 'activist' industrial policy (Richardson, 1986). A crucial perceptual factor supporting intense protectionist sentiments in the USA was and is the feeling that American manufacturing industries have fallen behind in international competition not because of lack of effort or ability, but because other countries are using 'unfair' means to propel their own industries. As a result, Americans became more interested in scrutinising the economic policies of their trading partners, and especially of Japan. Popular writings on the 'Japanese challenge' (C. A. Johnson, 1982; Borrus, 1983) painted a picture of the US economy becoming the cast-away residual of other countries' sectoral planning. To defend its economic prosperity, the USA would have to join the game and implement its own industrial policy, or would at least have to deter other countries from taking advantage of American *naiveté* and openness. Not surprisingly, the EC, spurred along by is traditionally more interventionist members, quickly claimed the new theories in support of European industrial policy ambitions (Pearce and Sutton, 1986). The continuing influence of these ideas on the policy discussions in major national capitals and in Brussels is reflected in the German Monopolies Commission's decision to devote an extensive chapter of its latest biennial report to a critical evaluation of strategic trade policies (Monopolkommission, 1992, ch. VII).[11]

The economics profession has responded forcefully with additional theoretical work to demonstrate the limitations of the pioneering efforts and has also attempted to test the new theories in empirical studies. The critical assessment of models of strategic trade policy has focused on weaknesses that cast doubt on the value of these models as guides for actual government policy: first, the apparent policy implications are highly sensitive to changes in the special assumptions of these models.

Second, it may be impossible to identify the real-world situations where the special assumptions apply, or even to identify potential rents that might be shifted. Third, policy-makers must consider general equilibrium effects because industries compete for scarce special factors within a country. Fourth, more than one country could intervene with respect to the same (or other) industries; thus policy-makers could be facing a prisoner's dilemma problem, and they also have to consider the effects of retaliation. Fifth, the potential beneficiaries of government intervention have the ability to capture policies in pursuit of their own interests that are not generally consistent with the interests of the community at large.

The use of oligopoly models in itself implies a lack of robust policy conclusions. As Grossman and Richardson (1985, p. 14) observed early on: 'The case for active trade policy in an imperfectly competitive environment rests crucially on the behaviour of oligopolistic firms. One might even say it rests uneasily, since the behaviour in question has to do with intrinsically subjective conjectures.' Eaton and Grossman (1986) demonstrated this point by providing a synopsis of models of strategic trade or strategic industrial policy for a variety of assumptions about market structure and firm behaviour. Assuming Cournot behaviour as Brander and Spencer (1985) did, an export subsidy should be used to shift oligopolistic profits towards the domestic firm; yet the optimal intervention changes to an export tax if one substitutes Bertrand conjectures for Cournot behaviour (Eaton and Grossman, 1986, pp. 391–3). Policy prescriptions derived from Brander–Spencer-type models also tend to be highly sensitive to the values of certain parameters, such as the number of firms assumed to exist in the acting country. If the number is greater than one there arises a conflict between the profit-shifting motive for intervention and the traditional terms-of-trade motive which would require an export tax to utilise the country's market power in the export market. The Brander–Spencer prescription of an export subsidy holds only if the number of domestic firms is 'not too large' (1986, p. 397). Furthermore, export subsidies or other measures promoting home production may cause the number of firms to increase. Such policy- induced entry can raise the industry's average cost and can cause the potential benefits of profit shifting to be dissipated (Horstmann and Markusen, 1986). Attempts at rent snatching might also be frustrated because the large firms involved play their own games with governments (Dixit and Kyle, 1985), and the motive for rent snatching can be shown to disappear if one country anticipates retaliation by the other (Collie, 1991). Finally critics have pointed out that a strategic trade policy designed to shift profits from foreign to domestic producers can increase national welfare only to the extent that the affected domestic producers are domestically owned. This condition is becoming more questionable every day as we witness the spread of multinational firms, international joint ventures and partnerships, particularly in industries that are typically considered targets for strategic intervention.

The authors of models of strategic trade policy have had a difficult time trying to identify real-world industries to which their policy prescriptions might apply. Barbara Spencer (1986) has suggested seven broad characteristics of industries for which 'targeting' by trade policy (or equivalent industrial policy) is most likely to lead to a national benefit. While consistent with the models from which they have been derived, her criteria are still too ambiguous to serve as a guide for practical policy. Take, for example, Spencer's first two requirements: (a) for an export subsidy to improve domestic welfare, the target industry 'must be expected to earn additional returns (expressed in profits or greater returns to workers) sufficient to exceed the total cost of the subsidy' (1986, p. 71); and (b) subsidisation of the domestic industry' should lead foreign rival firms to cut back capacity plans and output' (1986, p. 73).

The first requirement implies barriers to entry to preserve the gain in profits for a reasonable length of time. But as Grossman (1986) and others have pointed out, the Brander–Spencer argument applies only to truly 'natural' oligopolies where the opportunities for entry are limited at all stages of development. If entry (including policy-induced entry) increases competition at later stages, profits will be dissipated. Similarly, if lack of entry barriers allowed vigorous competition at earlier stages of industry development, seemingly abnormal profits of the successful firms might be only normal profits if one took account of those who tried but did not succeed. In other words, so-called 'excess profits' of firms that at later stages are protected by entry barriers, such as patent rights, goodwill or economies to scale, may in fact represent a risk premium required to reward risky large-scale investments which firms had to make to obtain those very patents, goodwill or economies to scale, and returns adjusted for risk would tend to be normal over the lifetime of the investment. A policy of targeting successful firms in Brander–Spencer–Krugman fashion would attract more investment at the early stages and would create 'a distortion of resource allocation akin to that ascribed to export subsidies in a fully competitive world, because the appropriate long-run view of the industry would indicate that the excess profits to be captured by one country or the other by means of strategic policy are nonexistent' (Grossman, 1986, pp. 57–8).

When presenting her second requirement for successful targeting, Spencer (1986, p. 72) shifts the emphasis towards policies that 'preempt the foreign competition' because she believes that pre-empting policies are less likely to be affected by ambiguity concerning oligopolistic conjectures discussed above. But a pre-empting strategy is even more vulnerable to the Grossman critique if entry barriers are insignificant at the early stages of development. A policy supporting all applicants could not capture any excess profits and, indeed, would result in a waste of the nation's resources. A more selective pre-empting policy, on the other hand, would have to contend with problems generally discussed under the heading of 'picking winners' (Streit, 1987). How would the government know what products might generate shiftable rents and which firms are likely to be the most successful innovators? How could it justify pre-emptive selective support of a particular firm on a scale large enough to matter for a strategic posture? What would be the right amount of support? How would inevitable mistakes be corrected if policy-makers derive 'credibility' from not admitting failure?

The problem of picking winners becomes more complicated when several potential target industries compete for the services of an essential factor of production for which supply is not perfectly elastic over the relevant period. The original profit-shifting models ignored this aspect because, in the established tradition of partial equilibrium analysis, they focused on one oligopolistic industry in an otherwise perfectly competitive economy. Dixit and Grossman (1986) have explored the implications of assuming several oligopolistic industries that are linked by a common resource in fixed supply, called 'scientists', and conclude that the case for Brander–Spencer–Krugman-type policies is weakened fatally in their scenario. An attempt to shift profits by inducing one domestic producer to expand output necessarily results in reducing the rents captured by others that must contract. But only differential subsidy rates affect allocation. 'If a general subsidy is applied, the real beneficiaries are the scientists whose wages rise' (Dixit and Grossman, 1986, p. 238), and even under the assumptions of the simplest model policy-makers would have to apply some subtle reasoning and would require practically unavailable information to select those industries that will create above-average rents in relation to their requirements of the fixed factor at the margin. In the absence of reliable discriminating information there is no case for intervention (Dixit and Grossman, 1986, p. 241).

Empirical work attempting to assess the practical significance of models of strategic trade policy has concentrated on three industries: civilian jet aircraft, microelectronics, and automobiles.[12] Adding steel (Harris, 1989), these are the manufacturing industries for which international commercial rivalry and policy-watching have been most intense. Empirical studies cannot test Brander–Spencer–Krugman type duopoly models directly because econometric testing of imperfect competition models is generally difficult and because the named industries are not duopolies, except for the case of large civilian jet aircraft (if one forces it a bit). The most pertinent work uses 'calibration' techniques similar to computable general equilibrium models (Venables and Smith, 1986; Dixit, 1988; R. Baldwin and Krugman, 1988a and 1988b; R. Baldwin and Flam, 1989; Harris, 1989; Klepper, 1990). The simulation results depend upon how well the computable model captures the actual market structure and behaviour and also upon the chosen values for parameters, such as elasticities. The calibrated models generate some support for the view that modest tariffs or subsidies, if used unilaterally, can increase national welfare. But these results cannot be generalised, and simulation studies do not tell us how governments could overcome the implementation problems discussed above.

The production of large civilian jet aircraft is often cited as the most plausible candidate for strategic government intervention because of the industry's structure and because of government-supported entry of the European Airbus Consortium in the 1970s. Airbus has managed to capture a substantial share of the world market at the expense of previously dominant US producers. There can be little doubt that government subsidisation has allowed Airbus to win a larger share than an unsupported European aircraft industry might have obtained. Indeed, it is unlikely that an unsupported private European firm would have entered the market at all. However, achieving a strategic effect is no guarantee that the interventions required to make Airbus a successful contender will enhance the national welfare of the countries bearing the costs of supporting the European consortium. Pomfret (1991), who has reviewed the literature on Airbus in detail, concludes that rent snatching is not a plausible motive to explain policies supporting European aircraft production. A summary of the professed policy motives

(GATT, 1991, Vol. I, pp. 224–5) emphasises technological spill-over effects and preventing monopolistic practices (presumably of Boeing). For these objectives, other policies might have been more efficient. Moreover, very large firms are involved and these play their own games against each other and against various other governments concerned. It should also be recognised that the example of Airbus points to additional theorical and practical problems because each strategic intervention is just one move in a repeated game for this industry (Dixit and Kyle, 1985, p. 151).

If opportunities for rent snatching are modest or non-existent, what remains uncertain is whether external benefits of home production should motivate strategic interventions. Krugman (1992, pp. 435–8) now believes that externalities are the key issue, especially if one defines external economies broadly, including market-size effects, technological spill-overs between industries, and coordination-failure effects. Although he acknowledges a lack of empirical research in this area, he 'would conjecture that the potential stakes are many times larger' than the opportunities for rent snatching (Krugman, 1992, p. 438). He now advocates a 'modest industrial policy' for the USA. spending 'say $10 billion of subsidies annually for industries for which a strong case for external economies can be made' (1992, p. 440). This is, of course, not a conclusion that would have required the long detour through models of strategic trade policy. External economies have always been recognised as a potential reason for government intervention. The difference is that the older 'domestic distortions' literature (Corden, 1986) was based on the traditional small country and small producer assumptions, whereas it is now understood that international strategic effects are inevitable when policies are made by large countries for large companies (Stegemann, 1989, pp. 97–8).

5.5 CONCLUDING COMMENTS

The research reviewed in this chapter has affected current international economics at three levels. First, models of strategic trade policy and the ensuing debate have expanded the scope of the positive theory of international trade. Second, they have modified the normative implications of trade theory, if only marginally. Third, these models have shifted the political economy of trade policy by seemingly providing intellectual support for increased government intervention.

Models of strategic trade policy and the profession's response have expanded the scope of positive trade theory by incorporating into it elements of strategic interaction and government power that had not previously been analysed in formal models. This enabled economic theorists to deal with circumstances that traditionally have concerned policy-makers and lobbyists, as well as our colleagues in political science, much more than the circumstances assumed for traditional trade models (Dillon, Lehman and Willett, 1990). However, it now seems agreed among economists that this strand of the new literature explains less of the real world than the strands reviewed in Chapters 1 and 4 above. Krugman (1989, p. 1207) calls the concept of strategic trade policy 'a clever insight', and adds: 'From the beginning, however, it has been clear that the attention received by that insight has been driven by forces beyond the idea's intellectual importance.'

The reason for the disproportionate share of attention was that models of strategic trade policy seemed to supply an intellectually respectable case for interventionist trade policy. Indeed, they seemed to model very well the motives for, and types of, intervening that policy activists in America and Europe were demanding. As reported in the previous section, the economics profession's critical response has established that the policy implications of models of strategic trade policy are not robust enough to serve as a basis for real-world policies. Moreover, empirical work has not succeeded in identifying situations where strategic trade policy could have increased an intervening country's national welfare significantly. Therefore, the normative implications of trade theory have changed only slightly. Economic theory now recognises a few new special cases in which free trade is not a country's optimal policy, yet, it is generally impossible for policy-makers to identify the special circumstances and to devise interventions that will actually increase their jurisdiction's welfare.

In spite of these negative conclusions, models of strategic trade policy may have made a permanent impact at the third level, the political economy of trade policy and related industrial policy. Economic theory is only part of the normative superstructure under which lobbyists and policy-makers take shelter when they justify government actions. Larger parts of this superstructure are crafted by political science and creative writing. The fact that mainstream economists have acknowledged the theoretical possibility of strategic trade policies may make it easier for interest groups to justify government interventions that have nothing in common with the new theories, except for the word strategic. On the positive side, mainstream economists are now able and willing to participate in the discussion of strategic international issues that previously were the almost exclusive domain of political science because traditional trade theory had little to say about these issues. The re-making of trade theory, combined with a generally increased interest in public choice theory, has opened up a dialogue between economists and political scientists, and both sides are now discovering broad areas of common ground (Richardson, 1990).

6 Economic Aspects of Voluntary Export Restraints

CARL HAMILTON and G. V. REED

6.1 INTRODUCTION

Protectionism has spread since the mid-1980s, and has increasingly taken the form of so-called 'voluntary' export restraints (VERs). The purpose of this chapter is to examine briefly this form of trade barrier and its effects. The focus is on aspects that are peculiar to VERs, and it is assumed that the reader is familiar with the standard analysis of tariffs and import quotas. (An overview of basic principles can be found in Williamson and Milner, 1991, Ch. 9, or Södersten and Reed, 1994, Ch. 10.)

Voluntary export restraints, also referred to as Voluntary Restraint Agreements (VRAs) and Orderly Marketing Arrangements (OMAs), have a long history; they were used to restrict Japanese exports of certain textiles to the USA from 1936 to 1940, and by France for a variety of products, but have only recently become prominent. In 1957 the only VER applied to Japanese textile exports to the USA, but it has been estimated that by 1986 there were about 130 VERs, covering about 10 per cent of world trade (Kostecki, 1987; Laird and Yeats, 1988, K. Jones, 1989). As Takacs (1991) notes, exports restraints tend to be concentrated in certain sectors (textiles and clothing, footwear, steel and steel products, automobiles, consumer electronics) and in certain bilateral trading relationships (notably between the USA, the EU and Japan).

Textiles, footwear and steel are examples of 'traditional, manufacturing sectors that are major providers of output, employment and exports for the developed countries, but which have faced increasing competition from newly established enterprises in more-recently-developed and still-developing countries. Although their relative importance in the developed countries has declined, they are still large enough to influence government policy making, particularly in international trade.

Trade in textiles and clothing has been regulated by successive international agreements. These agreements have been protectionist in the sense that they have prevented free trade, but up to the mid-1970s, for some importing and some exporting countries, the agreements may in fact have resulted in larger traded volumes than would otherwise have been the case (Wolf, 1983). However, since 1977, with the introduction of the second Multifibre Arrangement (MFA II), the European countries in particular have tightened their protection against imports from *developing* countries. The aim stated in MFA II was specified yearly increases in imports, but in the 1981 renewal of the MFA the European countries cut back the existing VER quotas of major developing country suppliers and the USA reduced the allowed growth in restricted imports. Subsequent MFAs were little less restrictive. However, under the Uruguay Round agreement, the MFA is to be phased out.

Protection in steel is more recent than in textiles and clothing. From 1968 to 1974 the USA imposed VERs on imports of Japanese and European steel. Then in 1976 a 'trigger price mechanism' was introduced which protected the US steel industry against imports sold in the USA below a stated reference price based on estimates of cost of production in Japan. In addition there seems to have been a tacit US–Japanese agreement since the late 1970s limiting Japanese steel exports to the USA. As a result of the higher prices in the USA and the protection against Japanese competition, the European steel producers found the US market attractive. The US steel industry subsequently pressed for VERs on European exports which they obtained in late 1982. VERs on European steel exports to the USA were maintained until 1992; since then steel has again become the subject of a trade dispute between the USA and EU, with US producers instituting anti-dumping proceedings.

The EU countries (and Sweden) have in the past protected their steel production by way of often massive government subsidies to obsolete steel plants. As a result of excess supply problems in Europe and the fact that Europeans have had to restrict their exports to the USA, the

EU has implemented controls of imports, prices and production of steel in Europe, passing on the protectionist consequences to countries like Brazil, Mexico, Taiwan and South Korea (Walter, 1983).

The most recent major protected industrial sector is automobiles. In 1981 the USA introduced VERs on imports of cars from Japan. This measure was followed by protection of the German automobile industry, prompted by fears of Japanese 'dumping' on the German market. However, even before the 1981 US VER on Japanese cars, highly protective regimes existed in Italy, France and the UK.

6.2   THE INCIDENCE OF VOLUNTARY EXPORT RESTRAINTS

It is difficult to obtain data on the incidence of VERs, partly because they are often not identified individually among the range of quantitative trade restrictions reported, and partly because their existence may not be officially acknowledged. Table 6.1 summarises estimates made by Laird and Yeats (1988) of the incidence in 1986 of quantitative restrictions by the USA, the EC and Japan on imports from developed and developing countries. The data distinguish between VERs and other quantitative restrictions on goods other than textiles and clothing, VERs negotiated under the MFA and quotas on textiles negotiated outside the MFA. It is interesting to note that Japan, the subject of

TABLE 6.1   Incidence of US, EC and Japanese quantitative restrictions on imports in 1986

	Developed countries				Developing countries			
	VER	QR	MFA	TEX	VER	QR	MFA	TEX
USA	15.5	0.8	0.4	0.0	2.1	4.5	9.7	2.8
EC(10)	6.3	2.3	0.0	0.0	1.7	5.4	9.9	2.5
Japan	0.0	20.5	0.0	0.0	0.0	5.0	0.0	0.0
OECD	7.4	4.8	0.1	0.0	1.5	5.1	7.6	2.0

Notes: VER = quantitative VERs other than under the MFA; QR = quantitative restrictions other than VER and MFA; MFA = quantitative restrictions negotiated under the MFA; TEX = textile and clothing quotas negotiated outside the MFA.

Source: Laird and Yeats (1988).

many VERs on its exports, makes (virtually) no use of them itself, but does rely heavily on other forms of quantitative restriction to limit its imports.

Developing countries are increasingly subject to VERs and other quantitative restrictions. This largely reflects the emerging importance of products to them that compete with those produced in the 'traditional sectors in many developed countries. The NICs in particular are subject to VERs on a wide range of products; e.g., Table 6.2 indicates the variety of restrictions affecting some or all of the exports of selected sectors in South Korea that were in place in November 1980. In addition to those identified in the table, Korea also faced export restrictions from some developed countries in a variety of goods, including motor vehicles, tyres, canned mushrooms, ski boots, baseball gloves and fish, dried fish and dried seaweed.

TABLE 6.2   Korea: restrictive trade measures affecting exports in selected sectors (as of November 1980)

	Sector affected				
Country	Cutlery	Electrical goods	Footwear	Iron/steel	Textiles/ clothing
Australia	–	GQ	GQ	GQ	TQ
Austria	–	–	–	–	BQ
Canada	–	–	GQ	–	BQ
EC	–	–	–	VER/MPS	BQ
Benelux	VER	–	–	–	–
Denmark	BQ	–	–	–	–
France	–	UQ	–	–	UQ
Germany	VER	–	–	–	–
Ireland	–	–	VER	–	–
UK	VER	BQ	VER	–	–
Finland	–	–	ID	–	BQ
Japan	–	–	IQ	–	IQ/VER
New Zealand	IL	IL	IL	IL	IL
Norway	BQ	–	–	–	BQ
Sweden	–	–	GQ	–	BQ/VER
USA	–	VER	BQ	TPS	BQ

Notes: BQ = bilateral quota; GQ = global quota; ID = import deposit; IL = import licence; IQ = import quota; MPS = minimum price system; UQ = unilateral quota; VER = voluntary export restraint

6.3   WHAT IS A VOLUNTARY EXPORT RESTRAINT?

A VER is the outcome of a negotiation, usually between two governments,[1] which results in the exporting country limiting its export supply
to the importing country. The agreement is not voluntary in the normal
sense of the word, but it is often preferred by exporting countries to
alternative forms of trade barrier – e.g., tariffs, import quotas or anti-
dumping duties – which the importing country implicitly or explicitly
threatens to use.

It is sometimes useful to consider a protectionist measure as a set of
constraints imposed on the free flow of international trade. Thus a VER
is a measure by which the importing home country negotiates the imposition of an upper limit on foreign supply (constraint I), defined by
commodity category (constraint II), defined by source of supply (III),
defined in volume rather than value terms (IV) and defined to cover a
stated period (V). In addition, the exporting country administers the
restriction on export supply. As we shall see, constraints II, III and IV
are particularly important in the analysis of VERs.

In comparison, tariffs and quotas also limit foreign supply. A tariff is
defined by commodity group, and such a commodity group is typically
more narrowly defined than a commodity category covered by a VER.
A tariff is not defined by source if it is a most favoured nation (MFN)
tariff, but it is defined by source if it is a preferential tariff. However, a
preferential tariff is very rarely export-country-specific, as a VER
always is. Typically a tariff is defined as a percentage of the value of
goods imported (*ad valorem* tariff) and is not related to the volume of
the traded goods as is the typical VER. Finally, a tariff is usually permanently imposed. The importing country administers the tariff and
collects the tariff revenue. The goods to which an import quota applies
may be defined as narrowly as a VER, and the quota is usually
specified in quantity terms, but it is not necessarily source-specific. The
importing country administers the quota, usually by issuing (or perhaps
selling) import licences.

In the next two sections we shall analyse first the importing country
and then the exporting country. As we shall see, the effects of VERs on
both importing and exporting countries depend very much on whether
there are other importing countries that do not impose VERs, and on
whether there are other exporting countries not subject to them. We

shall start by considering the most simple case, where there is only one importing country and one exporting country. We shall assume that the two countries are 'large' with respect to one another, so that the introduction of a VER changes prices in both countries.

6.4 A SIMPLE TWO-COUNTRY MODEL

The importing country

Figure 6.1 depicts the market for one good in the importing country. The importing country supply curve is S_m, and its demand curve D_m. The excess supply curve of the exporting country is S_x. With free trade the world market price is P_0, the volume consumed is Q_0, and this volume can be split into two parts: Q_1, which is produced domestically, and $Q_0 - Q_1$, which is imported. Suppose a VER is introduced limiting the import volume allowed to $Q_3 - Q_2 < Q_0 - Q_1$: the good becomes more scarce in the home country and its price rises from P_0 to P_1. In the exporting country there will be excess capacity forcing a reduction in

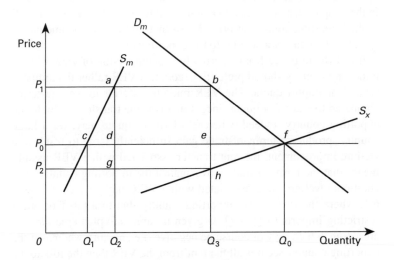

FIGURE 6.1   The effects of a VER on the importing country

production, with the remaining producers willing to supply at a lower price than before, i.e., the supply price falls to P_2.

Domestic production increases from Q_1 to Q_2, which may have been the government's motive for introducing the VER, but of course consumers suffer as a consequence of the price increase. These effects are similar to those we would observe from the imposition of an import tariff or quota. One particular distinction between those measures and the VER, however, lies in who captures the difference between the higher domestic price P_1 and the lower world supply price P_2. With a tariff the difference (area *abhg*) goes to the government of the importing country as tariff revenue, while with a quota it is likely to go to the (usually domestic) holders of import licences. However, with a VER it is likely that some, if not all, of the difference will go to the foreign suppliers. Why is this so?

Remember that it is the exporting country that administers the implementation of the export restriction. The right to export will be allocated to producers within the exporting country, who thus have some degree of monopoly power conferred upon them. This may be reinforced by the (formal or informal) establishment of a cartel among the exporters, or even by the institution of an official body such as a marketing board. In the simple case, it is usual to assume that the exporting firms will sell to the importing country at price P_1, so that all the rent income corresponding to area *abhg* accrues to the exporting country.

It is difficult to see from a narrowly economic point of view why an importing country should prefer to negotiate a VER rather than impose a tariff or import quota. The VER must be inferior in welfare terms compared to a tariff or quota since it involves the transfer of rent to the exporting country. Indeed, whereas a tariff or quota may, for a large country, produce a terms-of-trade gain sufficiently large to result in a welfare improvement, the rent transfer associated with a VER usually means that the terms of trade move against the importing country. The additional welfare costs associated with a VER may be seen in Figure 6.1, where the loss to the importing country due to a tariff or quota restricting imports to $Q_3 - Q_2$ is given by area *adc* plus area *bfe* less area *dehg*, which may of course be negative (i.e., a gain), whereas if the exporting country secures all the rent from the VER then the loss to the importing country is area *abfc*.

We must seek an answer to the use of VERs by importing countries in political economy arguments, which we shall pursue in more detail later on. For the moment, it suffices to note that VERs have not been illegal under the rules of the GATT whereas GATT rules more or less forbid import quotas and increases in tariffs, and that the rent transfer may persuade the exporting country to accept a VER rather than face another form of restriction. We shall discuss whether the exporting country actually *gains* from the VER in the next section.

The exporting country

In Figure 6.2 the market in the exporting country is depicted. Competitive producers have the export (excess) supply curve ES_x and the demand for exports curve is ED_m. In free trade the quantity R (equal to $Q_0 - Q_1$ in Figure 6.1) is exported at price P_0. Now suppose a VER is negotiated, limiting the export volume to Q (equal to $Q_3 - Q_2$ in Figure 6.1), so that the new export supply curve, ES_x' follows the original curve to point b and then becomes vertical. The price in the importing country rises to P_1 and the supply price falls to P_2. The price difference per unit is $P_1 - P_2$ and the ensuing rent income is represented by area *abgf*. (Thus a rent income can be illustrated either on the import side, as in Figure 6.1 or on the export side, as in Figure 6.2). Area *abgf* reflects the value of having access to the foreign market, and can be looked upon as the scarcity value of an 'entrance ticket' to the export market. Since VERs are administered by the exporting country, the rent income usually accrues to that country.

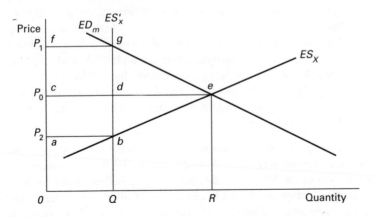

FIGURE 6.2   The effects of a VER on the exporting country

The welfare effect for the exporting country depends on the relative size of the rent income and the net loss on producer and consumer surplus, equal to area *abec*. Since area *abdc* is common, it is evident that the exporting country will gain from the VER if area *cdgf* (which we may regard as the *net* income transfer on the restricted volume of exports) is greater than area *bed* (the loss due to the reduction in exports). There is obviously a close parallel between the effects of a VER and an export tax. As we know, a large exporting country may gain from imposing an appropriate export tax; an export tax equal to $P_1 - P_2$ in Figure 6.2 would have the same effects as the VER, but with the revenue from the tax (area *abgf*) going to the government as revenue rather than to producers as rent. Export taxes are, however, illegal under GATT rules, so that agreement to a VER that restricts exports to the level that could have been obtained by a welfare-increasing export tax may be a tempting option to the exporting country. There may, of course, be other reasons for an exporting country to agree to a VER, and we shall return to these in the concluding section.

Figures 6.1 and 6.2 are a simplification even for the two-country case, and some complications should be noted.

1. VERs are typically used on top of tariffs, and the total trade barrier is then a combination of a tariff and the VER. A tariff allows the importing country to retain some of the rent as tariff revenue, but does not restrict the volume of trade unless the VER is not binding.
2. Figures 6.1 and 6.2 shows a situation where the domestically produced and the imported good are perfect substitutes in consumption. This may not always be true, of course, but does not change the essence of the analysis. For example, US and imported Japanese cars are not perfect substitutes, but a VER on Japanese cars still protects US production indirectly by driving up the price of the imperfect substitute (for an analysis with two imperfect substitutes, see Corden, 1971).

The wedge between the domestic price and the export supply price can be expressed as $(P_1 - P_2)/P_2$ and is then called the *ad valorem tariff equivalent* of the VER. The idea behind this labelling is that the same import reduction as the VER causes could alternatively have been achieved by an *ad valorem* tariff equal to $(P_1 - P_2)/P_2$. In Table 6.3 the combination of tariffs and import tariff equivalent is illustrated with clothing imported in 1981–83 to Europe and the USA from Hong Kong.

Members of the EU have a common external tariff against Hong Kong as they are members of a customs union, while European Free Trade Association (EFTA) members have different tariffs as they belong to a free trade area. The USA, EU members collectively, and EFTA members negotiate individually a bilateral three to four years' agreement with Hong Kong, stating exactly for a large number of commodity categories (EU, 114 categories plus sub-categories; USA, 108 categories) the different export quantities allowed per sub-period within the overall period; rules for substitution between commodity categories and for substitution between periods; export control certificates, etc.[2] Table 6.3 is based on average figures for the eight–twelve most important clothing categories.

TABLE 6.3 Trade barriers against clothing imports from Hong Kong, average 1981–83 (%)

(1) Country	(2) Import tariff equivalent of VERs, average	(3) Tariff rate	(4) Combined trade barrier*
Austria (EFTA)	4	33	38
Benelux (EEC)	14	17	33
Denmark (EEC)	14	17	33
Finland (EFTA)	6	35	43
France (EEC)	13	17	32
Germany (EEC)	14	17	33
Italy (EEC)	7	17	25
Sweden (EFTA)	29	14	47
Switzerland (EFTA)	n.a.[+]	13	n.a.[+]
UK (EEC)	15	17	35
Weighted average (import value)	15	17	35
USA	17	23	44

* Derived from columns (2) and (3), i.e., (1 + tariff equivalent rate) × (1 + tariff rate) yields the combined rate.

+ The tariff equivalent of the import licence system and of legal cartels is not known.

Source: C. Hamilton (1984), Table 1.

6.5   EXPANDING THE SIMPLE TWO-COUNTRY MODEL

The model used above has allowed us to identify the role of rent transfers between the importing and exporting country in two of the important aspects of VERs: the importing country necessarily loses and the exporting country may gain. However, it does not allow us to examine some other aspects, both connected with the fact that a VER is typically negotiated between one of several importing countries and one of several exporting countries. In these circumstances the VER may lead the importing country concerned to substitute goods from another exporting country for those from the restricted exporter, and the restricted exporter may seek to divert its exports to another importing country with which it has not negotiated a VER. We shall examine each of these possibilities in a world of three countries.

One importer, two exporters

The source-specific nature of a VER is particularly important to note when it comes to VERs applied by members of a customs union (like the EU) or of a free trade area (like EFTA), or when the importing country is a signatory to an international agreement such as the MFA. In this section we will analyse the effect of VERs in such a situation, using a three-country model in which all the countries are assumed to be large.

We assume that there are, first, an *importing country*, M; second, an *unrestricted exporting country*, U; and third, a *restricted exporting country*, R. Suppose the importing country government has as a target a given volume of domestic production, e.g., for perceived employment reasons. To achieve this, the importing country chooses to use neither direct subsidies nor tariffs, but a restriction on foreign supply from R in the form of a VER. The importing country's reduction of imports hits R only, *while U maintains free access to M's market*.

The left-hand panel of Figure 6.3 shows the excess demand curve for M, ED_m, and the excess supply curve for the unrestricted exporter, ES_u. The right-hand panel shows the net excess demand schedule for M and U, ED_{m-u}, and the excess supply curve for the restricted exporter, ES_r. Under free trade the world price will be P_0 and the importing country will import a quantity M_0 of which U_0 comes from U, and $R_0 = M_0 - U_0$ from R.

The importing country now negotiates a VER with R that restricts its exports to R_1. The price in M will increase to P_1, and imports will fall to

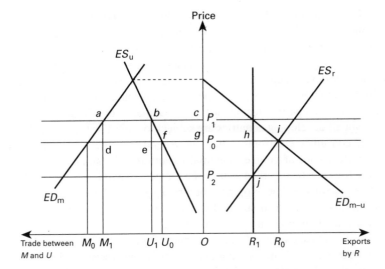

FIGURE 6.3   The effects of a VER when only one exporter is restricted

M_1. The unrestricted country can sell within M at the higher price, and so will increase its exports to U_1, where $U_1 = M_1 - R_1$. The VER has caused substitution of exports from the restricted exporter to the unrestricted one. Note that M's imports fall by less than the negotiated cut in R's exports.

As before, M must lose from the introduction of the VER. The loss to its consumers exceeds the gain to its producers, and the price paid for its imports has risen from P_0 to P_1. The unrestricted exporter makes a net gain equal to area *bcgf*. The restricted importer will make a net gain if the *net* rent transfer from M, equal to area *abed*, is greater than its loss on its reduced export volume, area *hij*.

An alternative policy for M would be to impose a multilateral import quota, shared between U and R in proportion to their original export volumes, that restricted imports to M_1. In this case M would be able to import price P_2, and would gain if the terms of trade effect exceeded the deadweight loss from the quota. Both exporting countries would of course lose from a quota (since there would be no rent income).

Most members of the EU and EFTA have VERs against outside countries, e.g., on clothing. This has encouraged exports of clothing from Italy and Finland to their partners in the EU and EFTA. This is a phenomenon known as *trade diversion*, i.e., the replacement of imports from a low-cost source with imports from a higher-cost source.

The US textile and clothing industry has proved quite competitive in some commodities in Europe. Had the USA received the same treatment as many developing countries, US exports would have been subject to import quotas or voluntary export restraints. However, no trade barriers except tariffs *vis-à-vis* the USA exist in Europe. Thus, for foreign policy reasons, Europe as a home country treats the USA as a trading club partner facing tariffs but not quotas or VERs.

Not all developing countries are subject to export restraints on clothing, consumer electronics, etc.; these tend to affect the very latest exporters and, of course, potential exporters. The situation of these countries can be regarded as that of a temporary partner in a trade club, with established developing country exporters being the outside countries. However, if successful in exporting, a late-coming exporter is also likely to become subject to VERs.

Actions taken against Japanese exports, for instance, have had effects on trade patterns, encouraging exports from non-restrained developing countries. This effect of VERs in stimulating industrialisation and exports from more developing countries ('quota jumping') is often regarded as a favourable effect (although the same effect could arguably be achieved more efficiently and more effectively by the deployment of other instruments).

One exporter, two importers

Suppose that there are two importing countries, one of which, R, negotiates a VER with the sole exporting country, X. The other importing country, U, maintains a policy of free trade. The left-hand panel of Figure 6.4 shows the excess supply curve of the exporting country, ES_x, and the excess demand curve of importing country R, ED_r. The right-hand panel shows the net excess supply for X given that it is exporting to R, ES_{x-r}, and the excess demand curve for U, the other importing country, ED_u. Under free trade the world market price will be P_0 with X exporting X_0, of which R_0 goes to R and U_0 to U.

R now negotiates a VER with the exporting country that restricts its volume of exports destined for R to R_1. As the exporting country now faces a perfectly inelastic demand from R for prices less than P_1, its excess supply to the unrestricted importer shifts to the dotted line jk for such prices, after which it follows the original excess supply curve ES_{x-r}. The world price will therefore fall to P_2. The restricting import-

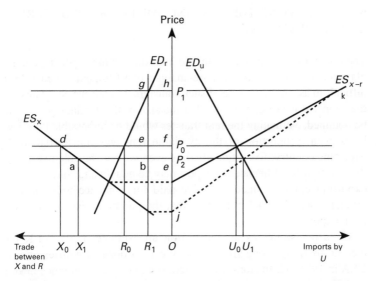

FIGURE 6.4   The imposition of a VER by one of two importing countries

ing country meets its import target, but imports by the other importing
country increase, so that *X*'s total export volume does not fall by the
full amount of its reduction in exports to *R*.

As in the simple case, the restricting importer suffers a fall in welfare
since its imports decrease and the terms of trade move against it. The
unrestricting importer's welfare increases since it is importing a greater
volume at a lower price. Whether the exporter gains or loses depends
on the relative size of its rent income from the restricting importer, are
abchg, and its net loss due to its exporting a lower total volume at a
lower price, *acfd*. That is whether or not its net rent income, *efhg*, is
greater than its loss on its exports over and above the VER amount, *abed*.

On the face of it, the government of the unrestricting importer, *U*,
should be satisfied with the effects of the VER since its aggregate
welfare has increased. But suppose that the government of *U* is concerned with the size of its own import-competing industry, whose output
has now decreased. It may then react by seeking to negotiate a VER in
its turn with the exporting country, perhaps restricting .its imports to
their previous level. Such an consequence, which has been identified in
practice (e.g., C. Hamilton, 1989), has been called the *domino effect*.

6.6   ESTIMATING THE RENT INCOME FROM VOLUNTARY
EXPORT RESTRAINTS

The transfer of rent income from the importing to the exporting country
plays a central role in the welfare analysis of VERs, but in general it is
difficult to ascertain the size of such transfers. Even if we could observe
the supply price of exports, so that the size of the available rent could
be obtained, estimating the rent transfer would be impossible unless we
knew what proportion of the available rent was transferred to the
exporting country. Exceptionally, however, we may be able to estimate
the rent transfer if licences to export may be bought and sold within the
exporting country, since the price paid for a licence will be, in an
efficient market, equal to the rent that the purchaser expects to obtain
from exporting.

Table 6.4 shows as an illustration an estimate of the VER rent
income to Hong Kong from some West European countries and the
USA in 1981–82. In Hong Kong there is a market for 'entrance tickets'
to different export markets for clothing and to arrive at the estimate of
Table 6.4, the price of 'entrance tickets', $P_1 - P_2$, was collected from
specialised brokers in 'entrance tickets'. Armed with these prices it was
then possible to estimate the Hong Kong rent income. The rent income
to Hong Kong corresponded to approximately 1 per cent of the city
state's GDP in 1981–82, or 16 per cent of the Hong Kong clothing
industry's value-added. However, a minor part of the rent income does

TABLE 6.4   **Rent income from VERs to Hong Kong from exports of
clothing**

Importing country	
Benelux	10
Denmark	7
France	6
Germany	94
Sweden	47
UK	100
USA	302
Total	566

Source: Calculated from Hamilton (1984), Table 2.

not accrue to Hong Kong nationals as some exporting firms are owned by importing country nationals.

The rent transfer is, as we have noted, only one element in the welfare effects of a VER for the importing country. Milner discusses the problems and the results of estimating the full welfare costs for importing countries in Chapter 7.

6.7   ALLOCATION OF THE VOLUNTARY EXPORT RESTRAINT QUANTITY BETWEEN DOMESTIC PRODUCERS

In the exporting country there must be some sort of mechanism for allocating among potential exporters the valuable 'entrance tickets' to foreign markets, i.e., export licences. In principle there are two approaches: the price mechanism with market prices for licences, i.e., auctioning licences and allowing an ongoing trade in them, or, on the other hand, an administrative decision-making process with civil servants deciding how large an export volume ('quota') applicants should receive, and when. Administrative allocation could be combined with the sanctioning of subsequent trade in export licences, which would then eventually approximate the first approach. However, the typical procedure is that there is no auctioning and no legally sanctioned trade. What mechanism is used has important implications for the efficiency with which resources are allocated in the exporting country, and for the distribution of the rent income. We shall consider the efficiency aspects first.

Efficiency of resource use

If there is auctioning of export licences and firms have different supply prices, the firms with the lowest supply prices will be the ones that are willing to pay most for an export licence. Think of the export supply curve as depicting rising production costs of a succession of increasingly inefficient small firms as we move to the right (in Figure 6.2). The more efficient firms offer to export at prices below P_2 along S_x. The higher cost firms – i.e., the less efficient ones – offering to export at prices above P_2 will turn to their domestic market or close down, and factors of production used in these firms can then be employed productively elsewhere, allowing for an adjustment period.

If there is no auction of export licences, but 'past performance' criteria are used in a first round of government allocation of export licences, then subsequent transferability is still desirable. This can be seen by assuming that transferability is not allowed. Because of the export restriction each firm would then have to cut back its export volume proportionally.[2] If firms originally produced at a cost-minimising scale, each of them would now have to move back up its average cost curve, producing at a sub-optimal scale. However, had trade in export licences been allowed, some firms would have sold all or part of their allocations of licences, or perhaps closed down, and factors of production would be freed for alternative employment. The firms which bought the licences could stay in business, producing at their now-optimal output level. Clearly this argument is more important for industries where economies of scale are substantial, such as automobiles and steel, and less so for clothing.

Finally, not permitting trade in licences and using 'past performance' criteria results in new and more efficient producers being discriminated against for the simple reason that they have no past record of export performance to refer to when applying for free government allocation of export licences. However, if trade in licences were allowed, a new firm that is more efficient than existing ones would be prepared to pay a higher price in the market for licences than existing, less efficient firms. Thus restricting trade in licences provides a breeding ground for inefficiency and high-cost production just like other forms of protection; in this case protection against the entrance of more efficient domestic firms.

Analyses of the effects of VERs traditionally concentrate on the importing country. Relatively little attention has been paid to the exporting country, save in the estimation where possible of the size of the rent transfer. De Melo and Winters (1990, 1993) have attempted to rectify this omission by considering the effects of VERs on resource allocation and welfare in the exporting country. They argue that a VER will cause the exporting sector to contract and result in a spill-over to unrestricted markets. In their 1990 paper they use an econometric model to study the effects of a US OMA on imports of footwear from Korea, and conclude that the Korean industry had limited ability to switch sales to unrestricted markets and that the marginal revenue products of factors employed in that industry fell sharply when the OMA was in force. In their 1993 paper they consider the consequences for the Taiwanese footwear industry of the American OMA, and conclude that the industry contracted; while profits rose, wages and employment fell. In both papers they suggest that it was possible that the US policy reduced welfare in the exporting countries, despite the rent transfer.

Rent distribution

If the licences are auctioned by the exporting country's government, the rent income is captured by this government. If the government allocates the export licences free of charge to a group of exporters (e.g., according to 'past performance') then it is this group of original receivers of licences that captures the rent income. Since there are often large incomes to be gained from receiving licences free from the government, existing exporters form a special interest group which has a strong incentive to oppose any change in existing allocation rules when based on past performance. Further, the use of administrative criteria can provide huge incentives for bribes to civil servants and offer politicians 'gains' in the political market place in return for an increased allocation of licences and no changes in rules favourable to the special interest group. Prohibition of trade in licences between exporters also reduces an exporting country's ability to utilise fully its given quota volumes.

As far as the authors are aware, government auctions of licences have been tried only with regard to clothing in Taiwan. The typical approach is that governments hand out licences according to some sort of 'past performance' criterion, or leave it to an industry cartel to sort out who should get what out of the limited export volumes. Trade in licences is typically not allowed. However, in Hong Kong trade in textile and clothing licences is permitted once the original 'past performance' allocation has been made. In addition, there are usually very complex and discriminating rules regulating entrance of new exporters.

6.8   OTHER ASPECTS OF VOLUNTARY EXPORT RESTRAINTS

Cartelisation

In considering the exporting country, we have assumed implicitly so far that there is competition among producers in the exporting country. However, even if this is a correct description of the situation before a VER is imposed, the VER itself may induce the creation of an export cartel. This is particularly so when there is no auctioning system for licences, when there is limited or no entry for new exporting firms, and 'past performance' is the criterion for allocating licences. A cartel must be instituted if it is left to the industry itself to decide on the licence allocation. For a profit-maximising cartel it can be rational to export less than the volume stated in the VER agreement. The mechanism is in principle no different from that in the standard analysis of an output-restricting monopoly. Then the fall in exports can have two elements: first, the fall imposed directly by the VER, and second, a fall imposed indirectly by the VER through its inducement of an exporters' cartel. Perhaps one could regard existing exporting country penalties for unused export licences as a way to force export cartels to export larger volumes than they would do from pure profit-maximising behaviour. Typical penalties for 'non-performing exporters' involve reduced free allocations to established exporters of export licences in the next period (C. Hamilton, 1985).

Upgrading

The typical VER is defined in physical units of a commodity category, e.g., number of cars or tons of meat. Within each commodity category there are often different grades or qualities with different world market prices. As the VER is defined in physical units, the price increase in money terms due to the VER will be equal for all units within the same commodity category regardless of grade. As a result, a high-cost grade or a high quality variety within a commodity category will have a lower *ad valorem* VER-tariff equivalent than the low-cost grade. Consider the following example:

Grade	World market price per physical unit VER	VER-rent per physical unit	*Ad valorem* tariff equivalent of the VER
High-cost grade	£100	£5	$\frac{5}{100}$ or 5%
Low-cost grade	£50	£5	$\frac{5}{50}$ or 10%

From the exporter's view it is, then, rational to gear the export mix of different grades towards more of those with the lower *ad valorem* VER-tariff equivalents. This means a tendency towards higher quality and more sophisticated exports. This effect of VERs has been given the label *upgrading*, or trading up.

Upgrading is often mentioned as one effect of VERs (Falvey, 1979; Rodriguez, 1979; Keesing and Wolf, 1980). Feenstra (1984, 1985) undertook the first detailed empirical investigations of quality upgrading, using hedonic price regression techniques. He considered imports of Japanese passenger cars to the USA in 1980–81 with and without the US VER. The price increase of Japanese cars on the US market is split into three parts: that which is due to inflation, the tariff equivalent of the VER, and that which is due to improved quality. Having corrected for inflation, two-thirds of the price increase is attributed to the fact that imported Japanese cars were upgraded in quality: e.g., they became longer and heavier, had increased horsepower, more often had automatic transmission, etc. Consumers received a quality increase in return for two-thirds of the price increase, but note that this quality upgrading was not necessarily something that was wanted by consumers. Indeed, had they asked for quality improvements in the earlier situation without the VER on imported cars, one would expect producers then to have already satisfied such consumer preferences, no doubt in return for a higher price (C. Hamilton, 1986b). Thus the net welfare change of consumers is ambiguous, even if the price had only increased by two-thirds of the actual rise.

Various authors have subsequently investigated quality upgrading, either following Feenstra in using the hedonic regression approach or using price index techniques. The motor vehicle sector is the most frequently studied (e.g., Dinopoulos and Kreinin, 1988, who also consider the spill-over effect of the US–Japanese VER on European prices: de Melo and Messerlin, 1988, on European–Japanese VERs; and Feenstra, 1988, again considering a US–Japanese VER, but this time on trucks). Other studies have considered footwear (Aw and Roberts, 1986, 1988, on the effects of American OMAs: de Melo and Winters, 1989, on the effects of restrictions on Korean exports), and textiles (Cline, 1987, and Faini and Heimler, 1991, on the MFA).

The broad conclusion to be drawn from these studies is that there is evidence of quality upgrading, but this result is not inevitable, as demonstrated by Bark and de Melo (1987). De Melo and Winters

(1989) also obtain results which suggest that VERs tend to be associated with less quality upgrading than would occur under free trade. Possible explanations that have been offered include the possibility that exporters are more interested in maximising foreign exchange rather than in maximising profits, and that the costs of upgrading were too high for exporters to attempt to adjust to what they see as a temporary effect (see C. Hamilton, de Melo and Winters, 1992).

Reactions to the threat of a VER

Producers in an exporting country may anticipate that an importing country will seek to negotiate a VER at some future time. This anticipation may be fuelled by various observations, such as that the importing country has already negotiated VERs with other exporter, that import-competing producers are lobbying their government for protection, or that their exports are already subject to surveillance (perhaps with a view to instigating anti-dumping action). This raises the interesting question of how rational exporting firms would react to the threat of a VER.

Yano (1989), who first modelled this problem explicitly, considered the case where VER quantities would be allocated proportionately to current exports, and the probability of VER introduction was exogenously determined, in a market with one domestic firm and two foreign exporters, all of whom had Cournot conjectures. He showed that if the future VER would generate rents then the foreign firms would increase their current export volumes. Variations on this work are due to Hariharan and Wall (1992), who demonstrated a similar effect with one exporting firm when future sales were positively related to current sales; Hoekman and Leidy (1990), who showed that rents were not a necessary condition for the Yano effect and made the probability of a VER endogenous: Ethier (1991), who considered these effects within a general equilibrium model; and Anderson (1992), who demonstrated the Yano effect for competitive exporters and an endogenised probability of a VER.

Winters (1994) has made the first attempt to determine econometrically whether the 'Yano effect' holds. He builds on earlier work (Winters 1990) that considered the effects on EC import volumes of import surveillance ('enhanced statistical monitoring of imports') on the grounds that 'its introduction is frequently justified in terms more appropriate to restriction than to monitoring'. In his applied study

Winters uses information on surveillance measures in the EC as an indicator of possible future VER negotiation. He concludes that 'exporters are [arguably] more likely to curtail their exports in response to a threatened VER the more collusive they are and the more discriminatory and restrictive the threatened restriction ... [and that] actual responses to EC import surveillance were consistent with this view'.

6.9 THE POLITICAL ECONOMY OF VOLUNTARY EXPORT RESTRAINTS

Compared to other instruments of protection, it seems difficult to understand from an economic point of view why VERs are used by importing country governments, rather than tariffs and quotas. With both tariffs and quotas the rent stays in the importing country, whereas VERs are selective and do not cover all sources of supply, and the importing country government must always be prepared to strike out at new suppliers. In addition VERs rank below both *ad valorem* tariffs and import quotas on welfare and efficiency grounds. What, then, is the explanation for governments' revealed preference for VERs over import quotas and tariffs, and for their continued renegotiation?

1. Members of GATT have agreed not to use quantitative import restrictions and discriminatory quotas and tariffs. By having the restriction on the export side through a VER, members of GATT avoid a clash with the letter of the GATT rules they have signed, although, of course, VERs in effect clash with the spirit of GATT. It seems that by restricting the possibilities of using traditional protectionist measures, new ones are stimulated to appear.

2. As was noted earlier, a VER acts as an export tax provided that all rents are transferred to the exporting country, so that a VER may increase both the profits of exporting firms and the welfare of the exporting country. Since export taxes are not sanctioned by GATT, an appropriate VER may be a tempting option for the government of an exporting country.

3. A special interest group is induced in the exporting country by the VER. This group presumably acts as a pressure group in the exporting country to maintain its rent income from the continuation of a VER. In this way the rent transferred to the exporting country can reduce the exporting country government's opposition

to a renewed VER, and from the importing country's point of view the rent transfer reduces the risk for retaliation and foreign policy frictions.

4. VERs are typically very easy to implement from a political point of view: 'While direct import restrictions such as tariffs and quotas must be implemented through legislative (US) or highly visible administrative (EEC) channels, a VER can be negotiated in secret, unhindered by open political process and public scrutiny' (K. Jones, 1984, p. 87).

5. An exporting country may prefer a VER because the agreement gives it an option every few years to pressure the importing country to eliminate the restriction, or at least to change or relax the definition of VER categories so as to fit in better with the export mix of the exporting country. This may of course be double-edged, in that the restrictions may be made more onerous. On these issues see K. Jones (1984).

6. Two groups are hurt by VERs, but they are both poorly organised as pressure groups for free trade. Consumers are hit by restrictions on foreign supply, but to each consumer the protected good is only one among many goods in the consumption basket, and to the typical consumer the cost increase caused by a VER is perceived (if at all) to constitute a fairly small part of his income. Even if the cost increase is small, it seems to be difficult for consumers to visualise and act upon an abstract alternative of reduced prices. Producers, on the other hand, receive the bulk of their income from the one good they produce, i.e., the prices means a lot more to their total income compared to the influence of protection on one consumer's cost of consumption of the same good. The pay-off to the producers from forming a protectionist pressure group could be substantial and easily cover the cost of organising an often rather small number of firms threatened by import competition. A large number of consumers with disparate main interests in life are much more costly to organise than producers, and to each one of them the pay-off from liberalisation is probably perceived as abstract and fairly small.

Late-coming (but existing) exporters are also hit by VERs. Importing countries typically allocate quotas among possible sources of supply by 'past-performance' criteria. As a result, late-coming exporters are 'locked in' at low levels of exports. These countries are typically small and often developing ones, so they would have a weak bargaining position if they were to try to get increased access to importing country markets at the expense of domestic producers and already established foreign suppliers subject to VERs with comparatively generous quotas. To sum up, the political economy of protectionism seems to work in the direction of VERs because of present GATT rules banning traditional forms of protectionism, and due to the asymmetric bargaining strength of groups having opposite interests for and against protectionism.

6.10 CONCLUDING COMMENTS

Are VERs here to stay? Even five years ago the answer might have been tentatively affirmative. Successive GATT rounds had failed to come to grips with non-tariff barriers in general, and the textiles trade had continued to be managed under successive MFAs, in which VERs and quotas are endemic. The Uruguay Round Agreement, however, commits GATT members to the integration of textiles and clothing within GATT disciplines, with import quotas being replaced by tariff quotas, followed by the progressive liberalisation of the tariffs. Non-tariff barriers in agriculture are also to be replaced by tariffs.

However, the history of governmental ingenuity in circumventing the letter of the GATT disciplines (VERs of course being a case in point), suggests that if VERs do disappear then they will probably be replaced with some other non-tariff barrier. Doubts have already been expressed about the role that may be played by the new anti-dumping and safeguards procedures agreed in the Uruguay Round.

7 Empirical Analysis of the Welfare Effects of Commercial Policy

CHRIS MILNER

7.1 INTRODUCTION

Empirical work on the welfare effects of commercial policy has prolifated in the last two decades. This is due to 'innovations' in trade theory, empirical methodology and in commercial policy instruments. Theoretical developments in the area of international trade and trade policy have widened our perspective as to the nature of the potential costs and benefits of trade policy interventions. In the context of the traditional models of trade we tend to focus on the static production, consumption and terms of trade effects of trade barriers. The new theories of trade under imperfectly competitive conditions have highlighted other possible impacts on economic welfare: changes in costs of production resulting from scale or learning effects, changes in consumer choice associated with imports of differing variety or higher quality goods, or changes in market structures. Similarly, greater awareness of second-best theory has resulted in increased attention being given to the welfare effects of market distortions and externalities (private costs being likely to give distorted measures of the social opportunity costs of resources). Empirical innovations, although often lagging behind theoretical developments, have also taken place in the case of commercial policy evaluation. Computing innovations now permit the computations that have facilitated the development of applied general equilibrium analysis. Finally, 'instrument innovation' has taken place with policy-makers relying less on the use of traditional border interventions (tariffs and overt quantitative import restrictions) and relying more on less overt forms of intervention (such as VERS and administrative protection) or on interventions that are less evidently at international borders (such as industrial support measures).

Faced with this diversity of issues and types of empirical analysis, it would be impossible to cover all aspects in a single chapter. The aim will be instead to illustrate recent developments or the focus of work in four broad areas. Section 7.2 will review the traditional partial equilibrium/costs of protection approach, and the more recent extensions to the instruments of the 'new protectionism'. It includes also work on factor market distortions and domestic resource cost analysis. In the third section the use of computable general equilibrium (CGE) models in trade policy evaluation is discussed. Work on tariff liberalisation in a multi-country context and on non-tariff liberalisation in a single, developing country context is illustrated. In Section 7.4 the focus shifts from a perfect to an imperfect competition framework. Simulations for specific imperfectly competitive markets are examined, as is the use of CGE analysis in this context. The fifth section reports on the limited empirical work into the adjustment costs associated with trade policy change. Finally, Section 7.6 offers some concluding comments and some thoughts on the possible direction of future empirical work in this area.

7.2 TRADITIONAL MODELS AND PARTIAL EQUILIBRIUM ANALYSIS

As shown in the previous section, the focus of any welfare or cost of protection study will be influenced both by the task at hand and by the circumstances prevailing in the country(ies) and sector(s) under consideration. The traditional triangles approach to measuring the net (static) welfare effects of tariff intervention is illustrated in Figure 7.1. It represents the demand (DD_h) and supply (SS_h) for a single importable good, where foreign supply (S_f) is perfectly elastic and the *ad valorem* tariff changes from t_1 to t_2 (or vice versa in the case of increased tariff protection). The production and consumption gains of a tariff reduction are represented by the areas a and b respectively; the former is the reduced resource cost of acquiring Q_3Q_1 through importing from lower cost foreign producers rather than from local producers, and the latter is the additional welfare derived over and above the cost of importation associated with the increased consumption Q_2Q_4.

From Figure 7.1 the net welfare (W) gain can be approximated as follows:

$$W = \tfrac{1}{2}(T_1 + T_2)\Delta M \tag{7.1}$$

where $T_i = P_w t_i$.

The ΔM can be estimated from information (econometrically estimated from time series data or 'borrowed' from other studies) on the price elasticity of demand for imports (n_m) and the initial level of imports. A constant value of n_m implies, however, that the import demand function is non-linear, contrary to the basis on which the expression was derived. The simultaneous assumption of linearity and constant elasticity is an expedient likely to induce some inaccuracy; in the case of multi-commodity studies this may be reduced by offsetting errors.

The appropriateness of the above methodology depends upon the extent to which the assumptions of the model conform to reality.

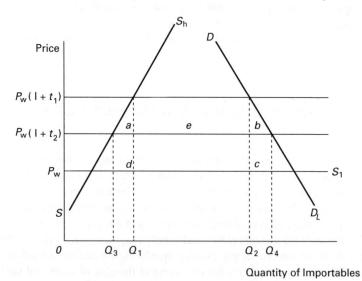

FIGURE 7.1   The effects of trade liberalisation

The absence of terms of trade effects

If the country is 'large' in the sense that it has market power in particular international markets, then it may not be appropriate to represent trading taking place at the same terms of trade (i.e., P_w) at all tariff-inclusive prices. Alternatively, terms of trade effects may be induced by trade policy interventions, where imported and import competing goods (or varieties) are not homogeneous (identical) and are produced under imperfectly competitive conditions.

The absence of tariff redundancy

The standard model above assumes that import-competing products will be priced fully up to the tariff-inclusive price of imports: i.e., that there is full information and that there is no differentiation in attributes or quality of the imported (M) and import-substitute (J) good. There may not be full information, for instance, in the case of remote or 'thin' markets for some goods in developing countries. In the case of industrialised countries then product differentiation is a common feature of many manufactured goods. In such circumstances we strictly need information on the elasticity of substitution between M and J.

The absence of intermediate inputs into importables production

Figure 7.1 represents both the production and consumption response to change in the tariff as being fashioned by changes in gross or nominal prices. Clearly consumers do base their decisions on gross prices, but producers will be concerned with the effects of tariffs on both the price of their final output and the cost of intermediate inputs (i.e., with net prices). Where intermediate inputs are important and where there is significant divergence between output and input tariffs (as is often the case in highly protected manufacturing sectors in some developing countries), then it is necessary to estimate the net or effective rates of protection.

The abstraction from dynamic effects

It may be appropriate to consider more than the static or once-and-for-all cost of a tariff (or tariff reduction). The cost of a tariff (or benefit of a tariff reduction) that is expected to be sustained should be the discounted value applying to a period of time. The estimation of the dynamic effects of commercial policies and the choice of appropriate discount rate is not without its difficulties.

The presence of 'static' expectations

If, as Saidi (1980) argues, decision-makers in tradable goods sectors form their expectations rationally, then their decision-making will change as commercial policy changes. The parameters of any model (e.g., import demand elasticities and elasticities of substitution) will therefore alter with policy change. This imposes a constraint on all empirical modelling of commercial policy effects, which have to rely on present rather than future (post-reform) parameter estimates. It must be hoped in such circumstances that parameter revisions are small or mutually offsetting.

The absence of distortions

The 'triangles' of Figure 7.1 are only valid measures of welfare change to the extent that first-best conditions apply. Where there are externalities which cause social and private valuations to diverge, or where there are other market and policy 'failures', then the valuations of any production and consumption changes induced by policy interventions will not be properly evaluated by the areas under DD_h and/or SS_h.

The absence of or abstraction from general equilibrium effects

By employing partial analysis we risk missing important indirect and feedback effects of commercial policy change. The larger is industry or sector J and, the larger the number of sectors under investigation, the more likely it is that income and relative price effects of commercial policy interventions will induce shifts in the supply and demand schedules of Figure 7.1.

The abstraction from adjustment costs

The traditional welfare or deadweight gains approach to the evaluation of trade policy tends to gloss over the important (from a policy viewpoint) problem of adjustment costs: the cost of switching resources from import-competing to export industries. In a neo-classical world of perfectly flexible prices and perfect factor mobility, a country stays on its production-possibility frontier. In practice the cost of resource re-allocation (often seen as a cost to labour only from adjustment) in the form of unemployment rather than also in the form of capacity under-utilisation should be substracted from the surplus triangles in order to provide a measure of *net* welfare gain or loss to society. This adjustment cost, which explains much of the political resistance to trade liberalisation, is frequently overlooked or unquantified by empirical studies.

Some evidence on tariff liberalisation

Cline *et al.* (1978) and Stone (1977) estimate the (expected) welfare effects of the Tokyo Round on tariff reductions for individual, and groups of, developed countries, using partial analysis.[1] Table 7.1 offers a general summary of these two studies.[2] Both studies provide results on a 1974 base (for Cline, a 1974 update from an earlier base year), without allowing for the effects of any induced exchange-rate changes. The estimates for export expansion are very similar at about $3 billion (in the US sense of thousand million), although the Stone estimates for import expansion and gross employment effects are somewhat smaller. In both cases the estimated gross changes are small compared to existing levels of trade and employment. Of course, the net effects are even smaller; indeed, they are so small for the USA as to be virtually insignificant. This type of conclusion agrees with earlier studies of trade liberalisation and might lead one to conclude that the costs of protection or gains of tariff liberalisation are not substantial.

However, the USA is a relatively closed economy and relatively larger effects may be expected for smaller and more open economies. In addition, the results reported in Table 7.1 are the static or once-and-for-all effects of tariff reduction for *one* year only: they take no account of cumulative gains from trade liberalisation accruing over time. A gain, relative to what would have happened without the tariff reduction, will in fact accrue in subsequent years as well. The results also take no account of possible dynamic gains from decreased X-inefficiency, scale economies or growth effects on investment for instance. Cline *et al.* (1978) do include a 'guesstimate' of these effects; they claim a conservative estimate to be about five times the static gains. These authors also take account of recurring gains over time. The net present value of the cumulative gains is shown to be much more significant relative to existing income and trade levels, even if some allowance for labour adjustment costs is made;[3] but the orders of magnitude reported must be viewed with great caution in the light of

TABLE 7.1   Partial equilibrium estimates of multilateral tariff reductions

(a) Scope of studies

	Cline *et al.* (1978)	Stone (1977)
Country coverage	USA; EEC; Japan; Canada;some results for 7 other DCs	USA; EEC; Japan
Number of tariff reduction formulae considered	12	2
Degree of disaggregation in estimation	About 500 tariff-line items for industrial countries	37 commodity categories
Base year for:		
trade data	1971, updated to 1974	1974
tariff data	post-Kennedy Round	post-Kennedy Round
input-output data	1970	1974

(b) Results of studies for USA (50% tariff cut)

	1974 update	1974 base
ΔX	+$3 210m	+$2 939m
ΔM	+$3 031m	+$2 155m
Direct Δ employment		
from ΔX	+71 000 man years	+32 000 man years
from ΔM	−55 000 man years	−23 000 man years
Δ welfare	+$436m	+$177m

DC = developed countries.
Source: Adapted from Kreinin and Officer (1979), Tables 1 and 3.

the methodological problems discussed above, and of the specific technical and data problems one faces in this type of empirical work.

'Equivalence' and non-tariff barriers

The 'new protectionism' has involved instruments that are non-tariff and non-transparent in nature. Empirical study has been confronted therefore with the problem of both identifying the extent of non-tariff barriers and with measuring their impact. There are likely to be deficiencies in information for the very reason that they are often intended to be non-transparent or hidden. Growing interest in the 1980s in this policy area generated greater efforts on the part of international agencies (IMF, UNCTAD, GATT, etc.) and of national governments (see, e.g., C. D. Jones, 1987, or Laird and Yeats, 1990) to improve their inventories of information on non-tariff barriers. However, we still face the problem of identifying the impact of a particular non-tariff barrier or combination of non-tariff barriers on price, in order to replicate the earlier model for estimating the 'deadweight' welfare effects of a tariff-equivalent of the non-tariff barrier.[4] The effect on price will not always be obvious. The most straightforward method of approximating the tariff equivalent $(\hat{t})$ of non-tariff barriers is to measure the differential between domestic (P_d) and international (P_w) prices:

$$\hat{t} = \frac{P_d - P_w}{P_w} = \frac{P_d}{P_w} - 1 \tag{7.2}$$

There are, however, a number of obvious problems associated with this approach. We must be able to adjust the domestic price for any actual tariffs and must assume that there is no tariff redundancy (pricing up by less than that permitted by the tariff and non-tariff barrier). We must also assume that there are no other distortions (besides the non-tariff barrier) or quality differences that are influencing the domestic price, and that the world price itself is not distorted in any way.

Yeats and Roningen (1977) used this price differentials approach (making some adjustments for the types of problems mentioned above) for a wide range of export commodities from less developed countries (LDCs) to fifteen developed market economies. They concluded that the average 'pure NTB residual' was generally considerably in excess of average tariff rates in industrial countries. This result is consistent with the results of the studies cited earlier on the effects of the Tokyo Round agreement on non-tariff barriers on specific industries. Cline *et al.* estimate that in the case of agriculture, a 60 per cent reduction in the *(ad valorem)* equivalent of the EEC variable import levies would cause imports to increase by more than half the total rise in manufacturing imports resulting from a 50 per cent tariff reduction.

There is usually no attempt in multi-country and sector studies to use the price differentials and elasticities approach to calculate deadweight gains from non-tariff barrier liberalisation (in the case of Cline *et al.* there is an estimate only for the reduction of EEC protection of agriculture). On the one hand, the scale of the task deters aggregate studies, while on the other hand the tariff equivalent residual is likely to be a compound of several influences when working at the aggregate level. It is for this reason that the work on non-tariff barriers tends to concentrate on specific industries and specific barriers.[5]

Industry studies of the 'costs' of the new protectionism

The management of trade in textiles (specifically of imports into the developed market economies from LDCs) since the 1960s (under the Short and then Long Term Arrangement on Cotton Textiles, and more recently under the MFA, which have 'legalised' the use of quantitative restrictions in response to market disruption) has generated a large potential source of information on the effects of non-tariff barriers. Keesing and Wolf (1980), for instance, provide a comprehensive examination of the global textiles market. They find widespread evidence of the price-raising effects of quotas, from which deadweight losses could be (but are not) calculated.

Several studies have attempted to infer the price-raising effects of quantitative restrictions. One approach has been based on a rather ingenious improvisation. Markets for quota licences have emerged in many of the countries where their exports are subject to quantitative restrictions in industrialised countries. To the extent that these markets are reasonably competitive and efficient, the prices paid for licences, the quota premia, serve to proxy the price-raising effects of the restrictions in the industrial markets. If we refer back to Figure 7.1, with the prevailing tariff set at level t_2 and a general import quota at the level Q_1Q_2, then a price rise is induced and required to reduce imports from Q_3Q_4 to Q_1Q_2. In this case the price must rise to $P_w(1+t_1)$, and this is equivalent to an increase in the *ad valorem* tariff of t_1-t_2. In the case of a country-specific quota or VER, the possibility of trade diversion to non-restricted sources of supply necessitates a larger country-specific quota than Q_1Q_2. Note also that in the case of a VER (ignoring the possibility of monopoly supply influences), that part of the maximum quota revenue[6] (area e in Figure 7.1) accrues to the affected exporters (since by definition the VER is administered by the exporting country).[7] This redistribution of 'rent' from home country authorities (as in the case for a tariff) to specific overseas suppliers therefore involves an additional loss from the national perspective. The redistribution may explain the willingness of the exporting countries to tolerate such hidden controls outside the GATT framework.

Variations in demand for licences over the year and cycle produce variability in premia, and therefore necessitates judicial use of the information. Nevertheless, in the case of Hong Kong, for instance, the market is legally sanctioned (and, given the size of Hong Kong's exports in specific areas, e.g., footwear and clothing, is clearly subject to competitive forces) and detailed data are officially published. (In other cases the markets are unofficial but tolerated, and data are available).

Following on work by Morkre and Tarr (1980) for the USA and Jenkins (1983) for Canada, Greenaway and Hindley (1985) have used such information to estimate the welfare costs of quantitative restrictions on imports of footwear and finished clothing into the UK, or the deadweight gains from their total removal.

C. Hamilton (1980b) develops a methodology to estimate the effects of partial lowering of VERs. It turns out to be important to distinguish between cases in which, from the exporter's point of view, the commodities involved are perfect or imperfect substitutes in export markets and, from the importing country's point of view, the commodities are perfect or imperfect substitutes to domestic production. Hamilton derives formulae for estimating the potential price changes (under alternative substitutional conditions), employing elasticity estimates from other empirical work, of an import increase into Sweden of 50 per cent of commodities under VERs from countries subject to VERs. He employs the maximum potential price falls for this import growth of textiles and clothing in the estimation of welfare and employment effects. Some results of this study are set out in Table 7.2. Significant potential consumer gains are identified, although the price effects are

TABLE 7.2 Maximum estimated deadweight gains and employment losses if VER imports increased by 50% in the case of Swedish textiles and clothing imports (1977)

	Average price fall (%)	Deadweight gain (US$ m)*	Man-years lost
Textiles	20	85.7	1290
Clothing	8.7	96.6	1580
Total	–	182.3	2870

* 1980 prices.

Source: Adapted from C. Hamilton (1980b).

modest for some commodity groups within clothing in particular (given that maximum potential price effects are identified). The potential unemployment is identified in the industry's marginal plants, where lower productivity is likely to express itself in higher labour inputs per unit of output than the industry average. By employing a model of the Salter (1960) type, Hamilton seeks to avoid a downward bias which he views as inherent in traditional estimates of the employment effects of trade policy adjustments. It is not average production units but more labour-intensive marginal units that have to close down as a result of increased import penetration. There is no attempt, however, in this particular study to evaluate the welfare costs of this unemployment. But, by way of comparison, Hamilton estimates the welfare and employment effects of a hypothetical withdrawal of the actual government subsidies given to the textiles and clothing industries during the 1973–77 period. The number of marginal man-years lost by the increase in restricted imports and by the withdrawal of subsidies turns out to be very similar.

It is possible to compare the cost of 'saving' each marginal man-year by the alternative non-tariff barriers. The average budget cost per man-year saved by subsidies is estimated at $8260, while the consumers' (deadweight) gain forgone per man-year by more restrictive VERs is $40 040 on average. In line with the theory of optimal intervention, job saving by a quantitative import restriction is much more expensive (in welfare terms) than through government subsidies. The idea of differences in the 'cost effectiveness' of alternative means of job protection is supported by other empirical studies (Pearson, 1983;

TABLE 7.3   A comparison of costs of alternative trade restrictions

	OMA	Tariff-equivalent*
Change in quantity of imports (in pairs)	25 m.	25 m.
Diversion to third countries	12.1 m.	0
US welfare loss	$68.8 m.	$10.1 m.
Global welfare loss	$12.2 m.	$10.1 m.
Quota premium to Taiwan	$43.6 m.	0
Tariff revenue effect	–$2.2 m.	+$56.6 m.
Increase in US employment	3132	3132
Annual US welfare cost per job protected	$21 967	$3224

* An *ad valorem* tariff set at 16.4% (10.4% above the initial tariff).

Source: Adapted from Pearson (1983), p. 51.

Wolf *et al.*, 1984). Some illustrative information from Pearson's study of the protection (by means of OMAs with Taiwan and South Korea) of the US footwear industry is set out in Table 7.3. The consumer loss in the USA for an equal net (of any trade diversion) reduction in the quantity of imports achieved by the alternative interventions is the same ($66.6 million). There are, however, significant differences in quota premium and tariff revenue effects between the two measures. For the (discriminatory) non-tariff restriction there is a tariff revenue loss on the reduced imports; tariff revenue increases substantially, by contrast, in the non-discriminatory, tariff-equivalent case. Thus US welfare loss (consumer loss minus revenue effect) is substantially different for OMAs and tariffs. (There is little difference, however, in terms of global welfare loss, because there is a substantial redistribution of welfare or rent from the USA to Taiwan in the form of quota premium.) The national (annual) welfare cost of protecting each of the estimated 3132 jobs is therefore nearly seven times greater for the OMA than for an equivalent tariff.

Factor market distortions and resource costs

Ironically there has been very little standard cost of protection analysis based on the 'triangles' method used in the context of developing countries, and this despite the fact that many developing countries have used an array of tariff and non-tariff barriers against imports in much of the post-war period. Indeed, even in the last decade when trade liberalisation has been pursued in many developing countries as part of Structural Adjustment Programmes, there has been little or no attempt to measure systematically the (static) potential gains from such liberalisation. The complexity of trade policy arrangements and data deficiencies (in particular in constraining econometric work to estimate the relevant elasticities) are no doubt part of the explanation for this gap in the empirical analysis.[8] But probably of more importance is the fundamental limitation on the use of the 'triangles method' where other product and factor market distortions are pervasive. Many developing countries experience a range of market imperfections and policy controls (e.g., price controls, minimum wage legislation, etc.) that can result in a divergence between market prices and shadow prices or social opportunity costs. This has led trade and industrial policy analysts working in a developing country context to use alternative tools which attempt to take account of distortions and eliminate them from the calculation of the 'costs' and 'benefits' of local production. A commonly used tool is the domestic resource cost (DRC) ratio, which seeks to measure the social opportunity cost or true domestic resource cost of a given local activity relative to the undistorted world resource cost.

Thus, the DRC coefficient of a commodity compares the opportunity cost of the primary factors (land, labour and capital) used in the production of that commodity with value-added in border prices. The coefficient shows the border price value of the resources in their best alternative use per unit of border priced return from the resources in their existing use. If the estimated coefficient exceeds unity, it can be concluded that, in principle, the resource could be put to better use in an alternative activity. In these terms the DRC ratio can be thought of as indicating activities of comparative advantage and disadvantage.

The DRC ratio for a given activity can be estimated as:

$$DRC_j = \frac{DC_j}{IVA_j} \qquad\qquad (7.3)$$

where:

DC_j = domestic cost of producing j with factors valued at their social opportunity costs

IVA_j = value-added in activity j at border prices

The higher is DRC_j the more costly in terms of domestic resources it is to produce this product. Another way of interpreting this ratio, which is infinitely more appealing, is to think of it as the costs to the economy of saving foreign exchange (through import substitution) or acquiring foreign exchange (through exporting). For example, if for a given activity the estimated DRC ratio comes out at 2, this tells us that the value of domestic resources used up in producing a unit of the relevant product is twice what it would cost to import it. Other things being equal the DRC ratio can therefore be thought of as an (*ex post*) index of comparative advantage. Ratios in excess of one indicate comparative disadvantage in the sense that the value of domestic resources used up in producing the product exceeds the value of foreign exchange required to import it. The higher the ratio the greater the domestic resources needed to produce it.

The operationalisation of the DRC concept requires that we are able to identify appropriate shadow prices or social opportunity cost measures. There is a vast literature on this subject (see Tower, 1991). In economies with long and extensive histories of government intervention, the need to have a set of prices which reflect as closely as possible the social gains and losses associated with actual policy, as well as the changes in that policy, is apparent. Ideally one would attempt to calculate 'first-best' shadow prices which assume that all government interventions will be dismantled. In this sense the shadow prices reflect true opportunity costs generated by a system completely free of distortions. In practice, however, one is frequently engaged in estimating 'second-best' shadow prices: i.e., those which prevail on the assumption that pre-existing non-optimal policies will remain in effect. The distinction matters for, as Findlay and Wellisz (1976) and Srinivasan and Bhagwati (1978) have shown, shadow prices will vary according to whether first-best or second-best conditions hold.

As we shall see later, CGE modelling techniques do offer a technology which can simulate the effect of removing a number of, or a subset of, or all, distortions in a given situation. Even here, though, the shadow prices one observes are driven by the model structure rather than the true structure of the economy. In the context of DRC analysis one is invariably estimating second-best shadow prices. Moreover, the exercise tends still to be constrained by data availability.

Despite these constraints there is a reasonable amount of empirical work that has used the DRC technique. Table 7.4 summarises the results of a study on a sample of firms from the manufacturing sector in Madagascar, taken from Greenaway and Milner (1990). The average DRC ratio for this sample of activities is in excess of 2; on

TABLE 7.4   Pattern of DRC ratios by industry in Madagascar, 1983

Industry	Number of firms	Average DRC	Industry range
1. Food and drink	5	3.99	0.82–9.35
2. Pharmaceuticals	3	2.49	0.79–3.68
3. Chemicals	4	1.40	0.78–2.38
4. Textiles	1	1.71	
5. Footwear and leather	2	1.65	1.39–1.91
6. Wood products	2	3.04	2.49–3.58
7. Metal products	5	2.15	1.33–3.02
8. Electrical products	1	1.40	
9. Paper products	2	0.64	0.60–0.68
10. Construction goods	1	1.70	
11. Miscellaneous	1	2.68	

Source: Greenaway and Milner (1990).

average, the value of resources required to earn/save a unit of foreign exchange is more than that suggested by the official exchange rate for tradable goods. Clearly this is the result of a highly protectionist and discriminatory (given the high average and variance of the ratios) trade policy. The 'triangles method' would have severely understated the production cost of this protection. Note, however, that the DRC ratios abstract from the potentially large consumption costs that would be identified by the triangles approach. DRC and 'triangles' measures can be viewed therefore as complementary tools of empirical analysis.

7.3   COMPUTABLE GENERAL EQUILIBRIUM MODELLING OF TRADE POLICY

The use of CGE models for policy analysis in general has become widespread in both developed and developing countries. In the case of developing countries this proliferation of CGE modelling has been driven by an interest in the impact of broad scale strategic or structural adjustment reforms (including commercial policy reforms), often in situations where econometric modelling techniques would be subject to severe data constraints. In the case of individual industrialised countries, applied CGE modelling has tended to address specific domestic policy issues relating in particular to taxation, although the application of CGE techniques to areas such as environmental analysis is growing. In the trade policy area, a large-scale modelling effort by Dixon *et al.* (1982) for Australia has been used to investigate trade policy options. More work in this area, however, has been multi-country in nature; studies to evaluate the effects of tariff liberalisation in the context of GATT negotiating rounds (F. Brown and Whalley, 1980; Whalley, 1985; Deardorff and Stern, 1986), and studies to evaluate the effects of regional trade liberalisation (D. K. Brown and Stern, 1987; Cox and Harris, 1992, on the North American Free Trade Area). These types of multi-country models tend to lose the detailed commodity or industry focus possible with the partial equilibrium approach, but they are able to capture income and terms of trade effects that are abstracted from by partial techniques. They also offer comprehensiveness, which is invariably not sought or is not possible with partial techniques.

Some principles and problems

An individual market is in equilibrium when the quantity of the particular good demanded is equal to the quantity supplied. General equilibrium analysis deals explicitly with the inter-relationships between different markets and different sectors of an economy or several economies. If there are c commodity markets and f factor markets, there will be $c + f = n$ markets and $n-1$ equilibrium prices to be determined if all markets are to be in equilibrium; when they are all in equilibrium, the economy will be in a state of general equilibrium. Walras' Law states that for a given set of prices the sum of the excess demands over all markets must be equal to zero. In other words, if one market has positive excess demand, some others must have excess supply; and if all but one are in balance, so is that one. If all economic agents are satisfying their budget constraints and $n-1$ markets are in equilibrium, then the nth market will also be cleared. These concepts about a Walrasian general equilibrium system were formalised and elaborated on in the 1950s by economists such as Arrow and Debreu (1954). With a specified number of consumers, each of which has an initial endowment of commodities and a given set of preferences, there are market demand functions for each commodity which are the sum of each individual's demand. These market demands for commodities are determined by all prices; the functions are well behaved and satisfy Walras' Law, i.e., the total value of consumers' expenditures equals consumer incomes. On the production side constant returns to scale and profit maximisation are assumed if a competitive solution is assumed. Given these model characteristics it is relative, not absolute, prices that are of significance. General equilibrium is characterised by a set of (relative) prices and pattern of production that clears the market for each commodity. (For an illustration and numerical example of the structure of a simple general equilibrium model see Whalley, 1991, or Greenaway and Milner, 1993.)

A range of problems are encountered in designing and using an applied CGE model. What type of model structure is required for the particular purpose at hand? For that general structure, how are functional forms and parameter values to be chosen? How is the model to be solved? How is the calibrated model to be used to evaluate policy change? Space constraints prevent a discussion of these issues separately (see Whalley and Shoven 1984, and Greenaway and Milner,

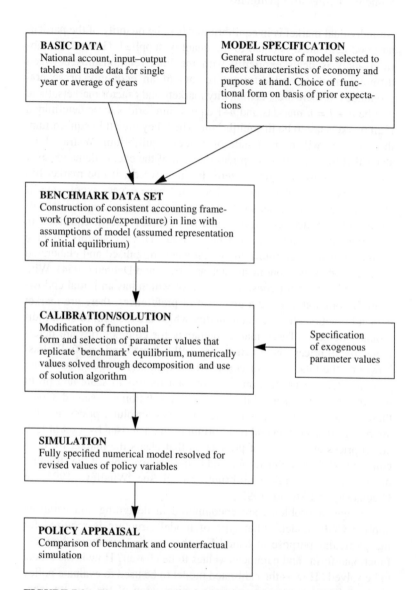

FIGURE 7.2   The process of applied general equilibrium analysis

1993, for a discussion of these issues). Figure 7.2 summarises the broad stages of the CGE modelling process. The important point to make is that there is no unique modelling form or solution procedure. This is a strength of CGE analysis: it has the ability to adapt the modelling purpose at hand and to the circumstances that are being represented. However, there is also the danger that the modelling approach will largely predetermine the conclusions of the analysis. But, as with all applied economic analysis, its robustness needs to be challenged through critical questioning and sensitivity analysis of the assumptions and parameter values used. Let us turn to an illustration of some trade policy applications of CGE modelling.

Multi-country evaluation

F. Brown and Whalley (1980) produce a general equilibrium model which incorporates four trading blocs, the (nine-member) EEC, the USA, Japan and the rest of the world. The model consists of thirty-three broad products groups, each of which is treated as being differentiated and produced solely in one of the trading blocs. Production and demand patterns in each trade area are influenced by domestic and world prices. An equilibrium is achieved where demands equal supplies in all products and there are zero abnormal profits. The effect of a tariff change in any country is to alter the relative prices of imported and domestically produced goods and to change import volumes. This, in turn, changes domestic demand patterns and indirectly product prices until equilibrium is restored. Comparison of equilibrium situations permits the measurement of changes in global welfare and the distribution of gains or losses by trading area.

The model was estimated by assembling a set of data (in this case for 1973) consistent with the conditions of the model (competitive equilibrium and zero trade balances). Data limitations abound, given the divergent sources of the material, but in addition corrections are necessary to adjust the data so that the equilibrium conditions are satisfied. From the benchmark/equilibrium data it is possible to estimate parameter values, e.g., point estimates of the price elasticities of demand for imports in each trading area. Once fully specified, the model can be solved for a general equilibrium, and this contrasted with the general equilibrium impact of a tariff-cutting formula. The estimated welfare effects by trading area for the Swiss formula (which was ultimately accepted as the general point of reference in the Tokyo round negotiations) are set

TABLE 7.5   General equilibrium welfare effects of Swiss tariff cutting proposal in Tokyo Round by trading bloc

Trading bloc	Welfare effect (1973 $USb.)
EEC	+1.45
USA	+0.79
Japan	+0.49
Rest of world	−1.75
World total	0.98

Source: Adapted from F. Brown and Whalley (1980).

out in Table 7.5. The (static) global gain is again small compared to the existing value of production (about $1200 billion for US GNP in 1973). This again applies to one year only. What is interesting about these results, however, is not so much the consistency of the absolute gains with other studies, but the distribution of the welfare effects. The major winner is the EEC and the major loser is the rest of the world. Brown and Whalley argue that this possibility of significant terms of trade effects can be explained in this instance by the exclusion of agricultural products from the tariff negotiations and by the fact that the rest of the world is an exporter of raw materials which already have low tariffs applied to them.

This study (like others) demonstrates that the global gains likely under any of the tariff-cutting proposals considered under the Tokyo Round of negotiations were small when estimated for a single year. However, the potential gains from the removal of all tariff and non-tariff distortions in the industrial camp are much larger, as are the discounted gains over longer time periods for a given reduction. Brown and Whalley suggest a figure in the region of $20 billion *per year* for complete liberalisation (and this is without considering the potential gains from liberalisation in the less developed countries).

Costs of protection and rent seeking in a developing country

Developing countries, especially prior to the trade policy reforms of the 1980s, typically used quantitative restrictions on imports, as well as tariffs, to protect domestic producers and ration foreign exchange. The regulation of imports in the late 1970s in Turkey, for instance, involved the classification of imports as follows: an unrestricted list of non-competing imports of raw materials and parts; a restricted list of competing intermediate and final goods imports for which an import licence was required; and a quota list (with quotas for specific commodities) of allocations between producers and consumers.

Grais, de Melo and Urata (1986) construct a tariff-quantitative restriction (TQR) model calibrated to 1978 Turkish data to estimate the welfare costs of such protection and of the extensive rent-seeking activity by industrialists associated with the import rationing induced by this trade policy regime.

The modelling of a trade regime like this is, of course, extremely difficult. The restrictiveness of the regime, and therefore the effects of any liberalisation, depends upon the extent to which the quantitative restrictions alone or QRs quantitative restrictions and tariffs combined have a binding effect before any policy change on the volume of imports. It is difficult to estimate with precision what the effects of the lowering of either policy instrument will be on import volumes, in particular of new products. This difficulty is compounded when, as might be expected, import restrictions induce smuggling and other illegal means of circumventing the controls. Thus, in order to simplify the model and analysis, the model sharply divides imports into three categories. It is assumed that investment and government goods are subject to tariffs only, consumer goods to both tariffs and quantitative restrictions but no rent-seeking activity, while intermediate goods are subject to tariffs, quantitative restrictions and rent-seeking activity. The authors estimate the welfare costs of quantity rationing and rent seeking; rationing of consumers in their purchase of imports of final goods and rationing and rent seeking by producers whose purchases of intermediate imports are restricted.

Rent-seeking activity is introduced into the model such that producers are induced to divert resources away from productive activities into acquiring import licences for intermediates and the rents associated with them. The model assumes that the entire value of the rents is spent on the production of rent-seeking activity. Thus the effect of rent seeking is to raise the price of intermediate inputs to the final user and to reduce the output of 'productive activities', but not to generate utility since the output of 'directly unproductive activities' is not an element in final demand.

The costs resulting from rationing and rent seeking can be illustrated by Figure 7.3 for a single sector. In the absence of rationing the

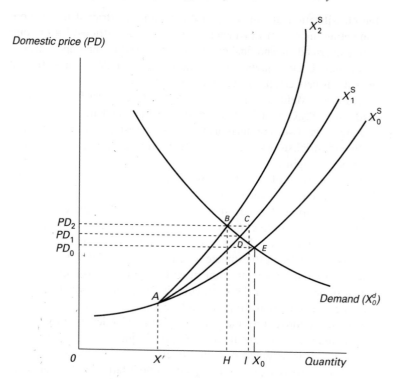

FIGURE 7.3   Welfare cost of rationing and rent seeking

domestic price is PD_0, which corresponds with the intersection of the initial domestic demand (X_0^d) and supply to the domestic market (X_0^s). Thus the 'traditional' output level (without rent-seeking activity) would be X_0. The rationing of intermediates causes the marginal costs of production to rise, and the supply schedule beyond X' (the level at which import rationing is binding) shifts leftward from X_0^s to X_1^s. At the resulting higher domestic price (PD_1) and reduced output of 'traditional' output associated with point D, there is a deadweight loss which can be represented by the area ADE. The effect of rent seeking is to push the supply curve further to the left, i.e., to X_2^s, as output is diverted from 'traditional' to rent-seeking activity. Relative to the numeraire, this raises the domestic price to PD_2 and the deadweight loss by the area

TABLE 7.6 Welfare gains from trade liberalisations* in Turkey
(% increase relative to base values in 1978)

	Real GDP	Real consumption	Real investment
Removal of QRs[+] on intermediate goods	+5.2	+3.8	+11.2
Removal of QRs[+] on intermediate and consumer goods	+5.4	+4.2	+11.0
Removal of all QRs[+] and a 50% cut in tariffs across the board	+5.5	+5.7	+7.1

* Assuming capital mobility across sectors.
[+] QRs = Quantitative restrictions.

Source: Grais, de Melo and Urata (1986), Table 7.

ABD. Thus the total deadweight loss associated with the restriction of output (*ABE*) can be broken down into a cost of rationing (*ADE*) and cost of rent seeking (*ABD*). At the final (distorted) domestic price (PD_2) producers would be willing to supply quantity *OI*, but only produce *OH* quantity of 'traditional' output because of rent-seeking production. *HI* 'production' of rent-seeking activity at price PD_2 values these rents at a level represented by the area *HBCI*.

The welfare effects of trade liberalisation in Turkey in 1978 using the eight-sector TQR model are reported in summary in Table 7.6. The gains of liberalisation (or, if the signs are reversed, the costs of rationing and rent seeking) are expressed as percentage increases over the base values. Overall gains in real GDP are estimated to be over 5 per cent. Interestingly the bulk of the potential gains (or costs) arise out of the rationing of imports of intermediate goods; eliminating quantitative restrictions on consumer goods and then lowering tariffs also across the board raises the total estimated gains by only 0.2 per cent and 0.1 per cent respectively. Clearly these results are sensitive to model specification (including the modelling of rent-seeking activity) and to the price-raising effects of quantitative restrictions incorporated into the calibrated solution for the base case. Nonetheless the results are indicative at least, and offer a richness that is unlikely to be available from partial equilibrium estimation techniques. The simulations will throw out new equilibrium values for all the endogenous variables in the model. In this case, for example, we are able also to comment on the costs of quantitative restrictions in terms of forsaken consumption and the reduced productive potential associated with lower investment levels.

7.4   IMPERFECT COMPETITION, TRADE AND WELFARE

In general the empirical work described in the previous sections has been based upon the traditional paradigms of trade theory; an assumed world of perfect competition, homogeneous goods and constant or decreasing returns to scale. The 1980s witnessed an explosion of theoretical interest in the determinants and implications of trade where there is imperfect competition, product differentiation and economies of scale of some form. Theory has indicated how trade can offer new potential sources of welfare gain – opportunities to reap increased economies of scale or greater access to variety – but it has also challenged some of the orthodox conclusions about the normative implications of commercial policy interventions. In this new 'second-best' world, more cases where trade interventions can increase national welfare have been suggested. The empirical robustness of these results has not yet been thoroughly investigated, partly because of the inherent problems of measuring or capturing the features of imperfectly competitive market structures and behaviour. There has, however, been some pioneering work on simulating specific markets, and CGE modellers have also begun to explore the implications of incorporating imperfect competition and non-constant returns into a general equilibrium framework.

Simulation studies

Using a specific model of imperfect competition for a particular industry or market, the analyst seeks to operationalise the model through a mixture of setting plausible elasticity values (through own estimation or as borrowed from other studies) and calibrating other behavioural parameters. With the empirical model reproducing specific values for the endogenous variables, the modeller can investigate the impact of policy(ies) by changing the values for the (exogenously-set) policy variables. The usefulness of any policy simulation results will be assessed on how well the model captures the actual market conditions (prior to policy adjustment). Good replication capability does not, of course, necessarily mean that the 'right' model is being used, and neither does it ensure that the simulated policy outcomes are robust. The Lucas critique applies: market structure and behaviour may change as policy changes. Indeed, we cannot check the stimulated results against real events; we can only investigate the logical consistency and plausibility of the model given its sensitivity or otherwise to changes in specification and parameter values.

R. Baldwin and Krugman (1988b) have modelled the market for 16K RAMs in order to investigate the role of Japanese protection of its domestic market in shifting comparative advantage from the USA to Japan. The model allows for increasing returns, oligopolistic interaction, and free entry. The cost function is defined by a technically determined yield coefficient, which is uniform across firms and set by inference from other published information. Two markets, with the same constant elasticity of demand (again borrowed from other literature), are assumed. The difference in revenue from foreign and home sales is fixed by an assumed percentage transport cost. The base-year market structure is approximated by six equal-cost US firms and three equal-cost Japanese firms. All Japanese firms are assumed to have the same conjectural variations (CVs) in the US market and the same (but higher) CVs in their home market, while all US firms have the same CVs in

TABLE 7.7   Simulation results of Baldwin and Krugman model

Variable	Base case	Free trade	Trade war
Welfare			
USA	1651.8	1827.5	335.3
Japan	698.4	738.9	725.6
Consumer surplus			
USA	1651.8	373.4	335.3
Japan	698.4	151.4	104.0
Price			
USA	1.47	1.30	1.49
Japan	1.47	1.37	2.19
Import shares			
USA in Japan	0.14	1.0	0.0
Japan in USA	0.19	0.0	0.0
Number of firms			
USA	6	7	7
Japan	3	0	5

Source: R. Baldwin and Krugman (1988b), Table 7.5.

both markets. This asymmetry arises out of the desire to have the size of the strategic trade barrier determined by the calibration exercise itself.

A comparison of alternative simulations, unrestricted US access to the Japanese market and a trade war (i.e., prohibitive tariffs in both markets), is set out in Table 7.7. With free trade seven US producers and no Japanese producers are predicted. Thus they conclude that Japanese trade policy did fashion the pattern of comparative advantage. Without a protected home market, Japanese firms would have had lower output and higher marginal costs, and would have been forced to exit from all markets. The welfare effects of Japanese protection policy are shown, however, to be negative for both the USA and Japan. Japanese consumers lose more than Japanese producers gain, and the world has higher costs with nine chip producers than with seven. Retaliation by the USA would, however, reduce US welfare still further; protected US firms would operate with smaller production runs and higher unit costs.

There are a number of potential theoretical and empirical weaknesses concerning this specific model. The results are plausible, however, and although there is no way of proving whether the model actually captures what happened in the early 1980s in this particular market, this type of empirical approach does indicate one important direction in which policy and welfare analysis is likely to evolve. Other single industry work of this type on strategic trade policy issues includes work on wide-bodied jet aircraft by Dixit and Kyle (1985) and R. Baldwin and Krugman (1988a), and on the car industry by Dixit (1988) for the USA and by Laussel, Montet and Peguin-Feissolle (1988) for the EC. Multi-industry simulations of imperfect competition models are also now being undertaken; Smith and Venables (1988), for instance, employ a ten industry/six country model to estimate the effects of completing the EC's internal market. They identify direct welfare gains from the lowering of intra-EC trade barriers, but interestingly show that larger welfare effects are available from the reduction of market segmentation. Clearly this new empirical work on the costs of protection is extending, as suggested earlier in this chapter, into aspects of cost that have been neglected by the traditional approaches.

New trade models and CGE analysis

As in the case of traditional partial equilibrium analysis, by focusing empirical investigations of strategic trade policy on a single or restricted set of industries we run the risk of missing important general equilibrium implications of policy intervention. Several studies have, however, incorporated features of the new trade theory into CGE models of the whole economy.

Cox and Harris (1985) predict substantially greater gains from Canadian trade liberalisation when imperfectly, rather than perfectly, competitive industries are assumed. This result strengthens the case for general free trade, especially if reciprocated with increased access to foreign markets. The Harris–Cox model has been criticised on a number of grounds. Firms are represented as either colluding in setting a 'focal price' equal to the world price plus tariff, or as monopolistically competitive ones setting price as a mark-up over marginal cost (with the size of the mark-up depending upon the firm's perceived market power). For their calculations, Harris and Cox assume that the actual price charged is a weighted average of these two prices rather than assuming either method when running the simulations. The Harris and Cox estimate of a net welfare gain from trade liberalisation equivalent to about 9 per cent of Canadian GDP (1976 base) must be viewed with caution as a result. Wigle (1988), for instance, using a specific rather than average pricing rule along with some other differences, actually estimates a net welfare loss (–0.1% of GDP).

Brown and Stern (1987, 1989) have applied the (Michigan) CGE model to the US–Canada free trade agreement. They also find that the estimated welfare gains to Canada are larger when imperfect competition is assumed, albeit with smaller magnitudes than the Cox–Harris model. But this series of papers shows that the results are sensitive to the nature of the market imperfection assumed. Brown and Stern (1989a) have run simulations of the model with three different types of competition assumed; imperfect competition between goods of different country of origin (the so-called Armington assumption); monopolistic competition as in the Harris–Cox model; and with segmented markets. Both the magnitudes of the net welfare effects and the sources of gains can differ significantly between the various market structures. Table 7.8 summarises some results from Brown and Stern (1989b) for Canada of free trade with the USA, with a best guess of the appropriate market structure for each industry (of the three above). The table shows a small terms of trade loss which is more than offset by efficiency gains to generate a net welfare increase (a positive equivalent variation of about $2 billion) for Canada equivalent to

TABLE 7.8   Summary of changes in a US–Canadian free trade area

Country	Imports*	Exports*	Exchange rates[+]	Terms of trade (%)	Equivalent variation[‡]
USA	6018.4	7348.0	–0.0	0.1	1540.6
Other	–8783.6	–3415.5	0.4	–0.1	–142.7
Canada	8272.6	8544.0	–1.1	–0.2	2077.0

* Dollar value of change in trade volume (US$ m.).
[+] (+) indicates depreciation of currency.
[‡] The income change valued at base period prices that yields the same change in welfare as the tariff reductions.

Source: Brown and Stern (1989b), Table 4.6.

1.1 per cent of GDP. Clearly much more work on refining the modelling of alternative sources of imperfection in markets is required before we can argue with any confidence about whether this more modest gain from trade policy reform or the more dramatic results of the Cox–Harris model apply.

7.5   ADJUSTMENT AND TRADE POLICY

In discussion of the partial and equilibrium empirical work in the previous sections there has been no discussion of the nature and speed of the adjustment processes associated with trade policy changes. As Table 7.1 shows many cost-of-protection studies estimate trade-induced employment displacement but often say little about the actual adjustment process.

The first task is to translate estimated changes in exports and imports into changes in domestic production. In the studies cited earlier, Cline *et al.* (1978) and Stone (1977) make arbitrary assumptions about the relationship between the trade changes and domestic production (a one-to-one relationship in the case of Cline *et al.*). R. E. Baldwin (1976), by contrast, uses the inverse of an inter-industry, input–output matrix to obtain trade-change (ΔX and ΔM separately) induced changes in domestic output. Output changes are then converted into changes in employment by multiplying the estimated output changes by average job/output coefficients. For Baldwin these coefficients relate to both direct and indirect employment. (The results are similar to those reported in Table 7.1.)

Although Baldwin's methodology overcomes the arbitrary nature of presumed relationships between trade change and domestic production, he achieves this by introducing a general equilibrium technique into what is otherwise a partial equilibrium analysis. The legitimacy of this depends on the appropriateness of partial analysis. It is most appropriate where we are satisfied with identifying and isolating impact effects of commercial policy changes. General equilibrium models may capture wider and longer-term effects. Stern (1978), for instance, treats eighteen industrial countries, with twenty-two tradable and seven non-tradable industries as a closed, general equilibrium system. Although with a full system of 6000 equations (finally reduced to thirty-nine) data problems are likely to be considerable and an assumption such as the law of one price is a helpful simplification, the methodology permits examination of long-run effects. Thus we may hesitate to attach great significance to the aggregate, net trade and employment effects estimated by Stern, but the disaggregated or cross-industry results may be instructive.

The appropriateness of the traditional partial equilibrium approach is also questioned by Pelzman and Bradberry (1980), who argue that the approach biases the estimated costs of redistributing resources from the import-competing sector following (unilateral) tariff reduction. They argue that it is inappropriate to assume that total expenditure on domestic-competing and imported goods will be constant in the move from one equilibrium to another; the possible responses in the disequilibrium process therefore induced by an increase in imports may consist of inventory changes and output changes, as well as changes in product price. The long-run import elasticity of output should, they argue, be estimated using a disequilibrium model of domestic supply which allows for both price and non-price rationing mechanisms. They also argue that multiplying estimated output changes by a set of labour requirements per unit of output ignores the fact that labour may be a quasi-fixed factor and the adjustment of labour to output changes may not be instantaneous or at a uniform rate. The adjustment of factor inputs towards their long-run equilibrium levels (i.e., the *long-run* output elasticity of employment) should be estimated from a set of partial adjustment equations.

These criticisms of traditional partial analysis are valid if the desire is to focus on the dynamic characteristics of the response to increasing imports (and this may be important for policy purposes). But Pelzman and Bradberry's conclusions – that the traditional approach significantly understates the costs of labour dislocation – must be viewed with some scepticism. Long-run elasticities are used to calculate impact effects in order to compare the traditional and their alternative approaches. If their criticisms are valid, then a dynamic model of adjustment to imports is required which would not be strictly comparable with the traditional, static model. But once dynamic factors are considered, we might also question the appropriateness of some methods used to calculate the costs to society of transitional unemployment. The loss to society is calculated as the product of the average hourly wage in the import-competing industry, the average hours worked and the average duration of unemployment, plus a negative wage differential over the displaced workers' lifetimes. This latter element is included on the presumption that trade liberalisation permanently reduces the productivity of those workers displaced. Even if this is the case, the full, possible dynamic effects are understated. Productivity growth in import-competing activities may be stimulated by liberalisation, or transfers of labour into higher productivity areas may be induced by liberalisation, but not necessarily in the form of transfers by labour directly displaced by imports. In fact there is empirical support for the view that trade liberalisation does encourage producitivity growth: see Blackhurst, Marian and Tumlir (1978).

More careful and detailed investigation is required into this aspect of the costs and benefits of trade liberalisation. Partial information is currently often presented in a potentially misleading manner, and often as points in the free trade versus protection debate. There is, for example, a considerable amount of evidence that, in the medium to long term, productivity change is in general a much more important source of job displacement than change in net trade positions (see Apan *et al.*, 1978; Cable, 1979). But, as we have already argued, productivity change is not independent of trade liberalisation. Thus the partial information (Bale, 1976; Lazear, 1976) about individual workers displaced by foreign competition can in turn be equally misleading. By merely deducting the transfer payments (unemployment insurance and any trade adjustment assistance) from the private losses to workers actually displaced, to obtain a measure of the loss to society or social cost (as measured earlier in this section), we ignore the wider or dynamic effects of trade expansion on productivity. Of course, it might be argued that many of these 'so-called' adjustment costs are in fact the product of other 'distortions' in product and factor markets and should therefore not be ascribed to trade policy adjustments.

7.6 CONCLUSIONS

The (static) gains from tariff and non-tariff liberalisation would appear to be relatively small from the viewpoint of the larger industrial countries in particular. This may help to explain in part why countries continue to 'protect' themselves and to use relatively inefficient instruments of protection. No doubt political economy factors also play an important role. Indeed, one of the interesting features of many of the empirical studies discussed in this chapter is that the distributional effects of commercial policies are often significant; the 'net' effects of intervention may be relatively small for a country or for the world, but there may be large redistributions from consumers to producers or to specific groups (e.g., to holders of import licences) or between countries. However, what is also clear from the recent work which incorporates imperfect competition, economies of scale and product differentiation is that there may be additional sources of gain from trade liberalisation which the traditional empirical work has failed to capture. Ironically the imperfect competition and the resulting second-best conditions have raised the theoretical possibility of strategic, welfare-raising trade policy interventions. The empirical work thus far does not find these results to be very robust, especially if retaliation is allowed for. But more applied work is required to test further the robustness of the results to model and parameter specification. In this regard, applied CGE analysis offers considerable scope for testing the ideas of strategic trade policy in a general rather than partial equilibrium setting. Practical limitations of strategic trade theory are likely to be exposed by such empirical testing, but that is not to say that the liberal case can claim robust empirical support for the view that the gains from trade are larger than are suggested by operationalisation of the static/traditional models. Clearly more empirical work is required on the testing of the 'new' trade theories, and on the dynamics of the trade expansion–productivity growth process. Similarly the lowering of resistance to trade liberalisation requires that further applied work is conducted on the costs of adjustment.

8 The Political Economy of Protection

BRUNO S. FREY and
HANNELORE WECK-HANNEMANN

8.1 INTRODUCTION

Economic theory argues convincingly that free trade leads to the most efficient allocation of resources and maximises a country's economic welfare. Empirical research shows that unilateral and bilateral tariff reductions yield significant welfare gains (see Greenaway 1983, ch. 6). Reality teaches us, however, that tariffs (and other trade restrictions) are prevalent in all periods and countries, and that there is a continual danger of ever-increasing protectionism in the world. The attempts made to reduce protectionism are based on the notion of reciprocity: that is to say, the propositions of trade theory about the welfare-increasing results of free trade do not seem to be accepted.

The glaring gap between theory and reality could be attributed to two causes. First, it might be argued that the policy-makers are misinformed and/or of limited intelligence and therefore do not know the welfare-increasing effect of unilateral tariff reductions. It may well be that producers and workers in some export sectors do not fully comprehend that higher import tariffs may threaten export sales because the costs of imports rise, other nations relatiate, or foreign income falls. The same may sometimes apply to consumers who are not fully aware that import barriers increase their cost of living. However, misperception and lack of intelligence can only explain a (small) part of protectionist activity; studies of debates over trade legislation reveal a rather remarkable degree of knowledge on the part of the groups affected.

The second explanation is more relevant. It notes that the assumptions underlying the pure theory of international trade do not fully obtain in reality. In particular, it should not be assumed that markets are perfect: real economies are subject to imperfect competition which distorts relative prices, and there are non-negligible costs of information, transactions and bargaining. Markets are thus not perfectly flexible, and it proves to be difficult, and sometimes impossible, to undertake the redistributions necessary to compensate the losers from a (potentially) Pareto-optimal trade-liberalising measure.

Once the world of perfectly competitive and frictionless exchange is left, *political* forces must be taken into account. This has been neglected in the established international trade theory. The traditional approach does away with the question of how the free trade optimum can be attained. Instead, it postulates the existence of a benign, omniscient government that can use non-distortionary taxes and subsidies to place society at a point on the utility-possibility frontier. If these assumptions are found not to hold in reality, a protectionist stand can be interpreted to be a *rational* policy for decision-makers in a democracy.

The optimum tariff argument states that under certain (rather restrictive) conditions a country may improve its material well-being by imposing restrictions on its exports or imports. More recently, the emphasis on increasing returns to scale in production and therewith imperfect competition has led to new arguments for government intervention in free trade ('strategic trade policy': see Krugman, 1987a). The corresponding welfare gains, however, can be achieved only at the expense of the economic welfare of the trading partners. As this policy is likely to lead to retaliations, the outcome may well be a general increase in tariffs and a general decline in welfare. As a consequence, even accepting the existence of (from the point of view of a particular country) an 'optimal' tariff, returns to scale and imperfect competition, free trade is still likely to be in the best interests of a country as a whole.

8.2 PROTECTIONIST PRESSURES IN A DEMOCRACY

In a democracy, the will of the majority should decide. As a unilateral shift to free trade increases welfare according to economic theory, it could be expected that the government would win votes by abolishing tariffs. By definition of Pareto optimality, either a majority of the electorate benefits directly, or the gains accruing to a minority can be redistributed so that a majority of the electorate is better off. In a system of direct simple majority rule in an assembly, the *median voter* (the one who makes a majority out of a minority) would cast his vote in favour of free trade. The median voter model is, however, based on a set of assumptions which in important respects do not represent reality. Their modification provides an explanation for the existence, and possibly growth, of tariffs in a democracy. There are five important modifications and extensions to consider (R. E. Baldwin, 1976).

1. The losers of a tariff reduction, the people engaged in the domestic production of the goods concerned, are not necessarily compensated. If they form a stable majority, they will obstruct the reduction and/or elimination of tariffs. The median voter model would then predict that protectionism prevails.

2. Prospective gainers have less incentive to participate in the vote, to inform themselves, and to organise and support a pressure group than do the losers. Tariff reductions are a 'public good' whose benefits are received by everybody, including those not taking the trouble and incurring the cost to bring about the reduction. The benefits for the gainers of a tariff reduction are moreover uncertain and take place in the future, and are therefore less visible. The losers of a tariff reduction, on the other hand, feel its effects much more directly, and will therefore engage more intensively in the political process.

3. It is possible that the prospective losers from free trade may be better represented in Parliament than the prospective winners. This is the case, for instance, when the prospective losers are favourably distributed regionally. If they have a 51 per cent majority in two out of three voting districts, they need only 33 per cent of the total votes to gain a majority in Parliament. If they have a 51 per cent majority in thirteen out of twenty-five voting districts, the group dominates Parliament on the basis of a vote share of 26 per cent.

4. Logrolling, or vote trading, can strongly affect the outcome of majority voting. Vote trading may happen if groups of voters have unequal preference intensities for two issues. Consider a group of voters, group I, engaged in domestic, import-competing activities. Their main preference is against the reduction of tariffs for their *own* products (proposition A) and weakly in favour of reduction of tariffs for some other products (proposition B). Assume another group of voters, group II, whose main interest lies in maintaining the tariff for the products concerned in B, and who have a weak preference for tariff reduction in A. If neither of the two groups has

a majority, and the other voters perceive the benefits of free trade, both propositions A and B would be accepted and free trade established. If, however, groups I and II combined have a majority, they can agree to exchange votes: group I votes against the tariff reduction which group II strongly opposes (i.e., votes *against* B), provided group II votes against the tariff reduction which group I strongly opposes (i.e., votes *against* A). This then leads to a majority vote against tariff reductions, so propositions A and B are both defeated.

5. Tariffs provide revenue for governments which, in their absence, would find it more difficult to finance public expenditure. This is especially true in developing countries where, due to the inefficiency of the tax system, there is little tax revenue. Table 8.1 shows that in many less developed countries, tariff revenues constitute a dominant part of total tax revenues. In Gambia the share was 67 per cent; in Swaziland, the Bahamas and Yemen the tariff revenues still accounted for more than half of total revenues. A government in such a country will have a keen interest in securing this income source, and for this reason would oppose free trade.

TABLE 8.1   Tariff revenue as a proportion of central government revenue, 1980–85, selected developing countries

Gambia	68%
Swaziland	63%
Bahamas	57%
Yemen	50%
Zaire	32%
Ecuador	24%

Source: *Government Finance Statistics Yearbook*, Vol. XII (Washington, DC, IMF, 1988).

The five modifications of the simple median-voter model combine to explain why free trade, which is optimal from the point of view of the country as a whole, is not actually found in reality. The discussion suggests that there is, on the contrary, a *political market* for protection (R. E. Baldwin, 1988; Nelson, 1988). Protection is demanded by particular groups of voters, firms and associated interest groups and parties, and supplied by politicians and public bureaucrats. Economic interests try to gain advantages and to improve their position by turning to the political system. They invest resources in order to influence political decisions in their favour. Such activities, which are directly unproductive because they do not increase the value of goods and services available, are a special form of profit-maximisation. Such profits can be gained by lobbying for trade barriers which generate rents that the particular actors can acquire for themselves (rent seeking); or they can be gained by appropriating the monetary revenues from tariffs (revenue seeking).

8.3   THE DEMAND FOR PROTECTION

In Figure 8.1 the horizontal axis measures the increase in the tariff level attained; the origin thus indicates the tariff level existing at the outset. The vertical axis measures the costs and benefits from such action in comparable monetary units. *OA* is the 'cost-of-lobbying' curve, showing the total cost in monetary terms of securing tariff protection by lobbying. This curve has a rising slope because it is reasonable to assume that it becomes increasingly difficult for a particular economic interest group to raise the tariff in its favour, i.e., there are rising marginal costs. The cost-of-lobbying curve reflects the willingness of political suppliers to grant additional protection to that particular economic

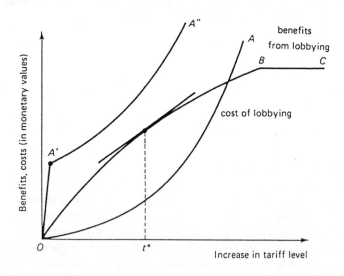

FIGURE 8.1   The optimal amount of lobbying for tariff protection

interest (sector or industry). The cost curve will be lower (a) the better the economic interest is organised (b) the more efficiently the lobbying activity is undertaken, and (c) the more the other groups in society feel that this particular economic interest should receive tariff protection. An example is farmers, whose protection against foreign competition is rather altruistically favoured for traditional reasons by many people in society. (A less altruistic reason for the willingness to favour a tariff increase may be that other interest groups think that such action will increase their own chances of receiving tariff protection themselves in the future, i.e., they endeavour to bring about a type of political exchange.)

Returning to Figure 8.1, *OBC* shows the 'benefits-from-protection' curve. It indicates the monetary value of tariff protection from the point of view of the group undertaking the lobbying activity. The larger the increase in the tariff, the higher the benefits accruing to the group, up to a maximum of *B*, which indicates the prohibitive tariff. The benefit curve's slope is not determined a priori; it is not inconceivable that increasing tariffs yield increasing marginal benefits, at least over a limited range. The curve shown in Figure 8.1 depicts decreasing marginal benefits over the whole range. The group's lobbying effort is optimal when it leads to an associated tariff increase t^*, at which point the 'rent' in the form of the difference between benefits and cost is maximised. The figure is able to illustrate that a lobbying activity to increase tariff protection need not necessarily be worthwhile for a particular economic interest group. Initial costs of lobbying (given by OA') may be so high that the cost curve $OA'A''$ lies above the benefit from lobbying curve *OBC* over the whole range.

This cost constellation may occur when the economic interests are difficult to organise, i.e., if there are high set-up costs to engage in political lobbying. The figure stresses the importance of having an established organisation to further one's interests in the political market for protection (or in any such market). If the cost of initial organisation were already covered (for instance, because the organisation already exists for other purposes, such as social gatherings), it would be advantageous to embark on lobbying. In that case, the cost of lobbying curve is *OA*, and the associated optimal tax increase is t^*. This explains why economic interests which are already organised have a tendency to get additional advantages, and so establish their privileged position even more strongly, while newcomers find it difficult to make their demands felt in the political struggle.

While the model is instructive, the extent of lobbying and protection achieved in reality can only be explained if the factors determining the position and slope of the cost and benefit curves can be empirically measured. This has indeed been done by comparing the conditions existing in various sectors or industries. We now turn to these aspects.

Pro-tariff groups

Domestic firms in competition with foreign firms supplying the home market have the strongest interest in *tariff protection*, and generally oppose free trade policies. They are joined by the workers and trade unions of the particular economic sector who know that they can share the rents achieved by tariff protection. Firms producing complementary products and supplying inputs to the import-competing firms also favour protection (provided they do not themselves strongly depend on imported raw materials). The protectionist groups usually have strong political interests because the effects of a change in protection are visible and direct, and therefore carry a lot of weight in the political debate. They can easily argue that a tariff reduction would result in a direct loss to them, reducing output and employment, while the foreign interests are favoured. Increased protection, on the other hand – so they will claim – obviously increases employment output and profits at home. These arguments are particularly forceful, and are actively promoted by trade unions when there is an abnormally high level of unemployment in the domestic economy.

Anti-tariff groups

The main group in society favouring trade-liberalising policies and opposing protection are the *export suppliers*. Firms offering their products on foreign markets realise that increased protectionism at home may lead to retaliation by foreign countries, threatening their sales. They cannot expect to widen their access to foreign markets if their own country is not prepared to reduce its own protection. It is, however, quite difficult to translate these export interests into effective political action. The damage suffered through import restrictions is indirect; it has the character of a forgone opportunity which is difficult to quantify. Among the firms opposing tariffs are the *multinationals*, who tend to favour free trade because they are able to compete efficiently on international markets. Protectionist tendencies may also lead to restrictions in their own activities, in the extreme leading to the nationalisation of their property in the foreign country in response to protectionist actions in the home country. Domestic firms using imported inputs for their production are also interested in trade liberalisation. Such firms, however, often belong at the same time to the import-competing sector with an interest in protection, so that their political position becomes equivocal or even pro-tariff.

Consumers and their organisations (as far as they exist) have an interest in low tariffs. Trade barriers burden consumers as they have a smaller choice of products and have to pay higher prices. Consumer groups have, however, little effect on trade policy. One reason is that consumers are normally also employees and workers. Their income is usually exclusively from this source, while their expenditure is distributed over many different goods, some of which are not (directly) affected by tariffs. As a consequence it is individually rational for consumers to pay most attention to their position on the producer side, which often benefits from import protection. Furthermore, consumers have little impact on trade policy as the loss of consumer welfare through the imposition of tariffs is rather difficult to identify. It is hard to see what the prices of the various products would be if tariffs were reduced or abolished, especially in an inflationary environment. The 'invisibility' and indirectness of the opportunity cost of tariffs hardly motivates consumers to fight politically for tariff reductions. This lack of engagement is only partially compensated for by the importers and distributors of foreign-produced consumption goods (such as retail chains, mail-order houses and discount firms) which have an obvious interest in low trade restrictions.

Political organisation

Whether pro-tariff or anti-tariff interests prevail depends on the political weight of the corresponding groups, and the intensity with which they raise their demands in the political process. A crucial factor is the ability and incentive to organise and to obtain the financing necessary for effective lobbying. As has been pointed out, protection constitutes a public good affecting all the members of a particular economic sector or occupation. There is an incentive not to join the interest group or to contribute financially because one may profit from the outcome by free-riding. Even if in an industry the benefits from further protection might be very large, it may be difficult or even impossible to raise the lobbying funds due to free-riding. The same problem holds even more strongly for anti-tariff interests, since the benefits of trade liberalisation are even more widely diffused.

There are three conditions under which interest groups are likely to form in the presence of public goods:

(a) when the group has been formed for some other reason than a lobby, or has been established by government decree (as, in some countries, the farmers' organisations);
(b) when group members only get specific private goods from belonging to the organisation, such as information or insurance;
(c) when there is a small group situation in which the members can impose sanctions on would-be free-riders.

Generally these conditions are more likely to obtain on the producer than on the consumer side. In a given sector, there are often only a few producers who find it easy to organise. As we have seen, import-competing and associated producers have on balance more to gain from protection than others. The opposite holds for those consumers interested in free trade. Because of their large number and diffuse interest, they are difficult to organise in an effective way, and it is almost impossible to raise funds for such general consumers' interests as low tariffs. Consequently, anti-tariff lobbying is comparatively weak.

We therefore have *two general propositions* concerning the demands for protection:

(a) pro-tariff interests have strong lobbies and mainly consist of import-competing producers (which includes the workers);
(b) anti-tariff interests have weak lobbies as consumers and exporters find it difficult, and have little incentive, to organise and to lobby effectively.

It should be noted that it is maintained throughout that the interests organise along *industry* or *sector*, and not along factor, lines as suggested by the Stolper–Samuelson (1941) approach (or much earlier, of course, by the Marxist theory of the struggle between capital and labour). This traditional theory of trade suggests that all capital interests would promote free trade (if that factor is internationally more competitive) and all labour interests would seek protection, or vice versa (if labour is internationally more competitive). It would not be expected that part of labour should be for protection, and the other part for free trade, and that capital interests should be similarly divided on the free trade issue. In contrast to the traditional Stolper–Samuelson view, the politico-economic approach emphasises the *rents* which the factors of production acquire through protection from foreign competition. In an industry which gains monopoly profits, the trade unions will attempt to get a share of these rents. As a result, the industry will be characterised by high wages and barriers to entry in the factor market of this industry. Factor mobility is curtailed by the actions of the interest groups, so that one of the basic assumptions of the traditional model of international trade no longer obtains. *Both* factors of production have an interest in defending the rent they share among themselves, and they will therefore act in concert. (For an empirical analysis of these contrasting views, see Magee, 1980).

8.4   THE SUPPLY OF PROTECTION

Tariff levels and changes are determined by political decisions in which politicians (in particular the government) and public officials (or bureaucracy) are dominant. Trade policy is not decided by direct referendum (this generally even holds for Switzerland). Protection versus free trade is only one of the issues over which an election is fought, and in most countries and periods trade policy is dominated by internal economic and political issues.

Every government may be assumed to pursue certain ideological goals, but is subject to a variety of constraints. One element among the ideological goals may be the position with respect of protection. The most important constraint perceived by most governments is the need to be re-elected. When a government fears it will lose a forthcoming election, it will undertake a policy which promises to raise its popularity with the voters. A party committed ideologically to free trade may be forced to resort to protectionism if it appears that such a policy may improve its re-election chances. We have seen that in the case of foreign trade, the consumer-voters interested in free trade are not very active, while the interest groups demanding protection try to exert as much influence as possible by lobbying. A government uncertain of re-election will therefore turn its attention to the demands for protection raised by the organised interests, hoping that they will deliver some votes, especially in marginal constituencies, and/or provide help in financing the election campaign.

The government has to act within the constraints set by the budget and the balance of payments. The extent to which these constraints restrict the government depends on the structure of the economy and on the prevailing economic conditions. A substantial balance of payments deficit may induce protectionist measures as an indication of willingness to act even if the politicians in charge are ideologically opposed to raising tariffs (or find this an ineffective remedial measure).

Another actor playing an important role in tariff formation is the *public administration*. This body has considerable influence on the 'supply side' of the tariff because it prepares, formulates and implements trade bills. The activity of public bureaucrats with respect to tariff may again be analysed with the help of the 'rational' model of behaviour, e.g., by assuming that they seek to maximise their utility subject to constraints set from outside. The main elements in the bureaucrats' utility function may be assumed to be the prestige, power and influence which they enjoy relative to the group of people they are officially designed to 'serve': their clientele. In most cases this clientele will be located in a specific economic sector. For example, in the case of public officials in the ministry of agriculture, the clientele would be those groups with agricultural interests. Public officials are moreover proud of being able to show that they are competent in their job ('performance excellence'). Public bureaucrats will therefore tend to fight for the interests of 'their' economic sector, and will work for tariffs and other import restrictions in order to protect it from outside competition. Furthermore, they will prefer to use instruments under their own control rather than to follow general rules imposed by formal laws, various kinds of non-tariff protection and support (subsidies, voluntary export restraints, etc.) rather than general tariffs.

The political constraints faced by public bureaucracy are imposed by Parliament and government. However, both of these actors have little incentive to control public administration tightly, because they are dependent on it in order to reach their own goals. In addition, political actors have less information available to them than the public bureaucracy, in particular with respect to the sometimes very complex issues of protection. The limited incentive of politicians to control the public administration gives bureaucrats considerable discretionary power which they can use to their own advantage in the area of trade policy.

The idea that public officials pursue the common interest or collective welfare and therefore fight for free trade has to be rejected. Indeed, it may be argued that they favour greater protection than politicians. As many public bureaux are organised along industry lines, they depend more on the relationship with this particular industry than the politicians. Moreover, bureaucracies have a more limited set of instruments available than the government, which has control over the whole range of economic policy. As a consequence, individual bureaucracies must reach their goals by using the instruments at hand *more intensively*: they strive to protect the economic sector they are associated with against foreign competition more strongly than do the government politicians, who have other means available to support the respective industry if it is in their interest to do so (Messerlin, 1981).

8.5   EMPIRICAL EVIDENCE

A number of studies provide interesting evidence about the quantitative aspects of tariffs and other protective devices, and provide strong support of the politico-economic approach (for a survey, see Marks and MacArthur, 1990). As is common practice today, econometric methods have been applied, in particular multiple regressions which take a number of influences into account and which are able to isolate the contribution of each determining factor to tariff formation, holding other influences constant. Empirical analyses have been used to explain both the differences of protection between industries (cross section) as well as the cyclical development of protection (time series).

Explaining protection between industries

Voting on tariffs

R. E. Baldwin (1976) seeks to explain the differences in political pressure for or against protection in the USA. The specific issue examined is the *trade-liberalising* bill introduced to the House of Representatives by a Republican President in 1973. The probability of a Congressman voting for or against the trade bill is explained by four determinants.

1.   The proportion of import-sensitive industries in the Congressman's constituency. A positive influence is expected here because the Congressman has an incentive to vote *against* the liberalising trade bill in order to please voters.

2. The proportion of export-orientated industries in his constituency. The more export-oriented a constituency is, the more likely it is that a Congressman supports the liberalising trade bill.
3. The financial contribution to the Congressman's campaign made by the three major trade unions opposing the bill. As a Congressman is sensitive to the size of monetary contributions received, it is expected that this induces him to vote against the bill.
4. The party affiliation.

As theoretically expected, the larger the weight of the industries in competition with imports in his constituency is, the more likely a Congressman is prepared to yield to their pressure and to vote against the trade-liberalising bill. (It is interesting to note that export-oriented industries do not have a statistically significant influence on the Congressman's vote decisions; this corresponds well with the theoretical notion that anti-tariff interests are politically less influential than pro-tariff interests.) Financial contributions of protectionist trade unions are able to influence a Congressman's behaviour: the more money he gets, the more likely he is to vote against the free trade bill. Finally, it stands to reason that due to party allegiance, a Republican Congressman is more likely to support the trade bill introduced by a President coming from his party than is a Democratic member of Congress. The result of this econometric analysis, as well as of more recent studies by Coughlin (1985), MacArthur and Marks (1988) and Tosini and Tower (1989) of the voting behaviour in the American Congress, accords very well with the political economy approach to tariff formation discussed earlier. The same holds for the results of an empirical analysis of referenda on trade policy issues in Switzerland (Weck-Hannemann, 1990): special interests are also able to bring about protectionism in a political system of direct democracy because of the way citizens cast their votes.

Actual tariff rates

Several studies have analysed the differences in *tariff rates* between industries as the outcome of the political struggle between demand and supply of protection in Canada. A particularly interesting contribution to explain the tariff structure (Caves, 1976) compares three competing models:

(a) the government sets tariffs to maximise the probability of winning the election given a geographically represented electorate;
(b) interest groups determine the structure of tariffs, the various industries having different benefits and costs of lobbying for protection;
(c) the government sets tariffs to effect a collective nationalistic feeling about the industrial composition of the economy ('national policy model').

These three models emphasise different aspects of the politico-economic processes behind tariff setting. A multiple regression was run for between twenty-nine and thirty-five industries. Explanatory variables were chosen which were intended to represent the typical features of each of the three models. The *interest group* model comes out best: the more low-skilled and low-wage workers are employed in an industry, the higher are the tariff rates, since the respective pressure groups have better arguments to ask for protection. When the firms buying a product are strongly concentrated, and when they are confronted with a high seller concentration, they are induced to organise more strongly and are (*ceteris paribus*) able to keep tariff rates low. The slower the growth of a industry, the more it seeks political assistance for tariff protection. This latter influence is, however, not statistically significant. By contrast, the national policy and rate maximisation models perform poorly.

An alternative interest group explanation of Canada's tariff structure stresses *international* political influences (Helleiner, 1977). A time-series analysis for the period 1961–70 suggests that labour and multinational firms have the largest influence on tariffs: labour seeks increased protection because of the rising supply of industrial products from low-wage countries, while multinationals are generally interested in free trade.

Similar studies on the determinants of the tariff structure between industries have been carried out for other countries such as France, West Germany, Japan, the UK and the USA in the context of a research project sponsored by the World Bank (R. E. Baldwin, 1984). The results suggest again that the import-competing industries tend to get higher tariff protection than the industries with export interests. It also turns out that labour-intensive, low-wage industries and sectors with few firms and large numbers of employees tend to be protected more because they can more convincingly argue in the political discussion that they are directly threatened by foreign suppliers; because of the large number of voters involved it is of particular interest to government to yield to their demands for protection.

Another study (Lavergne, 1983) distinguishes three sets of determinants of the level of, and the change over a time period in, tax rates. The first is 'political' and refers to the pressure group influences; the second contains 'mixed' economic and political influences such as the effort by decision-makers to minimise displacement cost, the comparative advantage of the industry relative to foreign competition, and tariff setting as a means of international bargaining; the third set of determinants includes 'principles' such as the maintenance of historical continuity, as well as miscellaneous aspects related to a public interest view of tariff setting. The econometric test is applied on 300 manufacturing industries in the USA from 1930 to the present. The estimates reveal that the most important influence on the tariff-setting process is conservatism: the structure of tariff rates between industries tends to be maintained over time. Of considerable importance is the possibility of using home tariffs in the international bargaining process over protectionism and free trade. It also turns out that the more competitive an industry is in the international field, the lower is its tariff level. Contrary to almost all the other econometric studies of tariff formation, the pressure groups do not seem to exert any systematic influence. The study is useful, however, because it shows that there are a great number of different factors which may influence the tariff-setting process.

Non-tariff barriers

Tariffs are not the only instrument for protection from foreign competition. There exist a great many forms of non-tariff barriers to international trade (see Greenaway, 1983). An explanation of the typical features of the formation of non-tariff barriers may be based on the economic theory of regulation (see, e.g., Peltzman, 1976). It argues that the regulators serve special interest groups. Government intervention in a market may be viewed as a politically optimal way of redistributing wealth from some constituents to others. When an outside interference takes place, the regulatory interventions have to be changed in order to re-establish political equilibrium. In the international trade area one such intervention was the Kennedy round, the purpose of which was to reduce tariffs across the board by 50 per cent (the so-called linear rule). The negotiations were quite successful. The simple average tariff reduction on US manufacturing products was 46.8 per cent between

1967 and 1972. The share of imports in domestic sales of manufactured products rose from an average value of 4.8 per cent in 1967 to 7.3 per cent in 1972. However, the structure of protection was not strongly affected by the Kennedy Round because the tariff reduction was *substituted* by other forms of protection, in particular by regulatory non-tariff barriers (Moser, 1990).

This interaction of tariffs and non-tariff barriers to international trade has been empirically tested for the year 1970 (when most of the Kennedy Round reductions had already materialised) by Marvel and Ray (1983). They confirm that non-tariff barriers are related to the historical political equilibrium before the Kennedy Round (in the form of the tariff rate of 1965). Furthermore, they found that those industries having the highest tariff protection *also* have the political influence to reach high non-tariff protection. The two forms of protection are, however, not equally attractive for specific industries. The estimates indicate that non-tariff barriers are more accessible than tariffs for low-concentration industries (which have greater difficulties in exerting political influence, mainly because of the free-rider problem). For firms in industries with a great number of suppliers, the rents generated by tariffs cannot easily be appropriated because they may be bid away through the rapid entry of new domestic firms into the industry. Non-tariff barriers are more advantageous because the rents generated can often be distributed selectively to punish free-riders, and can be withheld from new entrants. An example are import quotas based on historic sales of the firms already in the market.

Finally, Marvel and Ray suggest that *both* tariffs and non-tariff barriers tend to be high in consumer goods industries because the consumers who are burdened therewith find it difficult to organise themselves effectively.

On the whole, the estimates strongly support the political economy interpretation of the process of protectionism. They indicate that there is a systematic influence of special interest which undermine the linear type of trade liberalisation agreed to in such agreements as the Kennedy Round. It is shown that the factors which make it possible for industries to gain more protection than others can be empirically identified.

Voluntary export restraints

As we have seen in Chapter 7, in recent years international trade relations have witnessed the emergence and rapid expansion of VERs.

They have been applied to a large number of manufacturing goods, such as steel, colour television sets and automobiles. VERs differ in three main respects from global tariffs or global non-tariff barriers.

(a) VERs are discriminatory, lowering the import share of restraining suppliers;
(b) they lead to a deterioration in the importing country's terms of trade and a share in the rents created is appropriated by the restraining exporters;
(c) the agreements are reached in clandestine consultations.

These three characteristics offer specific incentives to certain decision-makers to favour such exports constraints (see K. Jones, 1984). The government and public bureaucracy in the importing country find it a suitable instrument to achieve protectionist ends with low political cost. Being 'voluntarily' agreed to by exporters, they do not violate international trade agreements, such as the GATT restriction on trade barriers. It is targeted at 'disruptive' suppliers, so that no retaliation has to be feared by other suppliers. (On the contrary, as they reduce the competition of the most efficient suppliers, they benefit from them.) VERs are quickly implemented and are in hands of the government and its administration, while Parliament need not be consulted. The import-competing producers reap the normal benefits from protection. They receive rents by being able to raise prices and increase output. They are not easily made responsible for the cost of such protection because attention is focused on the foreign exports which are said to have 'disrupted' the market. VERs are also beneficial to foreign exporting firms because the reduction in exports creates monopoly rents which they can appropriate (provided that exporters from other countries do not compensate the reduction). In order to implement this agreement, the foreign government must set up an export cartel which tends to favour the established firms in the economic sector concerned. Competition is weakened by the allocation of export market shares and the entry of new firms is prevented. Consumers are the group which has to carry the burden, as with all other kinds of protection from international competition. Compared to tariffs, they have to pay twice: once in the form of higher domestic prices, and again in the form of forgone tariff revenues. Consumers are excluded from the decision-making process; the agreements are negotiated by highly specialised experts on a technical level, removed from the public view. The costs involved in such voluntary agreements are not only difficult to understand and measure quantitatively, but they are so far not part of the political debate in which the opponents of this form of protectionism are capable of, and willing to, raise their voices. For these reasons it is not surprising that this new protectionist tool has gained in importance as a substitute for more open, and politically sensitive, protectionism by tariffs.

Explaining the cyclical development of protection

Protectionism is strongest when a country's economic position is weak; attempts at liberalising international trade have the best chances when economic conditions are good. These statements are almost commonplace; the question is, however, whether they are supported by serious empirical analyses.

Number of petitions

One way to measure the intensity of the *demand* for protection is the number of 'escape clause' petitions to the International Trade Commission under the trade legislation of the USA. It may be hypothesised that the number of such petitions is larger (a) the worse domestic economic conditions are (measured by the level of GNP, unemployment or unused capacity) because the industries threatened by foreign competition can establish a 'convincing case' that the bad state of the economy is due to 'unfair' competition by foreign suppliers, which raises the expected rate of return from political activity; (b) the worse the balance of trade is as an indicator of the (unsatisfactory) international competitive position of the country; (c) the larger import penetration is, because this is an obvious sign to which the domestic industries can point in order to 'prove' the damaging influence of foreign suppliers; (d) the larger the number of *successful* escape clause petitions is in recent years, because a firm considering making a petition takes this as a favourable element in its benefit–cost comparison.

Work by Takacs (1981) covering the thirty years from 1949 to 1979 in the USA supports the theoretical hypothesis: macroeconomic conditions significantly affect protectionist pressure. The number of escape clause cases rises the lower the level of real GNP, the higher unemployment, and the lower capacity utilisation are. Foreign trade conditions also have the expected influence: the worse the trade balance and the larger import penetration are, the more petitions will be filed which demand protection. Finally, the larger the share of successful petitions in the past, the more new ones will be made, *ceteris paribus*.

Dumping cases

In another study (Magee, 1982) protectionist pressure is measured by the number of dumping cases filed with the US Bureau of Customs. Protectionist pressure is again hypothesised to rise with unemployment. Increasing inflation, on the other hand, leads to pressure from households and consumer groups to liberalise imports.

The period covered is 1933–77, and Magee finds that a 10 per cent increase in the rate of unemployment (e.g., from 5 per cent to 5.5 per cent) is associated with a 9 per cent increase in protectionist pressure; each percentage point rise in the rate of inflation (e.g., from 7 per cent to 8 per cent) lowers the protectionist pressure by 5.7 per cent.

The econometric estimates of the cyclical influences on the tariff formation process are so far limited to the demand side. The difficulty is, of course, to find sufficiently long and comparable data series to perform a similar type of analysis on actual tariffs or on other protectionist measures as the outcome of the political struggle.

8.6   CONCLUDING COMMENTS

International trade theory proves that a (unilateral) move to free trade by a country maximises economic welfare. The corresponding welfare loss of protectionism can and has been calculated. In reality we observe intensive bargaining and reciprocity agreements for tariff reductions. Theory and reality can be reconciled by taking into account that information, transactions and bargaining are not free of cost and that not all interests are represented equally well in the democratic political process. Tariffs are decided in a *political market*; it pays to invest resources in order to gain the rents from protection. The pro-tariff groups mainly composed of import-competing industries (capital owners, management and workers) have a strong political position because their demands for protection are visible and understandable and the organisational problem is more easily manageable. The anti-tariff groups, mainly composed of consumers, find it difficult to organise effectively because of the free-riding effect. The level and structure of protection is the result of the interaction between the actors of the demand side (mostly interest groups organising along industry lines) and of the supply side (government and public bureaucracy). This political equilibrium can be modelled in various ways.

The unequal degree of protection of the various industries against foreign competition in the politico-economic process has been analysed by econometric methods, considering the demand side (voting on tariffs) and the political equilibrium outcome (actual tariff rates). Non-tariff barriers can be empirically explained by a similar set of determinants, because the two means for protection are partly used as substitutes. Tariffs and non-tariff barriers are found to be positively linked with the importance and degree of concentration of import-competing industries. Declining industries, and sectors with low-skilled, low-wage and a large number of employees have a good chance of getting protection. The more competitive an industry is (among them the multinational firms), the lower is protection, *ceteris paribus*. Important influences on tariffs and non-tariff barriers are also the historically given structure of protection and the possibilities for international bargaining. As theoretically expected, the export-oriented industries and consumers have little or no influence on issues of free trade and protection.

Recently, VERs have become important as a protectionist device. They are advantageous for both the home industry and the foreign suppliers (the latter can appropriate the monopoly rents of curtailed supply), as well as for the government and public bureaucracy, mainly because there is no possibility or incentive for consumers (who carry the burden) to oppose such agreements.

Protectionist pressure is empirically shown to be strongest when a country's economic conditions are weak, in particular if GNP is low and unemployment high, and when the foreign trade position is bad. Rising inflation, on the other hand, leads to pressure to reduce tariffs.

The econometric studies presented on the whole provide strong support for the political economy of protection.

9 International Economic Integration

ALI M. EL-AGRAA

9.1 INTRODUCTION

International economic integration is one aspect of 'international economics' that has been growing in importance in the past four decades or so. It is concerned with the discriminatory removal of all trade impediments between the participating nations and with the establishment of certain elements of cooperation and coordination between them. The latter depends entirely on the actual form that integration takes. Different forms of international integration can be envisaged, and some have actually been implemented:

1. *Free trade areas*, where the member nations remove all trade impediments among themselves but retain their freedom with regard to the determination of their policies *vis-à-vis* the outside world (the non-participants): e.g., EFTA and the Latin American Free Trade Area (LAFTA).
2. *Customs unions*, which are very similar to free trade areas except that member nations must conduct and pursue common external commercial relations; for instance, they must adopt common external tariffs (CETs) on imports from the non-participants, as is the case in the EU; the EU in this particular sense is a customs union, but it is much more than that.
3. *Common markets*, which are customs unions that also allow for free factor mobility across national member frontiers; i.e. capital, labour and enterprise should move unhindered between the

174

participating countries, as in the example of the East African Community (EAC) and the EU (but again it is far more complex).

4. *Complete economic unions*, which are common markets that ask for complete unification of monetary and fiscal policies; i.e., a central authority is introduced to exercise control over these matters so that existing member nations effectively become regions of one nation.

5. *Complete political integration*, where the participants become literally one nation: i.e., the central authority needed in point 4 not only controls monetary and fiscal policies but is also responsible to a central Parliament with the sovereignty of a nation's government. An example of this is the recent unification of the two Germanies.

It should be stressed that each of these forms of economic integration can be introduced in its own right: they should not be confused with *stages* in a *process* which eventually leads to complete political integration. It should also be noted that within each scheme there may be sectoral integration in particular areas of the economy, e.g., the EU's Common Agricultural Policy (CAP). Of course, sectoral integration can be introduced as an aim in itself, as was the case in the European Coal and Steel Community (ECSC), but sectoral integration is a form of 'cooperation' since it is not consistent with the accepted definition of international economic integration.

It should be pointed out that international economic integration can be *positive* or *negative*. The term 'negative integration' was coined by Tinbergen (1954) to refer to the removal of impediments on trade between the participating nations or to the elimination of any restrictions on the process of trade liberalisation. The term 'positive integration' relates to the modification of existing instruments and institutions and, more importantly, to the creation of new ones so as to enable the market of the integrated area to function properly and effectively, and also to promote other broader policy aims of the union.

9.2   ECONOMIC INTEGRATION AND GATT RULES

The rules of GATT allow the formation of regional groupings, on the understanding that, although customs unions, free trade areas, etc., are discriminatory associations, they may not pursue policies which increase the level of their discrimination beyond that which existed prior to their formation, and that tariffs and other trade restrictions (with some exceptions) are removed on substantially all trade among the participants. Hence, once allowance was made for the proviso regarding the external trade relations of the regional grouping (the CET level, or common level of discrimination against extra-area trade, in a customs union, and the average tariff or trade discrimination level in a free trade area), it seemed to the drafters of article XXIV that regional groupings did not contradict the basic principles of GATT – liberalism, stability and transparency – or more generally the principles of non-discrimination and reciprocity.

There are various arguments that article XXIV is in direct contradiction to the spirit of GATT. However, Wolf (1983, p. 156) argues that if nations decide to treat one another as if they are part of a single economy, nothing can be done to prevent them (witness the efforts needed to enable the unification of the two Germanies), and that regional groupings, particularly those such as the EU, have a strong impulse towards liberalisation; in the case of the EU, the setting of the CET happened to coincide with the Kennedy Round of tariff reductions.

Of course, these considerations are more complicated than is suggested here, particularly since there are those who would argue that nothing could be more discriminatory than for a group of countries to remove all tariffs and trade impediments on their mutual trade while at the same time maintaining the initial levels against outsiders. Moreover, as we shall see below, regional groupings may lead to resource reallocation effects which are economically undesirable. However, to have denied nations the right to form such associations, particularly when the main driving force may be political rather than economic, would have been a major setback for the world community. Hence, all that needs to be stated here is that as much as GATT's article XXIV raises problems, it also reflects its drafters' deep understanding of the future development of the world economy.

9.3 THE GLOBAL EXPERIENCE

Since the end of the Second World War various forms of international economic integration have been proposed and numerous schemes have actually been implemented. Even though some of those introduced were later discontinued or completely reformulated, the number adopted during the decade commencing in 1957 was so impressive that the period has been described as 'the age of integration'.

The EU is the most significant and influential of these arrangements since it comprises some of the most advanced nations of Western Europe: Belgium, Denmark, France, Germany, Greece, Ireland, Italy, Luxemburg, the Netherlands, Portugal, Spain and the UK. The EU was founded by six of these nations (usually referred to as the Original Six) under the Treaty of Rome in 1957, with three of the remaining six (Denmark, Ireland and UK) joining later in 1973. Greece became a full member in January 1981, and Portugal and Spain joined in January 1986 after a lengthy period of negotiation. Austria, Malta, Sweden and Turkey have submitted applications for membership. Although the Treaty of Rome relates simply to the formation of a customs union and provides the basis for a common market in terms of factor mobility, many of the originators of the EU saw it as a phase in a process culminating in complete economic and political integration. Thus the present efforts to achieve full harmonisation in member countries' monetary, fiscal and social policies, to accomplish a monetary union and to change the EC into a 'European Union', and to amend the Treaties in a way which will promote a democratic decision-making process (some of this has already been achieved in terms of the so-called Single European Act and European Union) can be seen as positive steps towards the attainment of the desired goals.

EFTA is the other major scheme of international economic integration in Western Europe. To understand its membership one has to learn something about its history. In the mid-1950s, when a European Community comprising the whole of Western Europe was being contemplated, the UK was unprepared to commit itself to some of the economic and political aims envisaged for that Community. For example, the adoption of a common policy for agriculture and the eventual political unity of Western Europe were seen as aims which were in direct conflict with the UK's interests in the Commonwealth, particularly with regard to 'Commonwealth preference' which granted preferential access to the markets of member nations of the Commonwealth. Hence the UK favoured the idea of a Western Europe which adopted free trade in industrial products only, thus securing the advantages of 'Commonwealth preference' as well as opening up Western Europe as a free market for her industrial goods. In short, the UK sought to achieve the best of both worlds for herself, which is of course quite understandable. However, it is equally understandable that such an arrangement was not acceptable to those seriously contemplating the formation of the EEC. As a result the UK approached those Western European nations who had similar interests with the purpose of forming an alternative scheme of international economic integration to counteract any possible damage due to the formation of the EEC. The outcome was EFTA, which was established in 1960 by the Stockholm Convention with the object of creating a free market for industrial products only; there were some arrangements on non-manufactures but these were relatively unimportant. The membership consisted of: Austria, Denmark, Norway, Portugal, Sweden, Switzerland (and Liechtenstein) and the UK. Finland became an associate member in 1961; Iceland joined in 1970 as a full member. But, as already stated, Denmark and the UK, together with Ireland, joined the EEC in 1973. This left EFTA with a membership consisting mainly of the relatively smaller nations of Western Europe. However, in 1972, due to the insistence of the UK prior to joining the EEC, the EEC and EFTA entered into a series of free trade agreements which have in effect resulted in virtual free trade in industrial products in a market which includes their joint membership. This outcome has, of course, provided the cynical observer of British attitudes towards Western Europe with a great deal to reflect upon!

International economic integration is not confined to the so-called 'free' nations of the world. Indeed, before the recent dramatic changes the socialist-planned economies of Eastern Europe had their own arrangement which operated under the Council for Mutual Economic Assistance (CMEA), or COMECON as it was generally known in the West. CMEA was formed in 1949 by Bulgaria, Czechoslovakia, the German Democratic Republic, Hungary, Poland, Romania and the USSR; they were later joined by three non-European countries: Mongolia (1962), Cuba (1972) and Vietnam (1978). In its earlier days, before the death of Stalin, the activities of the CMEA were confined to the collation of the plans of the member states, the development of a uniform system of reporting statistical data and the recording of foreign trade statistics. However, during the 1970s a series of measures were adopted by the CMEA to implement the 'Comprehensive Programme of Socialist Integration', hence indicating that the organisation was moving towards a form of integration based principally on methods of plan coordination and joint planning activity, rather than on market levers (Smith, 1977). Finally, attention should be drawn to the fact that the CMEA comprised a group of relatively small countries and one 'super power' (before its demise), and that the long-term aim of the organisation was to achieve a highly organised and integrated economic bloc, without any agreement having been made on how and when this was to be accomplished.

Before leaving Europe it should be stated that another scheme exists in the form of regional cooperation between the five Nordic countries (the Nordic Community): Denmark, Finland, Iceland, Norway and Sweden. However, in spite of claims to the contrary the Nordic scheme is one of cooperation rather than international economic integration since Denmark is a full member of the EU while the other countries are full members of EFTA; hence a substantial group of economists would argue that the Nordic Community has little practical relevance.

In Africa, there are several schemes of international economic integration (Robson, 1987). The *Union Douanière et Economique de l'Afrique Centrale* (UDEAC) comprises the People's Republic of the Congo, Gabon, Cameroon and the Central African Republic. Member nations of UDEAC plus Chad, a former member, constitute a monetary union. The *Communauté Economique de l'Afrique de l'Ouest* (CEAO), which was formed under the Treaty of Abidjan in 1973, consists of the Ivory Coast, Mali, Mauritania, Niger, Senegal and Upper Volta (renamed Burkina Faso); Benin joined in 1984. Member countries of CEAO, except for Mauritania plus Benin and Togo, are participants in a monetary union. In 1973 the Mano River Union (MRU) was established between Liberia and Sierra Leone. The MRU is a customs union which involves a certain degree of cooperation, particularly in the industrial sector. The Economic Community of West African States (ECOWAS) was formed in 1975 with fifteen signatories: its membership consists of all those countries which participate in UDEAC, CEAO, MRU plus some other West African States. In 1969 the Southern African Customs Union (SACU) was established between Botswana, Lesotho, Swaziland and the Republic of South Africa. The Economic Community of the Countries of the Great Lakes (CEPGL) was created in 1976 by Rwanda, Burundi and Zaire. Until its collapse in 1977, there was the EAC comprising Kenya, Tanzania and Uganda. In 1981 fifteen states from the Eastern and Southern African region adopted a Draft Treaty for a Preferential Trade Area (PTA): Angola, Botswana, the Comoros, Djibouti, Ethiopia, Kenya, Lesotho, Malawi, Mauritius, Mozambique, Swaziland, Tanzania, Uganda, Zambia and Zimbabwe. In August 1984 a treaty was signed by Libya and Morocco to establish the Arab-African Union, whose main aim is to tackle their political conflicts in the Sahara Desert. Several other schemes were in existence in the past but have been discontinued, while others never got off the ground. Hence a unique characteristic of economic integration in Eastern, Southern and Western Africa is the multiplicity and overlapping of the schemes. For example, in West Africa alone, there is a total of 32 schemes, which is why a Benin Union (BU) consisting of Benin, Ghana, Nigeria and Togo has been recommended recently in an attempt to try to rationalise economic cooperation arrangements in West Africa.

There are four schemes of international economic integration in Latin America and the Caribbean. Under the 1960 Treaty of Montevideo, the LAFTA was formed between Mexico and all the countries of South America except for Guyana and Surinam. LAFTA came to an end in the late 1970s but was promptly succeeded by the Association for Latin American Integration (ALADI) in 1980. The Managua Treaty of 1960 established the Central American Common Market (CACM) between Costa Rica, El Salvador, Guatemala, Honduras and Nicaragua. In 1969 the Andean Group was established under the Cartagena Agreement between Bolivia, Chile, Colombia, Ecuador, Peru and Venezuela; the Andean Group forms a closer link between some of the least developed nations of ALADI. In 1973 the Carribean Community (CARICOM) was formed between Antigua, Barbados, Belize, Dominica, Grenada, Guyana, Jamaica, Montserrat, St Kitts–Nevis–Anguilla, St Lucia, St Vincent, Trinidad and Tobago, replacing the Caribbean Free Trade Association (CARIFTA).

Asia does not figure very prominently in the league of international economic integration but this is not surprising given the existence of such large (either in population or GNP terms) countries as China, India and Japan. The Regional Cooperation for Development (RCD) is a very limited arrangement for sectoral integration between Iran, Pakistan and Turkey. The Association of South-East Asian Nations (ASEAN) comprises six nations: Brunei, Indonesia, Malaysia, the Philippines, Singapore and Thailand. ASEAN was founded in 1967 in the shadow of the Vietnam War. After almost a decade of inactivity 'it was galvanized into renewed vigour in 1976 by the security problems which the reunification of Vietnam seemed to present to its membership'. The drive for the establishment of ASEAN and for its vigorous reactivation in 1976 was both political and strategic. However, right from the start, economic cooperation was one of the most important aims of ASEAN; indeed most of the vigorous activities of the group between 1976 and 1978 were predominantly in the economic field, and they have recently decided on a firm timetable (10–15 years) for the dismantling of intra-area tariffs.

A scheme of integration-cum-cooperation that is presently being hotly discussed is that of 'Pacific Basin Integration/Cooperation'. However, given the diversity of countries within the Pacific region, it seems highly unlikely that a very involved scheme of integration will evolve over the next decade or so. This is in spite of the fact that there already exist:

(a) the PECC (Pacific Economic Cooperation Conference), which is a tripartite structured organisation with representatives from governments, businesses and academic circles, and with the secretariat work being handled between general meetings by the country next hosting a meeting;
(b) the PAFTAD (Pacific Trade and Development Conference), which is an academically oriented organisation;
(c) the PBEC (Pacific Basin Economic Council), which is a private-sector business organisation for regional cooperation; and
(d) the PTC (Pacific Telecommunications Conference), which is a specialised organisation for regional cooperation in this particular field.

The reason for the pessimism is that the region under consideration covers the whole of North America and South-east Asia, with Pacific South America, the People's Republic of China and the USSR all claiming interest since they are all on the Pacific. Even if one were to exclude this latter group, there still remains the cultural diversity of such countries as Australia, Canada, Japan, New Zealand and the USA, plus the diversity that already exists within ASEAN. It would therefore seem that unless the group of participants is severely limited, Pacific Basin *cooperation* will be the logical outcome; hence the recent drive for an East Asian Economic Area (EAEA) between ASEAN and Japan and Korea may be a more realistic goal, but Japan's interests may be closer to the USA's.

While discussing the Pacific area, it should be added that in 1965 Australia and New Zealand entered into a free trade area arrangement (the New Zealand-Australia Free Trade Area, NAFTA). NAFTA was replaced in 1985 by the more important Australia New Zealand Closer Economic Relations and Trade Agreement (CER): not only have major trade barriers been removed, but significant effects on the New Zealand economy have been experienced as a result. Canada and the USA have recently formed a free trade area and are presently negotiating the terms for Mexico's membership.

A scheme which covers more than one continent is the Arab League (AL), which consists of 21 independent nations, extending from the Gulf in the East to Mauritania and Morocco in the West. Hence, the geographical area covered by the group includes the whole of North Africa, a large part of the Middle East, plus Somalia and Djibouti. The purpose of the organisation is to strengthen the close ties linking Arab states, to coordinate their policies and activities and direct them to their common good and to mediate in disputes between them. These may seem like vague terms of reference, but the Arab Economic Council, whose membership consists of all Arab ministers of economic affairs, was entrusted with 'suggesting ways for economic development, cooperation, and organisation and coordination'. The Council for Arab Economic Unity (CAEU), which was formed in 1957, had the aim of establishing an integrated economy of all member states of the AL. Moreover, in 1964 the Arab Common Market was formed between Egypt, Iraq, Jordan and Syria, and the Gulf Cooperation Council (GCC) was established between Bahrain, Kuwait, Oman, Qatar, Saudi Arabia and the United Arab Emirates to bring together the Gulf states and to prepare the ground for them to join forces in the economic, political and military spheres.

There are two schemes of sectoral international economic integration. The first is the Organisation of Petroleum Exporting Countries (OPEC), founded in 1960 with a truly international membership. Its aim was to protect the main interest of its member nations: petroleum. The second is the Organisation of Arab Petroleum Exporting Countries (OAPEC), established in January 1968 by Kuwait, Libya and Saudi Arabia. These were joined in May 1970 by Algeria and the four Arab Gulf Emirates (Qatar, Abu Dhabi, Bahrain and Dubai). In March 1972, Egypt, Iraq and Syria became members.

OAPEC was temporarily liquidated in June 1971 and Dubai is no longer a member. The agreement establishing the organisation states that the principal objectives of OAPEC are: the cooperation of the member nations in various forms of economic activity, the realisation of the closest ties among them, the determination of ways and means of securing their legitimate interests, the use of joint efforts to ensure the flow of petroleum to its consumers and the creation of an appropriate atmosphere for the capital and expertise invested in the petroleum industry in the member nations. OAPEC was originally conceived as an example of sectoral integration, with the political objective of using petroleum as a weapon for international bargaining against the Israeli occupation of certain Arab areas. Recently, however, the organisation has undertaken a number of projects both internally and externally.

Finally, there are also the North Atlantic Treaty Organisation (NATO), the OECD and the Organisation for African Unity (OAU), but these and the AL are, strictly speaking, for political and economic cooperation only.

9.4   THE GAINS FROM INTEGRATION

In reality, almost all existing cases of economic integration were either proposed or formed for political reasons, even though the arguments popularity put forward in their favour were expressed in terms of possible economic gains. However, no matter what the motives for economic integration are, it is still necessary to analyse the economic implications of such geographically discriminatory groupings.

At the customs union (and free trade area) level, the possible sources of economic gain can be attributed to:

(a) enhanced efficiency in production made possible by increased specialisation in accordance with the law of comparative advantage;

(b) increased production levels due to better exploitation of economies of scale made possible by the increased size of the market;

(c) an improved international bargaining position, made possible by the larger size, leading to better terms of trade;

(d) enforced changes in economic efficiency brought about by enhanced competition; and

(e) changes affecting both the amount and quality of the factors of production due to technological advances.

If the level of economic integration is to proceed beyond the customs union level to the economic union level, then further sources of gain become possible due to:

(f) factor mobility across the borders of member nations;

(g) the coordination of monetary and fiscal policies; and

(h) the goals of near full employment, higher rates of economic growth and better income distribution becoming unified targets.

9.5   THE CUSTOMS UNION ASPECTS

The basic concepts

Before the theory of second-best was developed (Meade, 1955a; Lipsey and Lancaster, 1956–7) it used to be the accepted tradition that customs union formation should be encouraged. The rationale for this was that since free trade maximised world welfare, and since customs union formation was a move towards free trade, customs unions increased welfare even though they did not maximise it. This rationale certainly lies behind GATT article XXIV, which permits the formation of customs unions and free trade areas as the special exceptions to the principle of non-discrimination.

Viner (1950) challenged this proposition by stressing that customs union formation is by no means equivalent to a move towards free trade since it amounts to free trade between the members and protection *vis-à-vis* the outside world. This combination of free trade and protectionism could result in 'trade creation' and/or 'trade diversion'. Trade creation is the replacement of expensive domestic production by cheaper imports from a partner, and trade diversion is the replacement of cheaper initial imports from the outside world by more expensive imports from a partner. Viner stressed the point that trade creation is beneficial since it does not affect the rest of the world, while trade diversion is harmful; it is therefore the relative strength of these two effects that determines whether or not customs union formation should be advocated. It is therefore important to understand the implications of these concepts.

Assuming perfect competition in both the commodity and factor markets, automatic full employment of all resources, costless adjustment procedures, perfect factor mobility nationally but perfect immobility across national boundaries, prices determined by cost, and three countries H (the home country), P (the potential customs union partner) and W (the outside world), plus all the traditional assumptions employed in tariff theory, we can use a simple diagram to illustrate these two concepts.

In Figure 9.1, S_w is W's perfectly elastic, tariff-free supply curve for this commodity; S_H is H's supply curve, while S_{H+P} is the joint H and P tariff-free supply curve. With a non-discriminatory tariff imposed by H

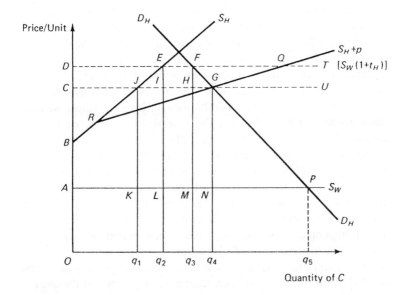

FIGURE 9.1   Trade creation and trade diversion

of AD (t_H), the effective supply curve facing H is $BREFQT$, i.e., its own supply curve up to E and W's, subject to the tariff [S_w (1 + t_H)], after that. The domestic price is therefore OD, which gives domestic production of Oq_2, domestic consumption of Oq_3 and imports of q_2q_3. H pays q_2LMq_3 for these imports, while the domestic consumer pays q_2EFq_3, with the difference ($LEFM$) being tariff revenue which accrues to the H government. This revenue can be viewed as a transfer from the consumers to the government, with the implication that when the government spends it, the marginal valuation of that expenditure should be exactly equal to its valuation by private consumers so that no distortions should occur.

If H and W form a customs union, the free trade position will be restored so that Oq_5 will be consumed in H and this amount will be imported from W. Hence free trade is obviously the ideal situation. But if H and P form a customs union, the tariff will still apply to W while it is removed from P. The effective supply curve in this case is $BRGQT$. Price falls to OC, resulting in a fall in domestic production to Oq_1, an increase in consumption to Oq_4 and an increase in imports to q_1q_4. These imports now come from P.

The welfare implications of these changes can be examined by employing the concepts of consumers' and producers' surpluses. As a result of increased consumption, consumers' surplus rises by *CDFG*. Part of this (*CDEJ*) is a fall in producers' surplus due to the decline in domestic production, and another part (*IEFH*) is a portion of the tariff revenue now transferred back to the consumer subject to the same condition of equal marginal valuation. This leaves the triangles *JEI* and *HFG* as gains from customs union formation. However, before we conclude whether or not these triangles represent *net* gains, we need to consider the overall effects more carefully.

The fall in domestic production from Oq_2 to Oq_1 leads to increased imports of q_1q_2. These cost q_1JIq_2 to import from P, while they originally cost q_1JEq_2 to produce domestically. (Note that these resources are supposed to be employed elsewhere in the economy without any adjustment costs or redundancies.) There is therefore a saving of *JEI*. The increase in consumption from Oq_3 to Oq_4 leads to new imports of q_3q_4, which cost q_3HGq_4 to import from P. These give a welfare satisfaction to the consumers equal to q_3FGq_4. There is therefore an increase in satisfaction of *HFG*. However, the *initial* imports of q_2q_3 originally cost the country q_2LMq_3, but these imports now come from P and cost q_2IHq_3. Therefore these imports lead to a loss equal to the loss in government revenue of *LIHM* (*IEFH* being a retransfer). It follows that the triangle gains (*JEI* + *HFG*) have to be compared with the loss of tariff revenue (*LIHM*) before a definite conclusion can be made regarding whether the net effect of customs union formation has been one of gain or loss.

It should be apparent that q_2q_3 represents, in terms of our definition, trade diversion, and $q_1q_2 + q_3q_4$ represents trade creation (it is now generally accepted that the consumption effect has to be included in trade creation as Viner was concerned with production effects only), or alternatively that areas *JEI* plus *HFG* are trade creation (benefits) while area *LIHM* is trade diversion (loss).[1] It is then obvious that trade creation is economically desirable while trade diversion is undesirable, hence Viner's conclusion that it is the relative strength of these two effects that should determine whether or not customs union formation is beneficial or harmful.

The reader should note that if the initial price is that given by the intersection of D_H and S_H (due to a higher tariff rate), the customs union would result in pure trade creation, since the tariff rate is prohibitive. If the price is initially OC (due to a lower tariff rate), then customs union formation would result in pure trade diversion. It should also be apparent that the size of the gains and losses depends on the price elasticities of S_H and S_{H+P}, and D_H and on the divergence between S_W and S_{H+P} (i.e., cost differences).

The Cooper/Massell criticism

Viner's conclusion was challenged by Cooper and Massell (1965a). They suggested that the reduction in price from OD to OC should be considered in two stages: first, reduce the tariff level indiscriminately (i.e., for both W and P) to AC, which gives the same union price and production, consumption and import changes; second, introduce the customs union starting from the new price OC. The effect of these two steps is that the gains from trade creation ($JEI + HFG$) still accrue, while the losses from trade diversion ($LIHM$) no longer apply since the new effective supply curve facing H is $BJGU$, which ensures that imports continue to come from W at the cost of q_2LMq_3. In addition, the new imports due to trade creation ($q_1q_2 + q_3q_4$) generate tariff revenue of $JILK$ plus $MHGN$. Cooper and Massell then conclude that *a policy of unilateral tariff reduction is superior to customs union formation.*

Further contributions

Cooper and Massell (1965b) and H. G. Johnson (1965b) utilise a 'public good' argument for customs union formation, with Cooper and Massell's expressed in practical terms and Johnson's in theoretical terms.

Johnson's method is based on four major assumptions:

(a) governments use tariffs to achieve certain non-economic, political, etc., objectives;
(b) actions taken by governments are aimed at offsetting differences between private and social costs-they are therefore rational efforts;
(c) government policy is a rational response to the demands of the electorate;
(d) countries have a preference for industrial production.

In addition to these assumptions, Johnson makes a distinction between private and public consumption goods, real income (utility enjoyed from both private and public consumption, where consumption is the sum of planned consumption expenditure and planned investment expenditure) and real product (defined as total production of privately appropriable goods and services).

These assumptions have important implications. First, competition among political parties will make the government adopt policies that will tend to maximise consumer satisfaction from both 'private' and 'collective' consumption goods. Satisfaction is obviously maximised when the rate of satisfaction per unit of resources is the same in both types of consumption goods. Second, 'collective preference' for industrial production implies that consumers are willing to expand industrial production (and industrial employment) beyond what it would be under free trade.

Tariffs are the main source of financing this policy, and protection will be carried to the main point where the value of the marginal utility derived from collective consumption of domestic and industrial activity is just equal to the marginal excess private cost of protected industrial production.

The marginal excess cost of protected industrial production consists of two parts: the marginal production cost and the marginal private consumption cost. The marginal production cost is equal to the proportion by which domestic cost exceeds world market cost. In a very simple model this is equal to the tariff rate. The marginal private consumption cost is equal to the tariff rate. The marginal private consumption cost is equal to the loss of consumer surplus due to the fall in consumption brought about by the tariff.

In equilibrium, the proportional marginal excess private cost of protected production measures the marginal 'degree of preference' for industrial production. This is illustrated in Figure 9.2, where S_W is the world supply curve; D_H is the free trade constant-utility demand curve; S_H is the domestic supply curve; and S_{H+u} is the marginal private cost curve of protected industrial production, including the excess private consumption cost. (*FE* is the first component of marginal excess cost – determined by the excess marginal cost of domestic production in relation to the free trade situation due to the tariff (*AB*) – and the area *GED* (=*IHJ*) is the second component which is the deadweight loss in consumer surplus due to the tariff.) The height of *vv* above S_W represents the marginal value of industrial production in collective consumption and its slope reflects the assumption of diminishing marginal utility.

The maximisation of real income is achieved at the intersection of *vv* with S_{H+u}, requiring the use of tariff rate *AB/OA* to increase industrial production from Oq_1 to Oq_2. Note that, in equilibrium, the government is maximising real income, not real product: maximisation of real income makes it necessary to sacrifice real product in order

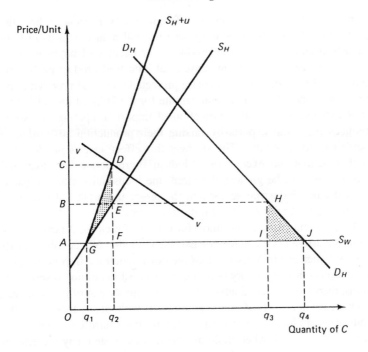

FIGURE 9.2   **Preference for industrial production**

to gratify the preference for collective consumption of industrial production.[2]

To make the model useful for the analysis of customs union issues it is necessary to alter some of the assumptions. Let us assume that industrial production is not one aggregate but a variety of products in which countries have varying degrees of comparative advantage; that countries differ in their overall comparative advantage in industry as compared with non-industrial production; that no country has monopoly/monopsony power (conditions for optimum tariffs do not exist); and that no export subsidies are allowed.

The variety of industrial production allows countries to be both importers and exporters of industrial products. This, in combination with the 'preference for industrial production', will motivate each country to practise some degree of protection. A country can gratify its preference for industrial production only by protecting import-competing industries. Hence the condition for equilibrium remains the same: $vv = S_{H+u}$. S_{H+u} is slightly different, however, because, first, the protection of import-competing industries will reduce exports of both industrial and non-industrial products (for balance of payments purposes). Hence in order to increase total industrial production by one unit it will be necessary to increase protected industrial production by more than one unit so as to compensate for the induced loss of industrial exports. Second, the protection of import-competing industries reduces industrial exports by raising their production costs (due to perfect factor mobility). The stronger this effect, *ceteris paribus*, the higher the marginal excess cost of industrial production. This marginal excess cost will be greater, the larger the industrial sector compared with the non-industrial sector and the larger the protected industrial sector relative to the exporting industrial sector.

In the event of customs union formation, if reciprocal tariff reductions are arrived at on an MFN basis, the reduction of a country's tariff rate will increase imports from *all* the other countries. If, however, the reduction is discriminatory (starting from a position of non-discrimination), there are two advantages: first each country can offer its partner an increase in exports of industrial products without any loss of its own industrial production by diverting imports from third countries (trade diversion); second, when trade diversion is exhausted, any increase in partner industrial exports to this country is exactly equal to the reduction in industrial production in the same country (trade creation), hence eliminating the gain to third countries.

Therefore discriminatory reciprocal tariff reduction costs each partner country less, in terms of reduction in domestic industrial production (if any) incurred per unit increase in partner industrial production, than does non-discriminatory reciprocal tariff reduction. On the other hand, preferential tariff reduction imposes an additional cost on the tariff-reducing country: the excess of the costs of imports from the partner country over their cost in the world market.

The implications of this analysis are:

(a) both trade creation and trade diversion yield a gain to the customs union partners;

(b) trade diversion is preferable to trade creation for the preference-granting country since a sacrifice of domestic industrial production is not required;

(c) both trade creation and trade diversion may lead to increased efficiency due to economies of scale.

Johnson's contribution has not achieved the popularity it deserves because of the alleged nature of his assumptions. It can, of course, be claimed that an

> economic rationale for customs unions on public goods grounds can only be established if for political or some such reasons governments are denied the use of direct production subsidies – and while this may be the case in certain countries at certain periods in their economic evolution, there would appear to be no acceptable reason why this should generally be true. Johnson's analysis demonstrates that customs union and other acts of commercial policy may make economic sense under certain restricted conditions, but in no way does it establish or seek to establish a general argument for these acts. (Krauss, 1972, p. 428)

While this is a legitimate criticism, it is of no relevance to the world we live in: subsidies are superior to tariffs, yet all countries prefer the use of tariffs to subsidies. It is a criticism related to a first-best view of the world. Therefore it seems unfair to criticise an analysis on grounds which do not portray what actually exists: it is what prevails in practice that matters. That is what Johnson's approach is all about, and that is what the theory of second-best tries to tackle. In short, the lack of belief in this approach is tantamount to a lack of belief in the validity of the distinction between social and private costs and benefits.

Dynamic effects

The so-called dynamic effects (Balassa, 1961) relate to the numerous means by which economic integration may influence the rate of growth of GNP of the participating nations. These include the following:

(a) scale economies made possible by the increased size of the market for both firms and industries operating below optimum capacity before integration occurs;

(b) economies external to the firm which may have a downward influence on both specific and general cost structures;

(c) the polarisation effect, by which is meant the cumulative decline either in relative or absolute terms of the economic situation of a particular participating nation or of a specific region within it, due either to the benefits of trade creation becoming concentrated in one region or to the fact that an area may develop a tendency to attract factors of production;

(d) the influence on the location and volume of real investment; and
(e) the effect of economic efficiency and the smoothness with which trade transactions are carried out due to enhanced competition and changes in uncertainty.

Apart from economies of scale,the possible gains are extremely long term in nature and cannot be tackled in orthodox economic terms: e.g., intensified competition leading to the adoption of best business practices and to an American-type of attitude, etc. (Scitovsky, 1958) seems like a naive socio-psychological abstraction that has no solid foundation with regard to both the aspirations of those countries contemplating economic integration and to its actually materialising.

Economies of scale that are internal to the industry can, however, be analysed in orthodox economic terms. In Figure 9.3, $D_{H,P}$ is the identical demand curve for this commodity in both H and P, and D_{H+P} is their joint demand curve; S_W is the world supply curve; AC_P and AC_H are the

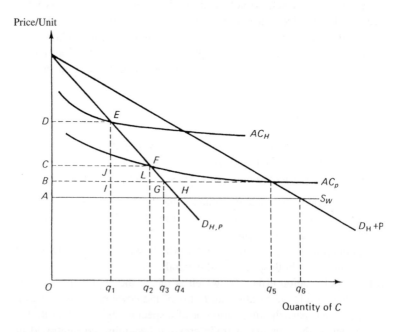

FIGURE 9.3   Scale economies and customs union formation

average cost curves for this commodity in P and H respectively. Free
trade is clearly the best policy, resulting in price OA with consumption
that is satisfied entirely by imports of Oq_4 in each of H and P, giving a
total of Oq_6.

If H and P impose tariffs, the only justification for this is that uncor-
rected distortions exist between the privately and socially valued costs in
these countries: see A. J. Jones (1979) and El-Agraa and Jones (1981).
The best tariff rates to impose are Corden's (1972) made-to-measure
tariffs which can be defined as those which encourage domestic production to a level that just satisfies consumption without giving rise to
monopoly profits. These tariffs are equal to AD and AC for H and P
respectively, resulting in Oq_1 and Oq_2 production in H and P respectively.

When H and P enter into a customs union, P, being the cheaper producer, will produce the entire union output, Oq_5, at a price OB. Note
that this requires a common external tariff rate of AB/OA, i.e., a lower
tariff than initially in the more efficient partner. This gives rise to consumption in each of H and P of Oq_3 with gains of $BDEG$ and $BCFG$ for
H and P respectively. Parts of these gains, $BDEI$ for H and $BCFL$ for P,
are 'cost-reduction' effects, i.e, the initial cost of this amount has been
reduced due to economies of scale. There also results a production gain
for P and a production loss in H due to abandoning production
altogether.

Whether customs union formation can be justified in terms of the
existence of economies of scale will depend on whether the net effect is
a gain or a loss (in this example P gains and H loses), as the loss from
abandoning production in H must outweigh the consumption gain in
order for the tariff to have been imposed in the first place. If the overall
result is net gain, then the *distribution* of these gains becomes an
important consideration. Alternatively, if economies of scale accrue to
an integrated industry, then the *locational distribution* of the production
units becomes an essential issue.

Domestic distortions

A substantial literature tried to tackle the important question of whether
or not the formation of a customs union may be economically desirable
when there are domestic distortions. Such distortions could be attributed to the presence of trade unions which negotiate wage rates in
excess of the equilibrium rates or to governments introducing minimum
wage legislation, both of which are widespread activities in most

countries. It is usually assumed that the domestic distortion results in *social* average cost curve which lies below the private one. Hence, in Figure 9.4, which is adapted from Figure 9.3, I have incorporated AC_H^S and AC_P^S as the *social* curves in the context of economies of scale and a separate representation of countries H and P.

Note that AC_H^S is drawn to be consistently above AP_W, while AC_P^S is below it for higher levels of output. Before the formation of a customs union, H may have been adopting a made-to-measure tariff to protect its industry, but the first-best policy would have been one of free trade, as argued in the previous section. Hence, the formation of the customs union will lead to the same effects as in the previous section, with the exception that the cost-reduction effect *(b)* will be less by DD' times Oq_1. For P, the effects will be: (a) as before, a consumption gain of area c; (b) a cost-reduction effect of area e due to calculations relating to social rather than private costs; (c) gains from sales to H of areas d_1 and d_2, with d_1 being an income transfer from H to P, and d_2 the difference between domestic social costs in P and P_W, the world price; and (d) the social benefits accruing from extra production made possible by the customs union – area f – which is measured by the extra consumption multiplied by the difference between P_W and the domestic social costs.

However, this analysis does not lead to an economic rationale for the formation of customs unions, since P could have used first-best policy instruments to eliminate the divergence between private and social cost. This would have made AC_P^S the operative cost curve and, assuming that D_{H+P+W} is the world demand curve, this would have led to a world price of OF and exports of q_3q_5 and q_5q_6 to H and W respectively, with obviously greater benefits than those offered by the customs union. Hence the economic rationale for the customs union will have to depend on factors that can explain why first-best instruments could not have been employed in the first instance (Jones, 1980). In short, this is not an absolute argument for customs union formation.

The terms of trade effects

So far the analysis has been conducted on the assumption that customs union formation has no effects on the terms of trade (t/t), which implies that the countries concerned are too insignificant to have any appreciable influence on the international economy. Particularly in the context of the EU and groupings of similar size, this is a very unrealistic assumption.

195

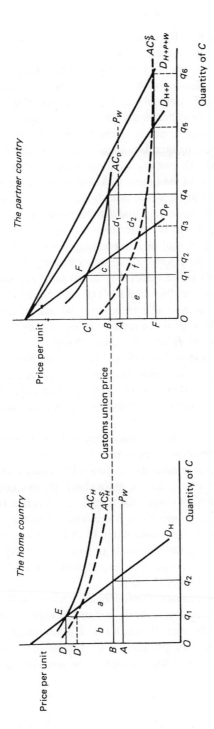

FIGURE 9.4 A customs union with economies of scale and domestic distortions

The analysis of the effects of customs union formation on the *t/t* is not only extremely complicated but is also unsatisfactory since a convincing model incorporating tariffs by all three areas of the world is still awaited: see Mundell (1964), Arndt (1968) and Wonnacott and Wonnacott (1981). To demonstrate this, let us consider Arndt's analysis, which is directly concerned with this issue, and the Wonnacotts' analysis, whose main concern is the Cooper/Massell criticism but which has some bearing on this matter.

In Figure 9.5, O_H, O_p and O_W are the respective offer curves of H, P and W. In section (a) of the figure, H is assumed to be the most efficient producer of commodity Y, while in section (b), H and P are assumed to be equally efficient. Assuming that the free trade *t/t* are given by OT_o, H will export q_6h_1 of Y to W in exchange for Oq_6 imports of commodity X, while P will export q_1p_1 of Y in exchange for Oq_1 of commodity X, with the sum of H and P's exports being exactly equal to OX_3.

When H imposes an *ad valorem* tariff, its tariff revenue-distributed curve is assumed to be displaced to $O'H'$ altering the *t/t* to OT_1. This leads to a contraction of H's trade with W and, at the same time, increases P's trade with W. In section (a) of the figure, it is assumed that the net effect of H and P's trade changes (contraction in H's exports and expansion in P's) will result in a contraction in world trade. It should be apparent that, from H's point of view, the competition of P in her export market has reduced the appropriateness of the Cooper/Massell alternative of a (non-discriminatory) union tariff rate (UTR).

Note, however, that H's welfare may still be increased in these unfavourable circumstances, provided that the move from h_1 to h_2 is accompanied by two conditions. It should be apparent that the larger the size of P relative to H and the more elastic the two countries' offer curves over the relevant ranges, the more likely it is that H will lose as a result of the tariff imposition. Moreover, given the various offer curves and H's tariff, H is more likely to sustain a loss in welfare the lower is her own marginal propensity to spend on her export commodity, X. If, in terms of consumption, commodity Y is a 'Giffen' good in country, H, h_2 will be inferior to h_1.

In this illustration, country H experiences a loss of welfare in case (a) but an increase in case (b), while country P experiences a welfare improvement in both cases. Hence, it is to H's advantage to persuade P to adopt restrictive trade practices. For example, let P impose an *ad valorem* tariff and, in order to simplify the analysis, assume that in

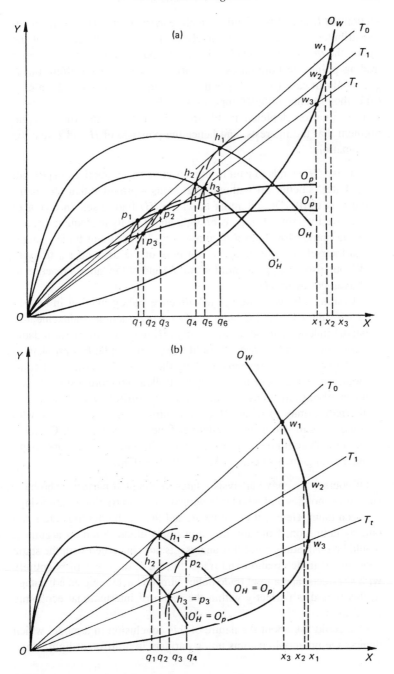

FIGURE 9.5   Customs unions and the terms of trade

section (b) *H* and *P* are identical in all respects such that their revenue-redistributed offer curves completely coincide. In both sections of the figure, the t/t will shift to OT_t, with h_3, P_3 and w_2 being the equilibrium trading points. In both cases, *P*'s tariff improves *H*'s welfare but *P* gains only in case (b), and is better off with unrestricted trade in case (a) in the presence of tariff imposition by *H*.

The situation depicted in Figure 9.5 illustrates the fundamental problem that the interests, and hence the policies, of *H* and *P* may be incompatible:

> Country *(H)* stands to gain from restrictive trade practices in *(P)*, but the latter is better off without restrictions – provided that *(H)* maintains its tariff. The dilemma in which *(H)* finds itself in trying to improve its terms of trade is brought about by its inadequate control of the market for its export commodity. Its optimum trade policies and their effects are functions not only of the demand elasticity in *(W)* but also of supply conditions in *(P)* and of the latter's reaction to a given policy in *(H)*.
>
> Country *(H)* will attempt to influence policy making in *(P)*. In view of the fact that the latter may have considerable inducement to pursue independent policies, country *(H)* may encounter formidable difficulties in this respect. It could attempt to handle this problem in a relatively loose arrangement along the lines of international commodity agreements, or in a tightly controlled and more restrictive set-up involving an international cartel. The difficulty is that neither alternative may provide effective control over the maverick who stands to gain from independent policies. In that case a Customs Union with common tariff and sufficient incentives may work where other arrangements do not. (Arndt, 1968, p. 978).

Of course, the above analysis relates to potential partners who have similar economies and who trade with *W*, with no trading relationships between them. Hence, it could be argued that such countries are ruled out, by definition, from forming a customs union. Such an argument would be misleading since this analysis is not concerned with the static concepts of trade creation and trade diversion; the concern is entirely with t/t effects, and a joint trade policy aimed at achieving an advantage in this regard is perfectly within the realm of international economic integration.

One could ask about the nature of this conclusion in a model which depicts the potential customs union partners in a different light. Here,

Wonnacott and Wonnacott's (1981) analysis may be useful, even though the aim of their paper was to question the general validity of the Cooper/Massell criticism, when the t/t remains unaltered as a result of customs union formation. However, this is precisely why it is useful to explain the Wonnacotts' analysis at this juncture: it has some bearing on the t/t effects and it questions the Cooper/Massell criticism.

The main point of the Wonnacotts' paper was to contest the proposition that UTR is superior to the formation of a customs union, hence the t/t argument was a side issue. They argued that this proposition does not hold generally if the following assumptions are rejected:

(a) that the tariff imposed by a partner (P) can be ignored;
(b) that W has no tariffs; and
(c) that there are no transport costs between members of the customs union (P and H) and W.

Their approach was not based on t/t effects or economies of scale and, except for their rejection of these three assumptions, their argument is also set entirely in the context of the standard two-commodity, three-country framework of customs union theory.

The basic framework of their analysis is set out in Figure 9.6. O_H and O_P are the free trade offer curves of the potential partners, whilst O_H^t and O_P^t are their initial tariff-inclusive offer curves. O_w^1 and O_w^2 are W's offer curves depending on whether the prospective partners wish to import commodity $X(O_w^1)$ or export it (O_w^2). The inclusion of both O_H^t and O_p^t meets the Wonnacott's desire to reject assumption (a) whilst the gap between O_W^1 and O_W^2 may be interpreted as the rejection of (b) and/or of (c): see Wonnacott and Wonnacott (1981, pp. 708–9).

In addition to the offer curves, I have inserted in Figure 9.6 various trade indifference curves for countries H and P (T_H... and T_P... respectively) and the pre customs union domestic t/t in H (O_t). $O_{W'}^2$ is drawn parallel to O_W^2 from the point c where O_P intersects O_t.

The diagram is drawn to illustrate the case where a customs union is formed between H and P with the CET set at the same rate as H's initial tariff on imports of X and where the domestic t/t in H remain unaltered so that trade with W continues after the formation of the customs union. With its initial non-discriminatory tariff, H will trade along O_W^2 with both P (Oa) and with W (ab). The formation of the customs union means that H and P's trade is determined by where O_P intersects O_t (i.e., at c) and that H will trade with W along $cO_{W'}^2$ (drawn parallel to OO_W^2). The final outcome for H will depend on the choice of

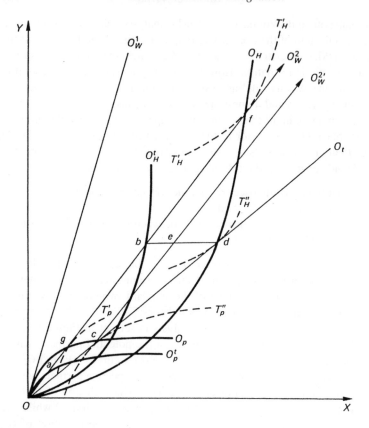

FIGURE 9.6   UTR versus customs unions

assumptions about what happens to the tariff revenue generated by the remaining external trade. If there is no redistribution of tariff revenue in *H*, then traders in that country will remain at point *d*. The tariff revenue generated by the external trade of the customs union with *W* is then shown to be equal to *ed* (measured in units of commodity *X*), which represents a reduction of *be* compared with the pre-customs union tariff revenue in *H*. Further, if procedures similar to those of the EU were adopted, the revenue *ed* would be used as an 'own resource' to be spent/distributed for the benefit of both members of the customs union whereas the pre-union tariff revenue (*bd*) would be kept by country *H*.

It can be seen that country *P* will benefit from the formation of the customs union even if it receives none of this revenue, but that *H* will undoubtedly lose even if it keeps all the post-union tariff revenue. This is the case of pure trade diversion and, in the absence of additional income transfers from *P, H* clearly cannot be expected to join the customs union even if it considers that this is the only alternative to its initial tariff policy. There is no rationale, however, for so restricting the choice of policy alternatives. UTR is unambiguously superior to the initial tariff policy for both *H* and *P* and, compared with the non-discriminatory free trade policies available to both countries (which take country *H* to T_H at *f* and country *P* to T'_P at *g*), there is no possible system of income transfers from *P* to *H* which can make the formation of a customs union Pareto-superior to free trade for both countries. It remains true, of course, that country *P* would gain more from membership of a customs union with *H* than it could achieve by UTR but, provided that *H* pursues its optimal strategy, which is UTR, country *P* itself can do no better than follow suit so that the optimal outcome for both countries is multilateral free trade (MFT).

Of course, there is no a priori reason why the customs union, if created, should set its CET at the level of the country *H*'s initial tariff. Indeed, it is instructive to consider the consequences of forming a customs union with a lower CET. The implications of this can be seen by considering the effect of rotating O_t anticlockwise towards O^1_W. In this context, the moving O_t line will show the post-union *t/t* in countries *H* and *P*. Clearly, the lowering of the CET will improve the domestic *t/t* for *H* compared with the original form of the customs union and it will have a trade-creating effect as the external trade of the customs union will increase more rapidly than the decline in intra-union trade. Compared with the original customs union, *H* would gain and *P* would lose. Indeed, the lower the level of the CET, the more likely is *H* to gain from the formation of the customs union *compared with the initial non-discriminatory tariff.* As long as the CET remains positive, however, *H* would be unambiguously worse off from membership of the customs union than from UTR and, although *P* would gain from such a customs union compared with any initial tariff policy it may adopt, it remains true that there is no conceivable set of income transfers associated with the formation of the customs union which would make both *H* and *P* simultaneously better off than they would be if, after *H*'s UTR, *P* also pursued the optimal unilateral action available: the move to free trade.

It is of course true that, if the CET is set at zero, so that the rotated O_t coincides with O^2_W, then the outcome is identical with that for the unilateral adoption of free trade for both countries. This, however, merely illustrates how misleading it would be to describe such a policy as 'the formation of a customs union, a customs union with a zero CET is indistinguishable from a free trade policy by both countries and should surely be described solely in the latter terms.

One can extend and generalise this approach beyond what has been done here: see Berglas (1983). The important point, however, is what the analysis clearly demonstrates: the assumption that the t/t should remain constant for members of a customs union, even if both countries are 'small', leaves a lot to be desired. But it should also be stressed that the Wonnacotts' analysis does not take into consideration the tariffs of H and P on trade with W, or deal with a genuine three-country model since W is assumed to be very large: W has constant t/t.

9.6   FURTHER EXTENSIONS OF THE BASIC ANALYSIS

Customs unions versus free trade areas

The analysis so far has been conducted on the premise that differences between customs unions and free trade areas can be ignored. However, the ability of the member nations of free trade areas to decide their own commercial policies *vis-à-vis* the outside world raises certain issues. Balassa (1961) pointed out that free trade areas may result in deflection of trade, production and investment. Deflection of trade occurs when imports from W (the cheapest source of supply) come via the member country with the lowest tariff rate, assuming that transport and administrative costs do not outweigh the tariff differential. Deflection of production and investment occurs in commodities whose production requires a substantial quantity of raw materials imported from W; the tariff differential regarding these materials might distort the true comparative advantage in domestic materials, therefore resulting in resource allocations according to overall comparative disadvantage.

If deflection of trade occurs, the free trade area effectively becomes a customs union with a CET equal to the lowest tariff rate, which is obviously beneficial for the world (see Curzon-Price, 1974 and 1982). However, most free trade areas seem to adopt 'rules of origin' so that only those commodities that originate in a member state are exempt from tariff imposition. If deflection of production and investment takes place, we have the case of the so-called 'tariff factories', but the necessary conditions for this are extremely limited (see El-Agraa in El-Agraa and Jones, 1981, ch. 3).

Common markets and economic unions

The analysis of customs unions needs drastic extension when applied to common markets and economic unions. First, the introduction of free factor mobility may enhance efficiency through a more rational reallocation of resources but it may also result in depressed areas and therefore creating or aggravating regional problems and imbalances: see Mayes (1983) and Robson (1987). Second, fiscal harmonisation may also improve efficiency by eliminating non-tariff trade barriers and distortions and by equalising their effective protective rates. Third, the coordination of monetary and fiscal policies which is implied by monetary integration may ease unnecessarily severe imbalances, hence resulting in the promotion of the right atmosphere for stability in the economies of the member nations.

These economic union elements must be tackled *simultaneously* with trade creation and diversion as well as economies of scale and market distortions. However, such interactions are too complicated to consider here: the interested reader should consult El-Agraa (1983a, 1983b; 1984). Hence, this section will be devoted to a brief discussion of factor mobility and monetary integration.

With regard to *factor mobility*, it should be apparent that the removal (or harmonisation) of all barriers to labour (L) and capital (K) will encourage both L and K to move. L will move to those areas where it can fetch the highest possible reward, i.e., 'net advantage'. This encouragement need not necessarily lead to an increase in actual mobility since there are socio-political factors which normally result in people remaining near their birthplace; social proximity is a dominant consideration, which is why the average person does not move. If the reward to K is not equalised, i.e., differences in marginal productivities (*mps*) exist before the formation of an economic union, K will move until the *mps* are equalised. This will result in benefits which can be clearly described in terms of Figure 9.7, which depicts the production characteristics in H and P. M_H and M_P are the schedules which relate the K stocks to their *mps* in H and P respectively, given the quantity of L in each country; assuming only two factors of production.

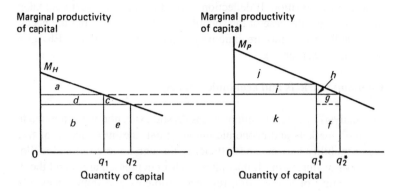

FIGURE 9.7   Factor mobility in a common market

Prior to economic union formation, the K stock (which is assumed to remain constant throughout the analysis) is Oq_2 in H and Oq_1^* in P. Assuming that K is immobile internationally, all K stocks must be nationally owned and, ignoring taxation, profit per unit of K will be equal to its *mp*, given conditions of perfect competition. Hence the total profit in H is equal to areas $b + e$ and $i + K$ in P. Total output is, of course, the whole area below the M_P curve but within Oq_2 in H and Oq^* in P, i.e., areas $a + b + c + d + e$ in H and $j + i + k$ in P. Therefore, L's share is $a + c + d$ in H and j in P.

Since the *mp* in P exceeds that in H, the removal of barriers to K mobility or the harmonisation of such barriers will induce K to move away from H and into P. This is because nothing has happened to affect K in W. Such movement will continue until the *mp* of k is the same in both H and P. This results in q_1q_2 ($= q_1^*q_2^*$) of K moving from H to P. Hence the output of H falls to $a + b + d$ while its *national* product, including the return of the profit earned on K in P ($= g + f$), increases by (g–c). In P, *domestic* product rises by ($f + g + h$) while *national* product (excluding the remittance of profits to H) increases by area h only. Both H and P experience a change in the relative share of L and K in national product, with K-owners being favourably disposed in H and unfavourably disposed in P.

Of course, this analysis is too simplistic since, apart from the fact that K and L are never perfectly immobile at the international level and multinational corporations have their own ways of transferring K (see Buckley and Casson, 1976; Dunning, 1977), the analysis does not take into account the fact that K may actually move to areas with low wages after the formation of an economic union. Moreover, if K moves predominantly in only one direction, one country may become a depressed area; hence the 'social costs' and benefits of such an occurrence need to be taken into consideration, particularly if the economic union deems it important that the economies of both H and P should be balanced. Therefore, the above gains have to be discounted or supplemented by such costs and benefits.

Monetary integration has two essential components: an exchange rate union and K market integration. An exchange rate union is established when member countries have what is in effect one currency. The actual existence of one currency is not necessary, however, because if member countries have *permanently* fixed exchange rates amongst themselves, the result is effectively the same.

Convertibility refers to the *permanent* absence of all exchange controls for both current and K transactions, including interest and dividend payments (and the harmonisation of relevant taxes and measures affecting the K market) within the union. It is of course absolutely necessary to have complete convertibility for trade transactions, as otherwise an important requirement of customs union formation is threatened, namely the promotion of free trade between members of the customs union, which is an integral part of an economic union. Convertibility for K transactions is related to free factor mobility and is therefore an important aspect of K market integration which is necessary in common markets, not in customs unions or free trade areas.

In practice, this definition of monetary integration should specifically include: (a) an explicit harmonisation of monetary policies; (b) a common pool of foreign exchange reserves; and (c) a single central bank. There are important reasons for including these elements. Suppose union members decide either that one of their currencies will be a reference currency, or that a new unit of account will be established. Also assume that each member country has its own foreign exchange reserves and conducts its own monetary and fiscal policies. If a member finds itself running out of reserves, it will have to engage in a monetary and fiscal contraction sufficient to restore the reserve position. This will necessitate the fairly frequent meeting of the finance ministers, or central bank governors, to consider whether or not to change the parity of the reference currency. If they do decide to change it, then all the member currencies will have to move with it. Such a situation could create the kinds of difficulty which plagued the Bretton Woods System.

In order to avoid such difficulties, it is necessary to include the above three elements in the definition of monetary integration. The central bank would operate in the market so as permanently to maintain the exchange parities among the union currencies and, at the same time, it would allow the rate of the reference currency to fluctuate, or to alter intermittently, relative to the outside reserve currency. For instance, if the foreign exchange reserves in the common pool were running down, the bank would allow the reference currency, and with it all the partner currencies, to depreciate. This would have the advantage of economising on the use of foreign exchange reserves, since all partners would not tend to be in deficit or surplus at the same time. Also surplus countries would automatically be helping deficit countries.

However, without explicit policy coordination, a monetary union would not be effective. If each country conducted its own monetary policy, and hence could engage in as much domestic credit creation as it wished, surplus countries would be financing deficit nations without any incentives for the deficit countries to restore equilibrium. If one country ran a large deficit, the union exchange rate would depreciate, but this might put some partner countries into surplus. If wage rates were rising in the member countries at different rates, while productivity growth did not differ in such a way as to offset the effects on relative prices, those partners with the smaller inflation rates would be permanently financing the other partners.

Therefore, monetary integration which explicitly includes the three requirements specified removes all these problems. Incidentally, this also suggests the advantages of having a single currency.

The benefits of monetary integration should by now be clear (see Robson, 1987). However, there is no consensus of opinion with regard to its costs, if any, simply because those who stress the cost entirely ignore the basic reality that although a member nation loses its individual ability to alter its exchange rate, the economic union's exchange rate can be altered. Moreover, the economic rationale for exchange rate flexibility depends heavily on Tinbergen's criterion of at least an equal number of policy instruments and policy objectives. Orthodoxy has it that there are two macroeconomic policy targets (internal and external equilibrium) and two policy instruments (financial instruments, which have their greatest impact on the level of aggregate demand, hence on the internal equilibrium; and the exchange rate, which operates mainly on the external equilibrium). Of course, financial instruments can be activated via both monetary and fiscal policies, and may have a varied impact on both the internal and external equilibria. Given this understanding, the case for maintaining flexibility in exchange rates depends entirely on the presumption that the loss of one of the two policy instruments will conflict with the achievement of both internal and external equilibria.

Assuming that there is a Phillips curve relationship (a negative response of rates of change in money wages, W, and the level of unemployment, U), Fleming (1971) and Corden (1972) can explain these aspects by using a simple diagram which was first devised by De Grauwe. Hence, in Figure 9.8 the top half depicts the position of H while the lower half depicts that of P. The top right and the lower left corners represent the two countries' Phillips curves while the remaining quadrants show their inflation rates $\dot{P}$. WI_H and WI_P are, of course, determined by the share of L in total GNP, the rate of change in the

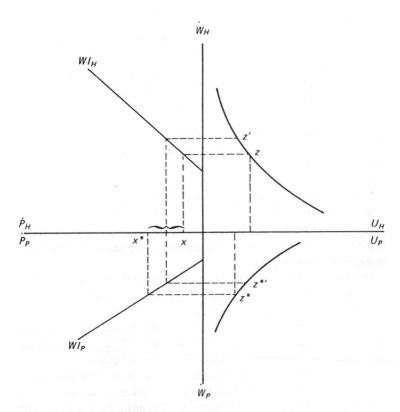

FIGURE 9.8   The traditional analysis of economic and monetary union

productivity of L and the degree of competition in both the factor and commodity markets, with perfect competition resulting in the *WIs* being straight lines. Note that the intersection of the *WIs* with the vertical axes will be determined by the rates of change of L's share in GNP and its rate of productivity change. The diagram has been drawn on the presumption that the L productivity changes are positive.

The diagram is drawn in such a way that countries H and P differ in all respects: the positions of their Phillips curves, their preferred trade-offs between $\dot{W}$ and $\dot{P}$, and their rates of productivity growth. H has a lower rate of inflation, x, than P, x^* (equilibria being at z and z^*) and hence, without monetary integration, P's currency should depreciate relative to H's; note that it is almost impossible that the two countries' inflation rates would coincide. Altering the exchange rates would then enable each country to maintain its preferred internal equilibrium: z and z^* for respectively countries H and P.

When H and P enter into an exchange rate union, i.e., have irrevocably fixed exchange rates *vis-à-vis* each other, their inflation rates cannot differ from each other, given a model without traded goods. Hence, each country will have to settle for a combination of U and P different from that which it would have liked. Therefore, the Fleming/Corden conclusion is vindicated.

It does not require much imagination to see that if this crude version of the Phillips curve is replaced by an expectations-adjusted one, i.e., the Phillips curves become vertical in the long run, the Fleming/Corden conclusion need no longer hold. Moreover, once non-traded goods are incorporated into the model and/or K and L mobility are allowed for, it follows that the losses due to deviating from internal equilibrium vanish into oblivion. Finally, this model does not allow for the fact that monetary integration involves at least three countries, so that W has to be explicitly included in the model.

In addition, one should point out a fundamental contradiction in the analysis of those who exaggerate the costs. If a nation decides to become a member of a monetary union, this implies that it accedes to the notion that the benefits of such a union must outweigh any possible losses and/or that it feels that a monetary union is essential for maintaining a rational economic union. It will want to do so because its economy is more interdependent with its partners than with W. Why then would such a country prize the availability of the exchange rate as a policy instrument for its own domestic purposes? The answer is that there is no conceivable rational reason for its doing so; it will want to have an inflation rate, monetary growth target and unemployment rate which are consistent with those of its partner. Also, the use of the union's exchange rate *vis-à-vis W* plus the rational operations of the common central bank and its general activities should ensure that any worries on the part of *H* are alleviated. Hence, for such a country to feel that there is something intrinsically good about having such a policy instrument at its own disposal is tantamount to its not having any faith in or true commitment to the economic union to which it has voluntarily decided to belong!

These common market and 'economic union' elements must be considered *simultaneously* with trade creation and trade diversion. However, such interactions are too complicated to consider here.

Economic integration among communist countries

Until recently, the only example of economic integration among communist countries was the CMEA. However, here the economic system perpetuated a fundamental lack of interest among domestic producers in becoming integrated with both consumers and producers in other member countries. The integration policies of member nations focused on the mechanism of state-to-state relations rather than on domestic economic policies which would have made CMEA integration more attractive to producers and consumers alike: i.e., integration was planned by the state at the highest possible level and imposed on ministries, trusts and enterprises. It should also be stated that the CMEA operated different pricing mechanisms for intra- and extra-area trade. Moreover, the attitude of the former USSR was extremely important, since the policies of the East European members of the CMEA were somewhat constrained by the policies adopted by the organisation's most powerful member, for economic as well as political reasons. CMEA integration, therefore, had to be approached within an entirely different framework and this is not the appropriate place for discussing it: the interested reader should consult Marer and Montias (1982).

Economic integration among developing countries

It has been claimed that the body of economic integration theory as so far developed has no relevance for the Third World since the theory suggested that there would be more scope for trade creation if the countries concerned were initially very competitive in production but potentially very complementary, and that a customs union would be more likely to be trade-creating if the partners conducted most of their foreign trade among themselves (see Meade,1955b and Lipsey, 1960). These conditions are unlikely to be satisfied in the majority of the developing nations. Moreover, most of the effects of integration are initially bound to be trade diverting, particularly since most of the Third World seeks to industrialise.

On the other hand, it was also realised that an important obstacle to the development of industry in these countries was the inadequate size of their individual markets (see Brown, 1961; Hazlewood, 1967 and 1975; and, Robson, 1980 and 1983). It was therefore necessary to increase the market size so as to encourage optimum plant installations, and hence the need for economic integration. This would result, however, in industries clustering together in the relatively more advanced of these nations, i.e., those that have already commenced on the process of industrialisation.

I have demonstrated elsewhere (El-Agraa, 1979 and Ch. 6 of El-Agraa and Jones, 1981) that there is essentially no theoretical difference between economic integration in the advanced world and the Third World, but that there is a major difference in terms of the *type* of economic integration that is politically feasible; the need for an equitable distribution of the gains from industrialisation and the location of industries is an important issue (see above). This suggests that any type of economic integration being contemplated must incorporate as an essential element a common fiscal authority and some coordination of economic policies. But then one could equally well argue that *some degree* of these elements is necessary in *any* type of integration (see the Raisman Committee recommendations for the EAC, 1961; El-Agraa, 1982; Hazlewood, 1982).

9.7 MEASURING THE IMPACT OF ECONOMIC INTEGRATION

Any sensible approach to the analysis of changes in trade shares following economic integration should have the following characteristics:

(a) it should be capable of being carried out at the appropriate level of disaggregation;
(b) it should be able to distinguish between trade creation, trade diversion and external trade creation;

(c) it should be capable of discerning the effects of economic growth on trade that would have taken place in the absence of economic integration;

(d) it should be 'analytic', i.e., it should be capable of providing an economic explanation of the actual post-integration situation; and

(e) it should be a general equilibrium approach capable of allowing for the effects of economic integration in an interdependent world.

The effects on trade

The general trend of the empirical work on economic integration has been to examine various specific aspects of integration, mainly the effects on trading patterns, and to analyse them separately. The most important practical distinction made is between 'price' and 'income' effects. This is largely because the main initial instruments in economic integration are tariffs, quotas and other trade impediments which act mainly on relative prices in the first instance. However, all sources of possible economic gain incorporate 'income' as well as 'price' effects.

The immediate difficulty is thus the translation of tariff changes and other agreed measures in the customs union treaty into changes in prices and other variables which are known to have an impact on economic behaviour. Such evidence as there is suggests that there are wide discrepancies among the reactions of importers benefiting from tariff cuts and also among competitors adversely affected by them (EFTA, 1968), and that reactions of trade to tariff changes are different from those to price changes (Kreinin, 1961). Two routes would appear to be open: one is to estimate the effect of tariff changes on prices and then estimate the effects of these derived price changes on trade patterns; the other is to operate directly with observed relative price movements. This latter course exemplifies a problem which runs right through the estimation of the effects of economic integration and makes the obtaining of generally satisfactory results almost impossible: it is that to measure the effect of integration one must decide what would have happened if integration had not occurred. Thus, if in the present instance any observed changes in relative prices were assumed to be the result of the adjustment to tariff changes, then all other sources of variation in prices would be ignored, which is clearly an exaggeration and could be subject to important biases if other factors were affecting trade at the same time.

The dynamic effects

While in the discussion of the exploitation of comparative advantage, the gains from a favourable movement in the terms of trade and often those from economies of scale are expressed in terms of comparative statics, it is difficult to disentangle them from feedback on to incomes and activity. The essence of the gains from increased efficiency and technological change is that the economy should reap dynamic gains. In other words, integration should enhance the rate of growth of GDP rather than just giving a step up in welfare. Again, it is necessary to explain how this might come about explicitly.

There are two generalised ways in which this can take place: first, through increased productivity growth at a given investment ratio, and second, through increased investment itself. This is true whether the increased sales are generated internally or through the pressures of demand for exports from abroad through integration. Growth gains can, of course, occur temporarily in so far as there are slack resources in the economy. Again, it is possible to observe whether the rate of growth has changed, but it is much more difficult to decide whether that is attributable to integration.

Krause (1968) attempted to apply a version of Denison's (1967) method of identifying the causes of economic growth, but suggested that all changes in the rate of business investment were due to the formation of the EEC (or EFTA in the case of those countries). Mayes (1978) showed that if the same contrast between business investment before and after the formation of the EEC (EFTA) were applied to Japan, there was a bigger effect observed than in any of the integrating countries! Clearly changes in the rate of business investment can occur for reasons other than integration.

Previous studies

A few general comments and a representative sample of recent studies may be helpful here: first, let us consider the general comments.

Most of the measurements can be broadly classified as *ex ante* or *ex post*. The *ex ante* estimates are based on a priori knowledge of the pre-integration period (i.e., structural models), while the *ex post* studies are based on assumptions about the actual experience of economic integration (i.e., residual-imputation models).

There are two types of *ex ante* study: those undertaken before the EEC and EFTA were actually operative, and those undertaken after they became operative. The most influential studies to use this approach are those of Krause (1968), who predicted the trade diversion that would be brought about by the EEC and EFTA on the basis of assumptions about demand elasticities, and Han and Leisner (1970), who predicted the effect on the UK by identifying those industries that had a comparative cost advantage/disadvantage *vis-à-vis* the EEC and finding out how they were likely to be affected by membership, on the assumption that the pattern of trade prior to UK membership provided an indication of the underlying cost conditions and that this would be one of the determinants of the pattern of trade and domestic production after membership. This approach is of very limited advantage, however, for the simple reason that 'it does not provide a method of enabling one to improve previous estimate on the basis of new historical experience' (Williamson and Bottrill, 1971, p. 326).

The most significant studies to use the *ex post* approach are those of Lamfalussy (1964) and Verdoorn and Meyer zu Schlochtern (1974), who all use a relative shares method; Balassa (1967 and 1975), who uses a income-elasticity of import demand method; the EFTA Secretariat (1969, 1972), who use a share of imports in apparent consumption method; Williamson and Bottrill (1971), who use a more sophisticated share analysis; Prewo (1974) who uses an input-output method; and Barten, d'Alcantra and Cairn (1976), who use a medium-term macroeconomic method. The advantage of the *ex post* method is that it can be constructed in such a way as to benefit from historical experience and hence to provide a basis for continuous research. However, the major obstacle in this approach concerns the difficulty regarding the construction of an adequate hypothetical post-integration picture of the economies concerned.

A critique of previous studies

There are some general and some specific points of criticism to be made of these studies. Let me start with the general points.

1. All the studies, excepting the Truman (1975) and Williamson and Bottrill (1971) studies and, to a certain extent, the Aitken (1973) and Mayes (1978) studies, assume that the formation of the EEC (or EFTA) has been the sole factor to influence the pattern of trade. Since the EEC and EFTA were established more or less simultaneously (there is a year's difference between them), it is unjustifiable

to attribute changes in the pattern of trade to either alone. After all, EFTA was established in order to counteract the possible damaging effects of the EEC! Moreover, as we have seen above, a number of other schemes soon followed.

2. Most of the recent studies ignore the fact that Britain used to be a member of EFTA before joining the EEC. Since the UK is a substantial force as a member of either area, it seems misleading to attempt estimates which do not take into consideration this switch by the UK. This point, of course, adds force to the previous one.

3. In the period prior to the formation of the EEC and EFTA, certain significant changes were happening on the international scene. The most significant of these is that the discrimination against the US dollar was greatly reduced. Is it at all possible that such developments had no effect whatsoever on the trade patterns of the EEC and EFTA? It seems unrealistic to assume that this should have been the case.

4. All the studies, except for Truman's (1975), deal with trade data, and this is in spite of the fact that a proper evaluation of the effects of economic integration requires analysis of both trade and production data. Trade creation indicates a reduction in domestic production combined with new imports of the same quantity from the partner, while trade diversion indicates new imports from the partner combined with fewer imports from the outside world and a reduction in the rest of the world's production.

5. Tariffs are universally recognised as only one of many trade impediments, yet all the studies except Krause's (1968) and Prewo's (1974) are based on the assumption that the only effect of economic integration in Western Europe is on discriminatory tariff removal. This is a very unsatisfactory premise, particularly if one recalls that the EEC had to resort to explicit legislation against cheap imports from India, Japan and Pakistan! Moreover, the level of tariffs and their effective protection is very difficult to measure (Waelbroeck, 1977, p. 89).

6. The Dillon and the Kennedy Rounds of tariff negotiations resulted in a global tariff reduction which coincided with the first stage of the removal of tariffs. This point lends support to the previous one.

More specifically, however, there are a host of factors which influence the difference between the post-integration position and that of pre-integration; hence to attribute the difference to integration only is very misleading.

It therefore seems inevitable to conclude that:

All estimates of trade creation and diversion by the EEC which have been presented in the empirical literature are so much affected by *ceteris paribus* assumptions, by the choice of the length of the pre- and post-integration periods, by the choice of benchmark year (or years), by the methods to compute income elasticities, changes in trade matrices and in relative shares and by structural changes not attributable to the EEC but which occurred during the pre- and post-integration periods (such as the trade liberalization among industrial countries and autonomous changes in relative prices that the magnitude of no ... estimate should be taken too seriously. (Sellekaerts, 1973, p. 548)

9.8   THE STUDY BY WINTERS

Winters' objective was to assess the changes in UK imports of manufactures brought about by membership of the EEC. His method took account of the substitutability of imports for domestic production with a consistent modelling of price effects. He applied Deaton and Muelbauer's 'Almost Ideal Demand System' (AIDS) to annual data on domestic UK sales and imports from ten supply sources, five of which were members of the EEC (Belgium/Luxemburg, France, Italy, the Netherlands and West Germany), the others being Canada, Japan, the USA, Sweden and Switzerland.

Winters found AIDS to be a very broad yet tractable demand system, which satisfied various a priori restrictions arising from the theory of demand. Assuming away problems of aggregation, simultaneity and lagged responses, he postulated that the allocation of demand over supply sources was governed by:

$$w_{it} = \alpha_i + \sum \gamma_{ij} \log p_{jt} - \beta_i \log(E_t / P_t^*) + u_{it} \quad i = 1, \ldots N \qquad (9.1)$$

where w was country i's share of E_t, E_t was total expenditure when domestic sales were included, t was a time trend, p_{jt} was the price of manufactures from country j, P_t^* was calculated over the group of countries included, and α_i, β_i and γ_{ij} were parameters.

In order to add up, it was necessary that

$$\sum_i \alpha_i = 1 \quad \text{and} \quad \sum_i \gamma_{ij} = \sum_i \beta_i = 0 \qquad (9.2)$$

which was satisfied automatically by any set of w_i which added up to unity. Homogeneity required that

$$\sum_j \gamma_{ij} = 0 \tag{9.3}$$

and symmetry that

$$\gamma_{ij} = \gamma_{ji} \tag{9.4}$$

Winters was certain that these could easily be imposed, although (9.4) did mean that all equations had to be estimated simultaneously with cross-section constraints. This adding-up constraint also meant that $\sum_i u_{it} = 0$, where the u_{it} were the errors in equation (9.1). This created some problems in estimating equation (9.1) as a system, since the variance-covariance matrix $\Omega \equiv E(uu')$ was singular. Indeed, Winters conceded that the estimation of Ω was very difficult, due to the fact that the deterministic part of equation (9.1) alone contained 75 parameters when $N = 11$, and the estimation of Ω would have added a further 55. Winters therefore decided to constrain it a priori. For the full model, he found evidence to suggest that random changes in the share of any imports were largely reflected by compensating changes in the UK share; hence he specified, where the UK was the last supplier:

$$\Omega = \begin{bmatrix} \sigma_{11}^2 & & & & -\sigma_1^2 \\ & \sigma_{22}^2 & & 0 & -\sigma_{22}^2 \\ & & \ddots & & \vdots \\ & 0 & & \sigma_{1010}^2 & -\sigma_{1010}^2 \\ -\sigma_{11}^2 & -\sigma_{22}^2 & \cdots & -\sigma_{1010}^2 & \eta \end{bmatrix}$$

where $\eta = \sum\limits_{i=1}^{10} \sigma_{ii}^2$.

Winters allowed for the non-singularity in this case by suppressing the equation for the UK, estimating its parameters from the adding-up constraints.

Winters then applied the AIDS models to UK imports. The full model consisted of 55 price parameters. Since over the pre-EEC membership period 1952–71 none of the countries in this sample experienced great inflation and there were very few exchange-rate adjustments, he concluded that there would be very little variation in the independent data to allow a reasonable estimation of the AIDS model; indeed, he found huge standard errors, implausible estimates and a lack of convergence. Therefore, he estimated the model over the whole data period, adding dummy variables (DVs) to account for the EEC effect. This was done in two experiments: (a) where he added $\partial_i D$ to equation (9.1) for each country, where D was zero until 1972 and unity after 1973 which implied that EEC membership was both immediate and complete, a most unlikely event; (b) where he replaced D by D' with a value of zero for the period of 1952–71, unity for 1972, 3 for 1973 and increased the value by one unit per year thereafter, i.e., D' was 9 in 1979.

Winters noted that the procedure of using DVs shifted his model from that of the 'residual imputation' to the 'analytic' class, i.e., the use of DVs attributed all structural shifts and random variations only to the factor specifically under consideration.

He then added two further DVs to allow for the Swiss diamond trade which strongly influenced the results for his 'imports only' model. These DVs were assigned a value of zero for all years except that it was unity for 1972–9 and 1978–9. These values raised the share of Switzerland, so he had to decide which country was to be held responsible for this. He opted for the UK, due to its predominant share of its own market (he found it impossible to estimate at which country's expense since that would have required an extra 18 independent parameters).

The results are given in Table 9.1 for the complete AIDS model under experiment (b). Note that the Swiss dummies were significantly positive: e.g., they had t-statistics of 3.74 (1972–9 dummy) and 6.28 (1978–9 dummy); these reduced the Swiss external trade creation (and consequent loss of domestic sales) from £2195 million to £542 million.

Winters then drew the reader's attention to the fact that the ten EEC-membership effects were jointly significantly different from zero. Also, that the main effect was 'internal' trade creation: the effects on the five members of the EEC were significant jointly (and nearly so individually) and involved a substantial amount of trade. Moreover, the effects on the five non-partners were insignificant and relatively small. He concluded that, at face value, these results suggested that accession to the EEC, by 1979, had led to internal trade creation of £10 billion and external trade creation of £2 billion and a consequent loss of domestic sales of £12 billion. In proportion to the 1979 magnitudes, these figures amounted to 70, 22 and 17 per cent respectively.

Finally, Winters was quick to caution the reader that his results may have been an overestimation because the external trade creation figures may have captured other non-integration effects; the second oil price shock may have affected the competitiveness of the EEC and non-EEC members differently (note that the oil problem was largely dismissed in his 1985 paper); and his model implied that the consumption of manufactures and all (tax-exclusive) prices would have been the same irrespective of economic integration. He suggested that if these considerations had been taken into account, by 1979, trade creation might have amounted to £6 billion or more.

Winter's approach no doubt represents a great improvement on most of the previous estimates since, by including the effects of economic integration on the level of home sales, his model comes nearest to incorporating production effects; most other models deal with only trade data. However, his results should be examined with a great deal of caution. First, there are limitations which he himself explicitly stated: the model treats manufactures as if they were a single homogeneous product; there are no dynamics in the price effects because of 'tractability – it is not clear how to incorporate sensible dynamics into allocation models like the AIDS'; simultaneity problems are ignored; there is the serious problem of the 'causation running from the UK share of [its] own market in manufactures to the UK price index and aggregate level of spending on manufactures'; and the data are not perfect. Second, and equally seriously, is the neglect of the basic reality that before joining the EEC in 1973 the UK was a founder member of EFTA, a bloc which came into existence just a year after the formation of the EEC. This might not have been a problem had it not been for the fact that two of Winter's non-partners are themselves members of EFTA (namely Sweden and Switzerland). However, Winters draws my attention to the fact that DVs can account for both 'preference' and 'loss of preference', leading to minor estimation problems. Third, as part of the accession negotiations, the EEC and EFTA established several agreements which made virtually the whole of Western Europe into a free trade area in manufactures. Finally, although the UK formally joined the EEC in 1973, it was subject to a transitional period of four years before its tariffs against other members were fully dismantled. Of course, it could be argued that DVs allow for this, but I remain sceptical. Is it not conceivable that the

TABLE 9.1 Integration effects in an AIDS model of trade*

	Actual sales in the UK 1979[+] (£m)	Imports only Value 1979			Complete model value 1979	
		Share[‡]	(£m)	Share[‡]	(£m)	*t*-statics[§]
France	3 100	0.0060[¶]	1 292	0.00225[¶]	1 934	2.25
Belgium/ Luxemburg	1 967	0.0024	517	0.00203[¶]	1 745	2.03
Netherlands	1 883	0.0015	323	0.00153	1 315	1.53
Germany	5 419	0.0080[¶]	1 723	0.00436[¶]	3 748	4.36
Italy	2 012	0.0059[¶]	1 270	0.00155	1 332	1.55
Sweden	1 301	−0.0067	−1 443	−0.00014	−120	−0.14
Switzerland	2 559	−0.0034	−732	0.00063	542	0.64
Japan	1 471	−0.0005	−108	−0.00084	722	0.84
Canada	529	−0.0019	−409	−0.00027	−232	−0.27
USA	3 684	−0.0112[¶]	−2 412	0.00138	1 186	1.38
UK	71 581	–	–	0.01416[¶]	−12 171	4.54

Notes: * Experiments B: AIDS plus dummy D' and two Swiss dummies.
+ Adjusted for tariffs.
‡ The effect on the share in any year is this coefficient times the value for the year (1973–9).
§ *t*-statistics of coefficients on D'. Wald-statistics on the joint significance of the integration effects in this model are:
   (a) on all ten independent effects 36.9 (critical value $x_{10}^2 = 18.3$)
   (b) on five EEC partner effects 33.5 (critical value $x_5^2 = 11.1$)
   (c) on five non-partner effects 3.1 (critical value $x_5^2 = 11.1$)
¶ *t*-statistics exceeding 1.96.

Source: L. A. Winters (1984) 'British Imports of Manufactures and the Common Market', *Oxford Economic Papers*, 36, p. 112.

inclusion of any or all of these considerations would have drastically affected Winters' estimates?

An alternative

It seems evident that there is nothing wrong with the methodology, but that the problems of actual measurement are insurmountable. However, I do believe that these difficulties are due to some basic misconceptions regarding the welfare implications of trade creation and trade diversion:

trade creation is good and trade diversion is bad, using the Johnson (1974) definition.

In an interdependent macroeconomic world, trade creation is inferior to trade diversion for the country concerned (see El-Agraa, 1978; El-Agraa and Jones, 1981; and A. J. Jones, 1983) and both are certainly detrimental to the outside world. This conclusion is also substantiated by Johnson's work which incorporates the collective consumption of a public good (Johnson, 1965a). It therefore seems rather futile, for estimation purposes, to attach too much significance to the welfare implications of the trade creation/diversion dichotomy.

For all these reasons I suggest that the measurement of the impact of economic integration should be confined to estimating its effect on intra-union trade and, if possible, to finding out whether or not any changes have been at the expense of the outside world. The statistical procedure for such estimates should be straightforward if one uses my interdependent global macro model and incorporates into it the import demand functions suggested by Dayal and Dayal (1977). One can then utilise the concepts of income and substitution effects (suggested by the Dayals) without some of the unnecessary detail created by using simple marginal utility functions.

9.9 CONCLUSIONS

The conclusions reached here are consistent with my (1979) conclusions and with those of A. J. Jones (1980) and Jones in El-Agraa and Jones (1981); the contributions by Dixit (1975), Berglas (1979), Collier (1979), Riezman (1979), Whalley (1979), McMillan and McCann (1981) and Wonnacott and Wonnacott (1981) do not affect these conclusions sufficiently to merit separate consideration.

They are as follows. First, the rationale for regional economic integration rests upon the existence of constraints on the use of first-best policy instruments. Economic analysis has had little to say about the nature of these constraints, and presumably the evaluation of any regional scheme of economic integration should incorporate a consideration of the validity of the view that such constraints do exist to justify the pursuit of second- rather than first-best solutions.

Second, that even when the existence of constraints on superior policy instruments is acknowledged, it is misleading to identify the results of regional economic integration by comparing an arbitrarily chosen common policy with an arbitrarily chosen national policy. Of course, ignorance and inertia provide sufficient reasons why existing policies may be non-optimal, but it is clearly wrong to attribute gains that would have been achieved by appropriate unilateral action to a policy of regional integration. Equally, although it is appropriate to use the optimal common policy as a point of reference, it must be recognised that this may overstate the gains to be achieved if, as seems highly likely, constraints and inefficiencies in the political processes by which policies are agreed prove to be greater among a group of countries than within any individual country.

Although the first two conclusions raise doubts about the case for regional economic integration, a strong general case for economic integration does exist, in principle at least. In unions where economies of scale may be in part external to national industries, the rationale for unions rests essentially upon the recognition of the externalities and market imperfections which extend beyond the boundaries of national states. In such circumstances, unilateral national action will not be optimal, while integrated action offers the scope for potential gain.

As with the solution to most problems of externalities and market imperfections, however, customs union theory frequently illustrates the proposition that a major stumbling block to obtaining the gains from joint optimal action lies in agreeing an acceptable distribution of such gains. Thus the fourth conclusion is that the achievement of the potential gains from economic integration will be limited to countries able and willing to cooperate to distribute these gains so that all partners may benefit compared to the results achieved by independent action. It is easy to argue from this that regional economic integration may be more readily achieved than global solutions, but as the debate about monetary integration in the EU illustrates, the chances of obtaining potential mutual gains may well founder in the presence of disparate views about the distribution of such gains and weak arrangements for redistribution.

With regard to the empirical work in this area, my conclusion is that its quality is on par with the most sophisticated of econometric exercises, but it still does not merit serious consideration simply because the nature of the integration problem makes the exercise an impossible one.

End-Notes

CHAPTER 1

1. See, e.g., Aquino (1978), Greenaway and Milner (1984).
2. See, e.g., Balassa (1979b).
3. For an intuitive explanation of the derivation of reaction functions see Gravelle and Rees (1981), pp. 312–16.
4. Interestingly enough, in the Cournot model high-cost producers are never driven out of the market.
5. For a critique of the simple Cournot assumption see Gravelle and Rees (1981), ch. 12, or indeed virtually any intermediate microeconomics text.
6. One could of course argue that foreign shoes are imported because domestic supply does not cover British demand, so there is a shortage of shoes made in Britain. That may well happen on occasion, but it would not be a sound idea to build a model of international trade based on commodity shortages. If markets work, shortages should disappear over time, which implies that this type of trade would eventually cease. It is clear, however, that intra-industry trade is a systematic and not a temporary phenomenon.
7. This is a crucial assumption and some authors have expressed very strong reservations about its realism. For this and other criticisms of the Krugman model see the comments by Mussa, Chipman and Lancaster in Bhagwati (1982).
8. Note an important implication of this model: the larger the country, the greater the variety of products. *Ceteris paribus*, one is therefore better off living in a large country.
9. The discussion which follows assumes that goods contain only one characteristic.
10. Note that we conveniently ignore the question of divisibility. If you are troubled by this, think of your favourite ice-cream as an example!
11. Lancaster uses the line specification whereas Helpman prefers the circle specification. The latter has the slight advantage of allowing all producers to be treated as if they were in the same situation in the sense of

facing competition from the 'left' as well as the 'right'. In the line specification the producers on the 'edges' of the taste spectrum face asymmetrical market situations.

12. For the same reason the distance between the producer of m_1 and m_2 will be equal to the distance between m_2 and m_3, etc.

13. It should be noted, however, that some producers will incur adjustment costs following the opening of trade as a consequence of being forced to alter their product's specification.

14. The model discussed in the following pages is that of Falvey and Kierzkowski (1984). See also Linder (1961), Falvey (1981) and Shaked and Sutton (1984).

15. Problems of distinguishing empirically between horizontal and vertical differentiation are considered in Greenaway (1984).

CHAPTER 2

1. Notice from equation (2.4) that w falls to zero when $r = (1 - a/a)$, so that each part of Figure 2.1 is drawn only for the economically significant range $0 < r < (1 - a/a)$.

2. Hayek (1941, pp. 93–4) has described such a value fund concept of capital as 'pure mysticism' and stated that he could not 'attach any meaning to this mystical "fund"'!

CHAPTER 3

1. The convenience of these curves as a shorthand device for representing demand patterns outweighs their well-known disadvantages. However, especially in drawing welfare conclusions from shifts between these curves, we should continually keep in mind that they completely gloss over many important questions, by assuming that problems of optimal income distribution within the country have been solved.

2. In other words, a rise in p has a less than magnified effect on the wage rate in the specific-factors model (see R. W. Jones, 1971). To see this, consider the effects of an equal increase in w and p (i.e., a movement outwards along a ray from the origin in Figure 3.3). Output of Y is unchanged, but sector X faces a higher real wage. Sector X employers therefore reduce employment, so giving rise to an excess supply of labour.

3. Point m' lies on the same ray from the origin as a', representing an unchanged real wage in sector Y.

4. The total derivative of c^N with respect to p is $c_p^N + c_z^N z_p$ The term z_p is the output of the non-traded good which must equal the demand for that good. Hence, by the Slutsky equation, the total derivative equals the compensated price derivative of demand, which must be negative.

5. The careful reader will note that the discussion of Figures 3.4 and 3.5 glosses over a number of issues that are stressed in recent writings on Keynesian (or 'disequilibrium') macroeconomics. Although not usually thought of as pertaining to international trade theory, these issues should be taken into consideration in a complete discussion of short-run adjustment. However, for reasons of space I have ignored these complications in the text, and the story is not seriously affected as a result. Dixit (1978) and Neary (1980 and 1982) discuss these issues further in models very similar to the present one.

6. Neary (1982) illustrates some of the issues that arise in this case. It is shown there that privately profitable capital reallocation may nevertheless induce temporary phases of immiseration (i.e., falls in aggregate real income) as a result of the wage stickiness.

7. The reason for this may be deduced from any textbook exposition of the Heckscher–Ohlin model. The production of more than two commodities imposes more than two constraints on the admissible values of the wage rate and the return to capital, which (provided the technologies for producing the three goods are independent of one another) must make the factor prices overdetermined.

8. The article by R. W. Jones (1974) shows exactly how this locus is determined. See also Caves and Jones (1981, first published 1977), section 7.2.

9. Corden (1974) has called this a 'conservative social welfare function': no change is acceptable if it is likely to hurt any significant group, even though all groups might gain from the cumulative effects of a number of such changes.

CHAPTER 4

1. The most important of these assumptions are: free trade in commodities; perfect competition in products and factor markets; international immobility of factors, but perfect intra-national mobility; similarity of production functions; constant returns to scale; and homogeneity of tastes.

2. Nevertheless, an enigmatic question raised by Morrall (1972) merits attention in this context. He points out that in certain high-income countries, although human capital is a relatively abundant factor of production on a quantity basis, it would not be so on a price basis. This phenomenon, which Morrall calls the *demand reversal* of human capital, consists not only of the fact that the price of the *abundant* human capital in the high-income countries is *higher* than that of the same factor in countries with relatively lower endowment of human capital, but also the ratio of returns to skilled labour as compared to unskilled labour is higher in the former than in the latter. If demand reversals are irreversible, then the possibility arises of particular low-income countries specialising in human capital-intensive products – especially those which are not physically capital-intensive – without vitiating the optimal

resource allocation implications of the neo-factor proportions theory. This possibility may prove relevant in policy considerations.

3. The results were supported by another exercise whereby relative export performance of a sample of countries, at different levels of income, were regressed on skill, capital, scale and resource variables.

4. There are alternative variants of the index of revealed comparative advantage used in empirical studies. One that is commonly used in H–O–S studies is

$$RCA_{ij} = \frac{(X_{ij} / X_j)}{(X_{iw} / X_w)}$$

where
RCA_{ij} = revealed comparative advantage of country j for the exports of commodity i
X_j = total commodity exports of country j
X_{iw} = world exports of commodity i
X_w = total world commodity exports

5. The probit model is associated with the cumulative normal probability function and is applicable when the values of a given dependent variable lie in the $(0,1)$ interval.

6. In an important contribution concerning the empirical debate around the Heckscher–Olin theory, Staiger (1988) states that in the case of the existence of a relation between factor endowments and additional knowledge not included in the strong Heckscher–Olin theory, the interpretation of the regression results of the Heckscher–Olin model is too complicated, since the orthogonality condition would be violated. According to the author, this fact emphasises 'the potential empirical importance of theories which explore alternative channels through which endowments can affect trade'. On this matter the author draws attention to the work of Hunter and Markusen (1988) on the kind of endowment-determined characteristics *à la* Linder, or Magee and Young (1987) concerning endowments and protection.

7. For a simple, clear proof of this statement see Yungho You (1979).

8. The Grubel and Lloyd formula for measuring intra-industry trade (*IIT*) in product i is:

$$IIT_i = \frac{(X_i - M_i) - |X_i - M_i|}{(X_i + M_i)} \cdot 100$$

where
X_i = exports of product i by a given country in a given year

9. M_i = imports of product i by the same country in the same year

10. Dummy variables are commonly used in econometric work to capture the effect of qualitative, or 'either/or' influences. Thus a dummy variable might be incorporated in a study to capture the effects of membership of a customs union. The variable is assigned a value of 1 for a country which is member of the customs union, and a value of 0 when the country is not a member.

11. The numerical representation of the models examined in Venables and Smith's works exceeds the strict framework of typical strategic trade issues. Besides the work of incorporating the features of oligopolistic interactions, they allow the possibility of product differentiation in the tradition of Krugman (1979), and follow the type of models of trade in identical products (Brander, 1981; Brander and Spencer, 1983; and Dixit, 1984). The model also presents evidences for the case of identical products with free entry (Venables, 1985).

12. The changes in the volume of Japanese imports and US sales are reinforced when optimal policies are estimated with US monopoly (union) labour rents.

13. Krishna, Hogan and Swagel (1989) have further examined the robustness of Dixit's model by trying a different specification in an attempt to compare policy recommendations and welfare implications. The authors introduce in their model product differentiation not only between US and Japanese cars, but also between cars made in each of these countries. In contrast to Dixit's results the authors find that a subsidy on both imports and domestic production is the optimal trade policy. Moreover, as opposed to Dixit's results, their results indicate an automobile industry behaving in a more competitive fashion. Similar to other calibrated models, welfare gains are fairly small. They also issue a warning concerning the interpretation of optimal trade policies derived from simple calibration models: 'the nature of the recommended policies may simply be an artifact of the model specification and calibration procedure.'

14. The case of semiconductors is a direct application of the type of 'import protection as export promotion models' presented in Krugman (1984).

15. The industries used in this investigation are: pharmaceutical products; artificial and synthetic fibres; machine tools; office machinery; electric motors; domestic electrical appliances; motor vehicles; carpets; and footwear.

16. In Smith, Venables and Gasiorek (1992), after modelling intra-EC trade liberalisation in a general equilibrium model, the authors came to the conclusion that 'general equilibrium effects enter the accounting of the welfare effects of trade policy change, but not with sufficient force to make the order of magnitude of welfare changes different from those that would be derived from a partial equilibrium approach.'

CHAPTER 5

1. Kierzkowski's survey in Chapter 1 above includes duopoly models that generate intra-industry trade with non-differentiated products. Those models are not part of either of the two major strands of the new literature as defined in the text.

2. The next two sections are similar to corresponding sections of my earlier survey (Stegemann, 1989).

3. All models of strategic trade policy are based on the assumption that it is the objective of any government's economic policy measures to enhance the welfare of its own jurisdiction. It should be understood that this assumption is by no means novel or restricted to models of strategic trade policy. Indeed, as Eli Heckscher (1955, pp. 13–14) has pointed out, the objective of national welfare maximisation was common to mercantilists and classical free traders; the free trade doctrine was cosmopolitan only in its consequences. Therefore, one should not conclude that the new theories of strategic trade policy can be characterised as 'nationalistic' or 'mercantilist' because their authors have assumed a different policy objective: they have not. The point of models of strategic trade policy is that the classical harmony between national and cosmopolitan welfare maximisation may disappear if one assumes opportunities for strategic manipulation of international oligopolistic industries. In other words, the authors of the new theories have demonstrated that a country could enhance national welfare at the expense of other countries' welfare in a range of circumstances not previously considered by traditional trade theory, which conceded an international policy conflict only for the optimum tariff case.

4. Stackelberg (1952, pp. 190–204). I am referring to Stackelberg's textbook because it presents the essence of his argument and because it is most accessible. Stackelberg first published his duopoly solution in various places in 1932–34. While Alan Peacock's translation used the literal equivalent of *Unabhangigkeitsangebot* and *Abhangigkeitsangebot*, the now common terms 'leader' and 'follower' were adopted earlier to describe Stackelberg's duopoly in English (Leontief, 1936).

5. Jacquemin (1987, p. 172) suggests that government intervention has credibility 'based on its reputation and/or resources or because of the expected inertia of policies, once adopted'.

6. The home firm's higher profit including subsidy payments would be represented by the iso-profit curve associated with its new reaction curve going through point S. On the relationship between reaction curves and iso-profit curves see Clarke (1985, pp. 45–7), or any appropriate microeconomics text.

7. The suggestion that other states had to use temporary protection for their manufacturing industries to overcome British retardation strategies was spelled out in greater detail by Friedrich List (1985). See especially pp. 86–7 (the case of Prussia), 94–103 (the USA), and 388–402 (the German *Zollverein*).

8. See, e.g., Caves and Jones (1973 edn, pp. 260–1, 556–7); Chacholiades (1978, pp. 525–30); Ethier (1983, pp. 200–2). An exception is Richardson, who in his 1980 textbook offered an 'old-fashioned' strategic interpretation of the infant-industry argument (Richardson, 1980, pp. 291–4). Grubel and Lloyd (1975, pp. 150–3) considered what would now be called strategic infant industry policy when they discussed why the Japanese automobile industry developed its competitive advantage.

9. For simplicity, Krugman assumes that home market protection takes the form of total exclusion of the foreign rival, thus allowing the domestic producer to attain a monopoly position at home. A non-prohibitive tariff or quota would have the same result, in principle, because the duopolists would move to a new Cournot equilibrium entailing a lower rate of sales for the foreign firm and a larger rate for the domestic firm in the protected market.

10. Making the appropriate assumptions, one can show that home market protection might force the foreign rival to go out of business or not to enter the industry in the first place. Thus home market protection would establish an international monopoly position for the domestic firm (Jacquemin, 1987, pp. 172–4).

11. Concepts of strategic policy are said to have influenced the decision at the Maastricht summit to insert industrial policy provisions (articles 130 and 130f) into the EC Treaty (Monopolkommission, 1992, p. 373).

12. Pomfret (1992, pp. 33–45) has a detailed survey of empirical work. See also Monopolkommission (1992, pp. 386–404) and Smith and Krugman (1993).

CHAPTER 6

1. VERs are not necessarily negotiated between governments. For example, the restrictions on footwear exports to the UK agreed by Korea and Taiwan were agreed between the producers in the three countries, with no official participation by governments.

2. A fixed export volume would be allocated efficiently between *existing* producers if the marginal costs of all producers were the same. Equiproportionate cuts in exports are unlikely to achieve this. Transferability of export licences may do so, particularly if the licences are divisible.

CHAPTER 7

1. Studies of this type were also undertaken for the earlier Kennedy Round: see, e.g., Balassa and Kreinin (1967) and Officer and Hurtubise (1969).

2. For comparability purposes, the results of Table 7.1 exclude the respending effect (distinctive to Cline's study), namely the increase in exports of developing countries attributable to LDCs.

3. Cline *et al.* (1978) allow for this cost by taking the product of the average wage rate, the number of unemployed induced by liberalisation, and the average duration of unemployment.

4. Equivalence is used here only to refer to the price-raising effect of the non-tariff barrier. There are several effects of a non-tariff barrier which

    may be non-equivalent with a tariff (see Williamson and Milner, 1991, ch. 8).

5.   There are a number of tariff equivalence studies on specific sectors (e.g., agriculture, steel and textiles) where there is a reasonable degree of product homogeneity: see, e.g., C. Hamilton (1986a) on Swedish agriculture, or Cable and Weale (1985) on clothing in the EEC.

6.   The share of quota premia accruing to the affected country depends on this country's share of total imports following imposition of the VER.

7.   Where a quota restriction is additional to an existing tariff there is a tariff revenue loss (i.e., consumer loss not offset by redistributions to the authorities) associated with the reduced volume of imports.

8.   Much more attention has been devoted to trying to catalogue trade policies (the nature and extent of tariffs and non-tariff restrictions and exemptions) and to measure nominal and effective rates of tariff protection. This work is comprehensively reviewed and analysed in Greenaway and Milner (1993).

CHAPTER 9

1.   The reader should note that we are using Johnson's (1974) definition to avoid the unnecessary literature relating to a trade-diverting, welfare-improving customs union promoted by R. G. Lipsey (1960), Gehrels (1956–7) and Bhagwati (1971).

2.   Note also that this analysis is not confined to net importing countries; it is equally applicable to net exporters.

References

Aitken, N. D. (1973) 'The Effects of the EEC and EFTA on European Trade: A Temporal Cross-section Analysis', *American Economic Review*, 43, pp. 881–92.

Anderson, J. E. (1992) 'Domino Dumping, I: Competitive Exporters', *American Economic Review*, 82, pp. 65–83.

Apan, J. *et al.* (1978) *The US Apparel Industry*, Georgia: World Congress Institute.

Aquino, A. (1978) 'Intra Industry Trade and Inter Industry Specialisation as Concurrent Sources of International Trade in Manufactures', *Weltwirtschaftliches Archiv*, 114, pp. 275–95.

Aquino, A. (1981) 'Changes Over Time in the Pattern of Comparative Advantage in Manufactured Goods: An Empirical Analysis of the Period 1962–74', *European Economic Review*, 15, pp. 41–62.

Arndt, S. W. (1968) 'On Discriminatory Versus Non-Preferential Tariff Policies', *Economic Journal*, 78, pp. 971–8.

Arrow, K. J. and Debreu, G.(1954) 'Existence of an Equilibrium for a Competitive Economy', *Econometria*, 22, pp. 265–90.

Aw, B. J. and Roberts, M. J. (1986) 'Measuring Quality Change in Quota-Constrained Import Markets', *Journal of International Economics*, 21, pp. 45–60.

Aw, B. J. and Roberts, M. J. (1988) 'Price and Quality Level Comparisons for US Footwear Imports: An Application of Multilateral Index Numbers', in Feenstra (1988).

Balassa, B. (1961) *The Theory of Economic Integration*, Homewood, II: Irwin.

Balassa, B. (1967) 'Trade Creation and Trade Diversion in the European Common Market', *Economic Journal*, 77, pp. 1–21.

Balassa, B. (1975) *European Economic Integration*, Amsterdam: North-Holland.

Balassa, B. (1979a) 'The Changing Pattern of Comparative Advantage in Manufactured Goods', *Review of Economics and Statistics*, 61, pp. 259–66.

Balassa, B. (1979c) 'Intra Industry Trade and the Integration of Developing Countries in the World Economy', in Giersch (1979).

Balassa, B. (1985) 'Intra Industry Trade Among Exporters of Manufactured Goods', in Greenaway and Tharakan (1985).

Balassa, B. and Kreinin, M. E. (1967) 'Trade Liberalisation under the Kennedy Round: The Static Effects', *Review of Economics and Statistics*, 29, pp. 125–47.

Baldwin, R. (1988) 'Evaluating Strategic Trade Policies', *Aussenwirtschaft*, 43, pp. 207–30.

Baldwin, R. and Krugman, P. (1988a) 'Industrial Policy and International competition in Wide-Bodied Jet Aircraft', in R. Baldwin (ed.) *Trade Policy Issues and Empirical Analysis*, Chicago: University of Chicago Press.

Baldwin, R. and Krugman, P. (1988b) 'Market Access and International Competition: A Simulation Study of 16K Random Access Memories, in R. Feenstra (ed.) *Empirical Methods for International Trade*, Cambridge, MA: MIT Press.

Baldwin, R. and Flam, H. (1989) 'Strategic Trade Policies in the Market for 30-40 Seat Commuter Aircraft', *Weltwirtschaftliches Archiv,* 125, pp. 484–500.

Baldwin, R. E. (1971) 'Determinants of the Commodity Structure of US Trade', *American Economic Review*, 61, pp. 126–46.

Baldwin, R. E. (1976b) 'Trade and Employment Effects in the US of a Multilateral Tariff Reduction', *American Economic Review*, 66, pp. 142–8.

Baldwin, R. E. (1979) 'Determinants of Trade and Foreign Investment: Further Evidence', *Review of Economics and Statistics*, 61, pp. 40–8.

Baldwin, R. E. (1984) 'Trade Policies in Developed Countries', in R.TW. Jones and Kenen (1984).

Baldwin, R. E. (1988) *Trade Policy in a Changing World Economy*, Chicago: University of Chicago Press.

Bale, M. D. (1976) 'Estimate of Trade-Displacement Costs for US Workers', *Journal of International Economics*, 6, pp. 245–50.

Bark, T. and de Melo, J. (1987) 'Export Mix Adjustment to the Imposition of VERs: Alternative License Allocation Schemes', *Weltwirtschaftliches Archiv*, 123, pp. 668–77.

Barten, A. P., d'Alcantra, G. and Cairn, G. J. (1976) 'COMET, a Medium-term Macroeconomic Model for the European Economic Community', *European Economic Review*, 7, pp. 63–115.

Batra, R. N. (1973) *Studies in the Pure Theory of International Trade*, London: Macmillan.

Berglas, E. (1979) 'Preferential Trading Theory: The n Commodity Case', *Journal of Political Economy*, 81, pp. 315–31.

Berglas. I (1983). The case for unilateral tariff reductions: foreign tariffs rediscovered. *American Economic Review*, 73, pp. 1141–2.

Bergstrand, J. H. (1983) 'Measurement and Determinants of Intra-Industry International Trade', in Tharakan (1983).

Bhagwati, J. N. (1971) 'Customs Unions and Welfare Improvement', *Economic Journal*, 81, pp. 580–7.

Bhaghwati, J. N. (ed.) (1982) *Import Competition and Response*, Chicago: University of Chicago Press.

Bharadwan R. and Bhagwati, J. (1967) 'Human Capital and the Pattern of Foreign Trade: The Indian Case', *Indian Economic Journal*.

Blackhura R., Marian, N. and Tumlir, J. (1978) *Adjustment Trade and Growth in Developed and Developing Countries*, Studies in International Trade No. 6, Geneva: GATT.

Borrus, M. (1983) 'Responses to the Japanese Challenge in High Technology: Innovation, Maturity, and the U.S.–Japanese Competition in Micro-Electronics', Berkeley: Berkeley Roundtable on the International Economy.

Bowen, H. P., Leamer, E. E. and Sveikauskas, L. (1987) 'Multicountry, Multifactor Tests of the Factor Abundance Theory', *American Economic Review*, 77, pp. 791–809.

Bowen H. P. and Sveikauskas L. (1989) 'Judging Factor Abundance', *International Economics Research Paper* No. 61, Catholic University of Leuven, Centre for Economic Studies.

Brander, A. (1981) 'Intra-Industry Trade in Identical Commodities', *Journal of International Economics*, 11, pp. 1–14.

Brander, J. A. (1986) 'Rationales for Strategic Trade and Industrial Policy', in P. R. Krugman (ed.) *Strategic Trade Policy and the New International Economics*, Cambridge, MA: MIT Press.

Brander, J. A. (1987) 'Shaping comparative Advantage: Trade Policy, Industrial Policy, and Economic Performance', in R. G. Lipsey and W. Dobson (eds) *Shaping Comparative Advantage* (Policy Study No. 2), Toronto: C. D. Howe Institute.

Brander, A. and Krugman, P. (1983) 'A Reciprocal Dumping Model of International Trade', *Journal of International Economics*, 13, 313–21.

Brander, A. and Spencer, B. J. (1984) 'Tariff Protection and Imperfect Competition, in Kierzkowski (1984).

Branson, J. H. (1971) 'U.S. Comparative Advantage: Some Further Results', *Brooks Papers on Economic Activity*, pp. 754–9.

Branson, J. H. (1973) 'Factor Inputs, US Trade and the Heckscher–Ohlin Model', Seminar paper No. 27, Institute for International Economic Studies, University of Stockholm.

Branson, J. H. and Monoyios, N. (1977) 'Factor Inputs in US Trade', *Journal of International Economics*, 7, pp. 111–31.

Brander, J. A. and Spencer, B. J. (1985) 'Export subsidies and International Market Share Rivalry', *Journal of International Economics*, 18, pp. 83–100.

Brown, A. (1961) 'Economic Separatism Versus a Common Market in Developing Countries', *Bulletin of Economic Research*, 13.

Brown, F. and Whalley, J. (1980) 'Equilibrium Evaluations of Tariff Cutting Proposes in the Tokyo Round and Comparisons with More Extensive Liberalisation World Trade', *Economic Journal*, 90, pp. 838–66.

Brown, D. K. and Stern, R. M. (1987) 'A Modelling Perspective' in R. M. Stern, P. H. Trezise and J. Whalley (eds), *Perspectives on a US–Canadian Free Trade Agreement*, Washington, DC: Brookings Institute.

Brown, D. K. and Stern, R. M. (1989) 'Computable General Equilibrium Estimates of the gains from US–Canadian Trade Liberalisation', in D. Greenaway, T. Hyclak and R. Thornton (eds) Economic Aspects of Regional Trading Arrangements, Hemel Hempstead: Harvester Wheatsheaf.

Buckley, J. and Casson, M. (1976) *The Future of the Multinational Enterprise*, London: Macmillan.

Cable, V. (1979) *World Textile Trade and Protection*, EIU Special Report No. 63, London: Economist Intelligence Unit.

Cable, V. (1983) *Protectionism and Industrial Decline*, London: Hodder & Stoughton.

Cable, V. and Weale, M. (1985) 'The Economic Costs of Sectoral Protection', *The World Economy*, 8, pp. 421–38.

Caves, R. E. and Jones, R. W. (1981) *World Trade and Payments*, Boston: Little, Brown first edition 1973.

Chacholiades, M. (1978) *International Trade Theory and Policy*, New York: McGraw-Hill.

Clarke, R. (1985) *Industrial Economics*, Oxford: Basil Blackwell.

Cline, W. (1983) *Trade Policy in the 1980s*, Institute for International Economics, London/Cambridge, MA: MIT Press.

Cline W. (1987) *The Future for World Trade in Textiles and Apparel*, Washington, DC: Institute for International Economics.

Cline, W., Kronsjo, N., Kawanabe, T. and Williams, T. (1978) *Trade Negotiations in the Tokyo Round: A Quantitative Assessment*, Washington, DC: Brookings Institution.

Collie, D. (1991) 'Export Subsidies and Countervailing Tariffs', *Journal of International Economics*, 31, pp. 309–24.

Collier, P. (1979) 'The Welfare Effects of Customs Union: an Anatomy', *Economic Journal*, 89, pp. 84–95.

Cooper, C. A. and Massell, B. F. (1965a) 'A New Look at Customs Union Theory', *Economic Journal*, 75, pp. 742–7.

Cooper, C. A. and Massell, B. F. (1965b) 'Towards a General Theory of Customs Unions in Developing Countries', *Journal of Political Economy*, 73, pp.

Corden, W. M. (1971) *Theory of Protection* (Oxford, Clarendon Press.

Corden, W. M. (1972) 'Economies of Scale and Customs Union Theory', *Journal of Political Economy*, 80, pp. 465–75.

Corden, W. M. (1974) *Trade Policy and Economic Welfare*, Oxford: Clarendon Press.

Coughlin, Cletus C. (1985) 'Domestic Content Legislation: House Voting and the Economic Theory of Regulation', *Economic Inquiry*, 23, pp. 437–48.

Cox, D. and Harris, R. G. (1985) 'Trade Liberalisation and Industrial Organisation: Some Estimates for Canada', *Journal of Political Economy*, 93, pp. 115–45.

Cox, D. and Harris, R. G. (1992) 'North American Free Trade and its Implications for Canada: Results from a CGE model of North American Trade', *World Economy*, 15, pp. 31–44.

Curzon-Price, V. (1974) *The Essentials of Economic Integration*, London: Macmillan.

Curzon-Price, V. (1982) 'The European Free Trade Association', in El-Agraa (1982).

Daltung, S., Eskeland, G. and Norman, V. (1987) 'Optimun Trade Policy Towards Imperfectly Competitive Industries: Two Norwegian Examples', Discussion Paper No. 218, London: Centre for Economic Policy Research.

Dayal, R. and Dayal, N. (1977) 'Trade Création and Trade Diversion: New Concepts, New Methods of Measurement', *Weltwirtschaftliches Archiv*, 113, pp. 125–69.

Deardorff, A. V. (1979) 'Weak Links in the Chain of Comparative Advantage', *Journal of International Economics*, 9, pp. 197–209.

Deardorff, A. V. (1980) 'The General Validity of the Law of Comparative Advantage', *Journal of Political Economy*, 88, pp. 941–57.

Deardorff, A. V. (1982) 'The General Validity of the Heckscher–Ohlin Theorem', *American Economic Review*, 72, pp. 683–94.

Deardorff, A. V. (1984) 'Testing Trade Theories and Predicting Trade Flows' in R. W. Jones and Kenen (1984).

Deardorff, A. V. and Stern, R. M. (1986) *The Michigan Model of World Production and Trade: Theory and Applications*, Cambridge, MA: MIT Press.

Denison, E. F. (1967) *Why Growth Rates Differ: Post-war Experience in Nine Western Countries*, Washington, DC: Brookings Institution.

Diab, M. A. (1956) *The United States Capital Position and the Structure of its Foreign Trade*, Amsterdam: North-Holland.

Digby, C., Smith, A. and Venables, A. (1988) 'Counting the Cost of Voluntary Export Restrictions in the European Car Market', Discussion Paper No. 249, London: Centre for Economic Policy Reserch.

Dillon, P., Lehman, J. and Willett, T. D. (1990) 'Assessing the Usefulness of International Trade Theory for Policy Analysis', in J. S. Odell and T. D. Willett (eds) *International Trade Policies: Gains from Exchange between Economics and Political Science*, Ann Arbor: University of Michigan Press.

Dinopoulos, E. and Kreinin, M. (1988) 'Effects of the U.S-Japan Auto VER on European Prices and U.S. Welfare', *Review of Economics and Statistics*, 70, pp. 484–91.

Dixit, A. K. (1975) 'Welfare Effects of Tax and Price Changes', *Journal of Public Economics*, 4, pp. 103–23.

Dixit, A. K. (1978) 'The Balance of Trade in a Model of, Temporary Equilibrium with Rationing', *Review of Economic Studies*, 35, pp. 393–404.

Dixit, A. K. (1984) 'International Trade Policy for Oligopolistic Industries', *Economic Journal*, 84, Supplement, pp. 1–16.

Dixit, A. (1988) 'Optimal Trade and Industrial Policy under Oligopoly' in R. Feenstra (1988), *Empiricel Methods for International Trade*, Cambridge, MT: MIT Press, pp. 141–69.

Dixit, A. K. and Grossman, G. M. (1986) 'Targeted Export Promotion with Several Oligopolistic Industries', *Journal of International Economics*, 21, pp. 233–49.

Dixit, A. K. and Kyle A. S. (1985) 'The Use of Protection and Subsidies for Entry Promotion and Deterrence', *American Economic Review*, 75, pp. 139–152.

Dixit, A. K. and Norman, V. (1980) *Theory of International Trade*, Cambridge: Cambridge University Press.

Dixit, A. K. and Stiglitz, J. (1977) 'Monopolistic Competition and Optimum Product Diversity', *American Economic Review*, 77, pp. 297–308.

Dixon, P., Parmenter, B., Sutton, J. and Vincent, P. (1982) ORANI: A Multi-Sectoral Model of the Australian Economy, Amsterdam: North-Holland.

Dre`ze, J. (1960) 'Quelques reflexions sereines sur l'adaptation de l'industrie Belge au Marché Commun', *Comptes Rendus de Travaux de la Société Royale d'Economie Politiques de Belgique*, No. 275, December.

Dre`ze, J. (1961) 'Les exportations intra-CEE en 1985 et la position Belge', *Recherches Economiques de Louvain*, pp. 717–38.

Dunning, J. H. (1977) 'Trade, Location of Economic Activity and the MNE: A Search for an Eclectic Approach', in B. Ohlin, P. O. Hesselborn and P. K. Wijkman (eds) *The International Allocation of Economic Activity*, London: Macmillan.

Eaton, J. and Grossman, G. (1983) 'Optimal Trade and Industrial Policy Under Oligopoly', Discussion Paper, Cambridge, MA: National Bureau of Economic Research.

Eaton, J. and Grossman, G. M. (1986) 'Optimal Trade and Industrial Policy under Oligopoly', *Quarterly Journal of Economics*, 101, pp. 383–406.

EFTA Secretariat (1968) *The Effects on Prices of Tariff Dismantling in EFTA*, Geneva: EFTA.

EFTA Secretariat (1969) *The Effects of EFTA on the Economies of Member States*, Geneva: EFTA.

EFTA Secretariat (1972) *The Trade Effects of EFTA and the EEC*, pp. 1959–1967, Geneva: EFTA.

El-Agraa, A. M. (1978) 'Can Economists Provide a Rationale for Customs Union Formation?', Leeds Discussion Paper, No. 68.

El-Agraa, A. M. (1979) 'Common Markets in Developing Countries', in J. K. Bowers (ed.) *Inflation, Development and Integration: Essays in Honour of A. J. Brown,* Leeds: Leeds University Press.

El-Agraa, A. M. (ed.) (1982) *International Economic Integration*, London: Macmillan.

El-Agraa, A. M. (ed.) (1983a) *Britain within the European Community: The Way Forward*, London: Macmillan.

El-Agraa, A. M. (1983b) *The Theory of International Trade*, London: Croom Helm.

El-Agraa, A. M. (1984) *Trade Theory and Policy: Some Topical Issues* London, Macmillan.

El-Agraa, A. M. and Jones, A. J. (1981) *Theory of Customs Unions*, Oxford: Philip Allan.

Ethier, W. J. (1979) 'The Theorems of International Trade in Time Phased Economies', *Journal of International Economics*, 9, pp. 225–38.

Ethier, W. J. (1983) *Modern International Economics*, New York: Norton.

Ethier, W. (1991) 'Voluntary Export Restraints', in A. Takayama, M. Ohyama and O. Michiro (eds), *Trade Policy and International Adjustments*, New York: Academic Press.

Faini, R. and Heimler, A. (1991) 'The Quality and Production of Textiles and Clothing and the Completion of the Internal Market', in Winters and Venables (1991).

Falvey, R. (1979) 'The composition of Trade Within Import Restricted Product Categories', *Journal of Political Economy*, 87.

Falvey, R. (1981) 'Commercial Policy and Intra-Industry Trade', *Journal of International Economics*, 11, pp. 495–511.

Falvey, R. and Kierzkowski, H. (1984) 'Product Quality, Intra-Industry Trade and (Im)perfect Competition', Discussion Paper, Graduate Institute of International Studies, Geneva.

Feenstra, R. (1985) 'Automobile Prices and Protection: The U.S.–Japan Trade Restraint', *Journal of Policy Modeling*, 7, pp. 49–68.

Feenstra, R. (1988) 'Quality Changes under Trade Restraints in Japanese Autos', *Quarterly Journal of Economics*, 103, pp. 131–46.

Feenstra, R. (1984) 'Voluntary Export Restraint in US Autos, 1980–81: Quality Employment, and Welfare Effects', in R. Baldwin and A. Krueger (eds) *The Structure and Evolution of Recent US Trade Policy*, Chicago: University of Chicago Press, NBER.

Fels, G. (1972) 'The Choice of Industry Mix in the Division of Labour Between Developed and Developing Countries', *Weltwirtschaftliches Archiv*, 108, pp. 71–121.

Findlay, R. and Wellisz, S. (1976) 'Project Evaluation, Shadow Prices and Trade Policy', *Journal of Political Economy*, 84, pp. 543–52.

Finger, J. M. (1975) 'Trade Overlap and Intra-Industry Trade', *Economic Inquiry*, 13, pp. 581–9.

Fleming, J. M. (1971) 'On Exchange Rate Unification', *Economic Journal*, 81, pp. 467–88.

Forstner, H. and Ballance, R. (1990) *Competing in a Global Economy: An Empirical Study on Specialization and Trade in manufactures*, Chapter 9 (prepared for the United Nations Industrial Development Organization), London; Unwin/Hyman.

Fukasaku, K. (1992) 'Economic Regionalisation and Intra-industry Trade: Pacific-Asian Perspective', Technical Papers no. 53, OECD Development Centre.

GATT (1991) *Trade Policy Review: The European Communities 1991, Vols I and II*, Geneva: GATT.

Gehrels, F. (1956–7) 'Customs Unions from a Single Country Viewpoint', *Review of Economic Studies*, 24, pp. 61–4.

Giersch, H. (ed) (1979) *On the Economics of Intra-Industry Trade*, Tübingen: J. C. B. Mohr, Paul Siebeck.

Glejser, H., Goossens, K. and M. Vanden Eede (1982) 'Inter-Industry versus Intra-Industry Specialisation in Exports and Imports', *Journal of International Economics*, 12, pp. 363–9.

Grais, W., de Melo, J. and Urata, S. (1986) 'A General Equilibrium Estimation of the Effects of Reduction in Tariffs and Quantitative Restrictions in Turkey in 1978', in Srinivasan and Whalley (1986).

Gravelle, H. and Rees, R. (1981) *Microeconomics*, London: Longman.

Greenaway, D. (1982) 'Identifying the Gains from Pure Intra-Industry Trade', *Journal of Economic Studies*, 9, pp. 40–56.

Greenaway, D. (1983) *International Trade Policy: From Tariffs to the New Protectionism*, London: Macmillan.

Greenaway, D. (1984) 'The Measurement of Product Differentiation in Empirical Analyses of Trade', in Kierzkowski (1984).

Greenaway, D. and Hindley, B. V. (1985) *Costs of Protection in the UK*, Thames Essay No. 43, London: Trade Policy Research Centre.

Greenaway, D. and Milner, C. R. (1981) 'Trade Imbalance Effects and the Measurement of Intra-Industry Trade', *Weltwirtschaftliches Archiv*, 67, pp. 756–62.

Greenaway, D. and Milner, C. R. (1983a) 'Commercial Policy and Intra-Industry Trade: A Rationale for Infant Product Protection?, Discussion Paper 25, Buckingham: University of Buckingham.

Greenaway, D. and Milner, C. R. (1983b) 'On the Measurement of Intra-Industry Trade', *Economic Journal*, 94, pp. 900–8.

Greenaway, D. and Milner, C. R. (1984) 'A Cross-Section Analysis of Intra-Industry Trade in the UK', *European Economic Review*, 26, pp. 319–44.

Greenaway, D. and Milner, C. R. (1990) 'Industrial Incentives, Domestic Resource Costs and Resource Allocation in Madagascar', *Applied Economics*, 22, pp. 805–22.

Greenaway, D. and Milner, C. R. (1993) *Trade and Industrial Policy in Developing Countries*, London: Macmillan.

Greenaway, D. and Tharakan, P. K. M. (eds) (1985) *Imperfect Competition and International Trade: The Policy Aspects of Intra Industry Trade*, London: Wheatsheaf Books.

Grossman, G. M. (1986) 'Strategic Export Promotion: A Critique', in P.R. Krugman (ed.) *Strategic Trade Policy and the New International Economics*, Cambridge, MA: MIT Press.

Grossman, G. M. and Richardson J. D. (1985) *Strategic Trade Policy: A Survey of Issues and Early Analysis*, Special Papers in International Economics, No. 15, Princeton, NJ: International Finance Section.

Grubel, H. G. and Lloyd, P. J. (1975) *Intra Industry Trade*, London: Macmillan.

Gruber, W. H. and R,.Vernon (1970) 'The Technology Factor in a World Trade Matrix', in R. Vernon (ed.) *The Technology Factor in International Trade*, New York: Columbia University Press.

Gunasekera, H. D. B. H. (1989) 'Intraindustry Specialization in Production and Trade in Newly Industrialized Countries: A Conceptual Framework and Some Empirical Evidence from East Asia', *World Development*, 17, pp., 1279–87.

Hamilton, A. (1966) 'Report on the subject of manufactures' (1791) in H. C. Syrett (ed.) *The Papers of Alexander Hamilton*, Vol. X, New York and London: Columbia University Press.

Hamilton, C. (1980b) 'A New Approach to Estimation of the Effects of Non-tariff Barriers to Trade: An Application to the Swedish Textile and Clothing Industry', *Weltwirtschaftliches Archiv*, 119, pp. 298–325.

Hamilton, C. (1984) 'Voluntary Export Restraints on Asia: Tariff Equivalents, Rents, and Trade Barrier Formation', revised version of Seminar Paper No. 276, Institute for International Economic Studies, Stockholm.

Hamilton, C. (1986a) 'Agricultural Protection in Sweden, 1970–1980', *European Review of Agricultural Economics*, 13, pp. 75–87.

Hamilton, C. (1986b) 'The Upgrading Effect of Voluntary Export Restraints', *Weltwirtschaftliches Archiv*, 122, pp. 235–47.

Hamilton, C. (1989) 'The Political Economy of Transient "New" Protectionism', *Weltwirtschaftliches Archiv*, 125, pp. 522–46.

Hamilton, C., de Melo, J. and Winters, L. A. (1992) 'Who Wins and Who Loses from Voluntary Export Restraints? The Case of Footwear', *World Bank Research Observer*, 7, pp. 17–33.

Hamilton, C. and Svensson, L. E. O. (1984) 'Do Countries' Factor Endowments Correspond to the Factor Contents in their Bilateral Trade Flows?', *Scandinavian Journal of Economics*, 86, pp. 84–97.

Han, S. S. and Leisner, H. H. (1970) 'Britain and the Common Market', Occasional Paper No. 27, Cambridge: Department of Applied Economics, University of Cambridge.

Hansson, P. and Lundberg, L. (1989) 'Comparative Costs and Elasticities of Substitution as Determinants of Inter-and Intra-Industry Trade' in P. K. M. Tharakan and J. Kol (eds) *Intra-Industry Trade: Theory, Evidence and Extension*, London: Macmillan.

Hariharan, G. and Wall, H. J. (1992) 'Intertemporal Optimization under Threat of VER', *Journal of International Economic Integration*, 7, pp. 45–57.

Harkness, J. (1978) 'Factor Abundance and Comparative Advantage', *American Economic Review*, 68, pp. 784–800.

Harkness, J. and Kyle, J. F. (1975) 'Factors Influencing United States Comparative Advantage', *Journal of International Economics*, 5, pp. 153–65.

Harris, R. G. (1989) 'Trade and Industrial Policy for a "Declining?" Industry: The Case of the U.S. Steel Industry', Discussion Paper No. 766, Department of Economics, Queen's University at Kingston, Canada.

Havrylyshyn, O. and Civan, E. (1983) 'Intra-Industry Trade and the Stage of Development: A Regression Analysis of Industrial and Developing Countries', in Tharakan (1983).

Hayek, F. A. (1941) *The Pure Theory of Capital*, London: Routledge & Kegan Paul.

Hazlewood, A. (1967) *African Integration and Disintegration*, Oxford: Oxford University Press.

Hazlewood, A. (1975) *Economic Integration: The East African Experience*, London: Heinemann.

Hazlewood, A. (1982) 'The East African Community', in El-Agraa (1982).

Heckscher, E. F. (1995) *Mercantilism*, translated by M. Shapiro, revised edition, 2nd impression, edited by E. F. Soderlund, Vol. II, London: Allen & Unwin.

Helleiner, G. K. (1977) 'The Political Economy of Canada's Tariff Structure: An Alternative Model', *Canadian Journal of Economics*, 10, pp. 318–36.

Helpman, E. (1981) 'International Trade in the Presence of Product Differentiation, Economies of Scale and Monopolistic Competition', *Journal of International Economics*, 11, pp. 305–40.

Helpman, E. (1987) 'Imperfect Competition and International Trade: Evidence From Fourteen Industrial Countries', *Journal of the Japanese and International Economies*, 1, pp. 62–81.

Herman, B. (1975) *The Optimal International Division of Labour*, Geneva: International Labour Office.

Hirsch, S. (1974) 'Capital or Technology? Confronting the Neo-Factor Proportions and Neo-Technology Accounts of International Trade', *Weltwirtschaftliches Archiv*, 110, pp. 535–63.

Hoekman, B. M. and Leidy M. P. (1990) 'Policy Responses to Shifting Comparative Advantage: Designing a System of Emergency Protection', *Kyklos*, 43, pp. 25–52.

Horstmann, I. and Markusen, J. R. (1986) 'Up the Average Cost Curve: Inefficient Entry and the New Protectionism', *Journal of International Economics*, 20, pp. 225–47.

Hufbauer, G. C. (1970) 'The Impact of National Characteristics and Technology on the Commodity Composition of Trade in Manufactured Goods', in R. Vernon (ed.) *The Technology Factor in International Trade*, New York: Columbia University Press.

Jenkins, G. P. (1983) 'Costs and Consequences of the New Protectionism', in *Canada in a Developing World Economy*, Oxford: Oxford University Press.

Johnson, C. A. (1982) *MITI and the Japanese Miracle: The Growth of Industrial Policy, 1925–1975*, Stanford, CA: Stanford University Press.

Johnson, H. G. (1965a) 'Optimal Trade Intervention in the Presence of Domestic Distortions', in R. Baldwin *et al., Trade, Growth and the Balance of Payments*, Chicago: Rand McNally.

Johnson, H. G. (1965b) 'An Economic Theory of Protectionism, Tariff Bargaining and the Formation of Customs Unions', *Journal of Political Economy*, 73.

Johnson, H.G. (1974) 'Trade Diverting Customs Unions: A Comment', *Economic Journal* 84, pp. 618–21.

Jones, A. J. (1979) 'The Theory of Economic Integration', in J. K. Bowers (ed.) *Inflation, Development and Integration: Essays in Honour of A. J. Brown*, Leeds: Leeds University Press.

Jones, A. J. (1980) 'Domestic Distortions and Customs Union Theory', *Bulletin of Economic Research*, 32.

Jones, A. J. (1983) 'Withdrawal from a Customs Union: A Macroeconomic Analysis', in El-Agraa (1983a).

Jones, C. D. (1987) *Tariff and Non-tariff Barriers to Trade*, London: Government Economic Service Working Paper No. 97.

Jones, K. (1984) 'The Political Economy of Voluntary Export Restraint Agreements', *Kyklos*, 37, pp. 82–101.

Jones, K. (1989) 'Voluntary Export Restraint: Political Economy, History and the Role of the GATT', *Journal of World Trade*, 23, pp. 125–40.

Jones, R. W. (1971) 'A Three-Factor Model in Theory, Trade and History', in J. N. Bhagwati *et al.* (eds) *Trade, Balance of Payments and Growth: Essays in Honour of C.P. Kindleberger*, Amsterdam: North-Holland.

Jones, R. W. (1974) 'The Small Country in a Many Commodity World', *Australian Economic Papers*, 13, pp. 225–36.

Jones, R. W. (1979) *International Trade: Essays in Theory*, Amsterdam: North-Holland.

Jones, R. W. and Kenen, P. B. (eds) (1984) *Handbook of International Economics, Vol. I*, Amsterdam: North-Holland.

Keesing, D. B. (1965) 'Labour Skills and International Trade: Evaluating Many Trade Flows with a Single Measuring Device', *Review of Economics and Statistics*, 47, pp. 287–94.

Keesing, D. B. (1968) 'Labour Skills and the Structure of Trade in Manufactures', in P. B. Kenen and R. Lawrence (eds) *The Open Economy: Essays on International Trade and Finance*, New York: Columbia University Press.

Keesing, D. B. and Wolf, M. (1980) *Textile Quotas Against Developing Countries*, Thames Essay No. 23, London: Trade Policy Research Centre.

Kierzkowski, H. (ed.) (1984) *Monopolistic Competition and International Trade*, Oxford: Oxford University Press.

Klepper, G. (1990) 'Entry into the Market for Large Transport Aircraft', *European Economic Review*, 34, pp. 775–803.

Kostecki, M. (1987) 'Export Restraint Arrangements and Trade Liberalization', *The World Economy*, 10, pp. 425–53.

Krause, L. B. (1968) *European Economic Integration and the United States*, Washington, DC: Brookings Institution.

Krauss, M. B. (1972) 'Recent Developments in Customs Union Theory: An Interpretative Survey', *Journal of Economic Literature*, 10, pp. 413–36.

Kreinin, M. (1961) 'Effects of Tariff Changes on Imports', *American Economic Review*, 51, pp. 310–24.

Kreinin, M. and Officer, L. (1979) 'Tariff Reductions under the Tokyo Round: A Review of Their Effects on Trade Flows, Employment and Welfare', *Weltwirtschaftliches Archiv*, 115, pp. 543–72.

Krishna, K., Hogan, K. and Swagel, P. (1989) 'The Non-Optimality of Optimal Trade Policies: The U.S. Automobile Industry Revisited: 1979–1985', *National Bureau of Economic Research,*. Working Paper No. 3118.

Krueger, A. O. (1977) *Growth, Distortions and Patterns of Trade Among Many Countries*, Princeton Studies in International Finance, No. 40.

Krugman, P. (1979) 'Increasing Returns, Monopolistic Competition and International Trade, *Journal of International Economics*, 9, pp. 469–79.

Krugman, P. (1980) 'Scale Economies, Product Differentiation and the Pattern of Trade', *American Economic Review*, 70, pp. 950–9.

Krugman, P. (1982) 'Trade in Differentiated Products and Political Economy of Trade Liberalisation', in Bhagwati *et al.*, *Import Competition and Response,* Cambridge, MA: MIT Press.

Krugman, P. (1984) 'Import Protection as Export Promotion: International Competition in the Presence of Oligopoly and Economies of Scale', in Kierzkowski (1984).

Krugman, P. R. (1987a) 'Strategic Sectors and International Competition', in R. M. Stern (ed.) *U.S. Trade Policies in a Changing World Economy*, Cambridge, MA: MIT Press.

Krugman, P. R. (1987b) 'The Narrow Moving Band, the Dutch Disease, and the Competitive Consequences of Mrs. Thatcher', *Journal of Development Economics*, 27, pp. 41–55.

Krugman, P.R. (1989) 'Industrial Organization and International Trade', in R. Schmalensee and R. D. Willig (eds) *Handbook of Industrial Organization*, Vol. III, New York: North-Holland.

Krugman, P.R. (1992) 'Does the New Trade Theory Require a New Trade Policy?', *The World Economy*, 15, pp. 423–41.

Krugman, P. R. and Smith, A. (1993) *Empirical Studies of Strategic Trade Policy*, Chicago: Chicago University Press.

Laird, S. (1981) 'Intra-Industry Trade and the Expansion, Diversification and Integration of the Trade of the Developing Countries', *Trade and Development: An UNCTAD Review*, 3, pp. 79–101.

Laird, S. and Yeats, A. (1988) *Quantitative Methods for Trade Barrier Analysis*, Washington, DC: The World Bank.

Laird, S. and Yeats, A. (1990) *Quantitative Methods for Trade Policy Analysis*, London: Macmillan.

Lamfalussy, A. (1964) 'Intra-European Trade and the Competitive Position of the EEC', *Manchester Statistical Society Transactions*, March.

Lancaster, K. (1979) *Variety, Equity and Efficiency*, Oxford: Blackwell.

Lancaster, K. (1980) 'Intra-Industry Trade Under Perfect Monopolistic Competition', *Journal of International Economics*, 10, pp. 151–75.

Lary, H. B. (1968) *Imports of Manufactures from Less Developed Countries*, New York: Columbia University Press.

Laussel, D., Montet, C. and Peguin-Feissolle, A. (1988) 'Optimal Trade Policy under Oligopoly: A Calibrated Model of the Europe-Japan Rivalry in the EEC Car Marker', *European Economic Review*, 32, pp. 1547–65.

Lavergne, R. P. (1983) *The Political Economy of US Tariffs: An Empirical Analysis*, Toronto: Academic Press.

Lazear, E. (1976) 'Age, Experience and Wage Growth', *American Economic Review*, 66, pp. 548–58.

Leamer, E. (1974) 'The Commodity Composition of International Trade in Manufactures: An Empirical Analysis', *Oxford Economic Papers*, 26, pp. 351–74.

Leamer, E. (1980) 'The Leontief Paradox Reconsidered', *Journal of Political Economy*, 88, pp. 495–503.

Leamer, E. and Bowen, H. P. (1981) 'Cross-Section Tests of the Heckscher–Ohlin Theorem', *American Economic Review*, 71, pp. 1040–3.

Lee, Y. S. (1987) 'Intra-Industry Trade in the Pacific Basin', *International Economic Journal*, 1, pp. 75–89.

Lee, Y. S. (1989) 'A Study of the Determinants of Intra-Industry Trade among the Pacific Basin Countries', *Weltwirtschaftliches Archiv*, 125, pp. 346–58.

Leontief, W. W. (1936) 'Stackelberg on Monopolistic Competition', *Journal of Political Economy*, 44, pp. 554–9.

Leontief, W. W. (1953) 'Domestic Production and Foreign Trade: The American Capital Position Re-examined', reprinted in R. E. Caves and H. G. Johnson (eds) *Readings in International Economics*, London: Allen & Unwin, 1968.

Leontief, W. W. (1956) 'Factor Proportions and the Structure of American Trade: Further Theoretical and Empirical Analysis', *Review of Economics and Statistics*, 38, pp. 386–407.

Leontief, W. W. (1964) 'An International Comparison of Factor Cost and Factor Use', *American Economic Review*, 54, pp. 335–45.

Linder, S. B. (1961) *An Essay on Trade and Transformation*, New York: Wiley.

Lipsey, R. E. (1976) 'Review of H. G. Grubel and P. J. Lloyd's Intra-Industry Trade', *Journal of International Economics*, 6, pp. 312–14.

Lipsey, R. G. (1960) 'The Theory of Customs Unions: A General Survey', *Economic Journal*, 70, pp. 496–513.

Lipsey, R. G. and Lancaster, K. (1956–7) 'The General Theory of the Second Best', *Review of Economic Studies*, 24, pp. 11–32.

List, F. (1885) *The National System of Political Economy*, translation by S. S. Lloyd, London: Longmans, Green.

Loertscher, D. and Wolter, F. (1980) 'Determinants of Intra-Industry Trade Among Countries and Across Industries', *Weltwirtschaftliches Archiv*, 116, pp. 280–93.

Lundberg, L. and Hansson, P. (1985) 'Product and Country Patterns of Intra-Industry Trade: Causes and Comsequences for Adjustment. An Empirical Analysis Based on Swedish Data', in Greenaway and Tharakan (1985).

MacArthur, John, and Marks, Stephan V. (1988) Constituent Interest vs. Legislator Ideology: The Role of Political Oppurtunity Cost', *Economic Inquiry*, 26, pp. 461–70.

McMillan, J. and McCann, E. (1981) 'Welfare Effects in Customs Unions', *Economic Journal*, 697–703

Magee, S. P. (1980) 'Three Simple Tests of the Stolper–Samuelson Theorem', in P. Oppenheimer (ed.) *Issues in International Economics*, London: Routledge & Kegan Paul.

Magee, S. P. (1982) 'Protectionism in the United States', mimeo, Dept of Finance, University of Texas at Austin.

Magee, S. P. and Young, L. (1987), 'Endogenous Protection in the United States, 1900–1984', in R. M. Stern (ed.) *U.S. Trade Policy in a Changing World Economy,* Cambridge, MA: MIT Press.

Marer, P. and Montias, J. M. (1982) 'The Council for Mutual Economic Assistance' in El-Agraa (1982).

Marks, Stephen V. and MacArthur, John (1990) 'Empirical Analyses of the Determinants of Protection: A Survey and Some New Results' in John S. Odell and Thomas D. Willett (eds) *International Trade Policies: Gains from Exchange between Economics and Political Science*, Ann Arbor: University of Michigan Press.

Marvel, H. P. and Ray, E. J. (1983) 'The Kennedy Round: Evidence on the Regulation of International trade in the United States', *American Economic Review*, 75, pp. 190–7.

Marvel, H. P. and Ray, E. J. (1987) 'Intra-Industry Trade: Sources and Effects on Protection', *Journal of Political Economy*, 95, pp. 1278–91.

Mayes, D. G. (1978) 'The Effects of Economic Integration on Trade', *Journal of Common Market Studies,* 17, pp. 1–25.

Mayes, D. G. (1983) 'EC Trade Effects and Factor Mobility' in El-Agraa (ed.) (1983a).

Meade, J. E. (1955a) *The Theory of International Economic Policy, Vol. II: Trade and Welfare* Oxford: Oxford University Press.

Meade, J. E. (1955b) *The Theory of Customs Unions*, Amsterdam: North-Holland.

Melo, J. de and Messerlin, P. A. (1988) 'Price, Quality and Welfare Effects of European VERs on Japanese Autos', *European Economic Review*, 7, pp. 1527–46.

Melo, J. de and Winters, L. A. (1989) 'Price and Quality Effects of VERs – Revisited. A Case Study of Korean Footwear Exports', PRE Working Paper 26, Washington, DC: World Bank.

Melo, J. de and Winters L. A. (1990) 'Voluntary Export Restraints and Resource Allocation in Developing Countries', *World Bank Economic Review*, 4, pp. 209–33.

Melo, J. de and Winters, L. A. (1993) 'Do Exporters Gain from VERs?', *European Economic Review*, 37, pp. 1331–50.

Messerlin, P. A. (1981) 'The Political Economy of Protectionism: The Bureaucratic Case', *Weltwirtschaftliches Archiv*, 117, pp. 469–96.

Metcalfe, J. S. and Steedman, I. (1972) 'Reswitching and Primary Input Use', *Economic Journal*, 82, pp. 140–57, reprinted, with minor corrections, in Steedman (1979).

Metcalfe, J. S. and Steedman, I. (1973) 'Heterogeneous Capital and the Heckscher–Ohlin–Samuelson Theory of Trade', in J. M. Parkin (ed.) *Essays in Modern Economics*, London: Longman, reprinted in Steedman (1979).

Minhas, B. A. (1963) *An International Comparison of Factor Costs and Factor Use*, Amsterdam: North-Holland.

Monopolkommission (1992) *Wettbewersbspolitik oder industriepolitik,* Hauptgutachten 1990/1991, Baden-baden: Nomos.

Montet, C. (1979) 'Reswitching and Primary Input Use: A Comment', *Economic Journal*, 89, pp. 642–7.

Morkre, M. and Tarr, D. (1980) *Staff Report on Effects of Restrictions on United States Imports: Five Case Studies and Theory*, Washington, DC: Federal Trade Commission.

Morrall, J. F. (1972) *Human Capital, Technology and the Role of the United States in International Trade*, Gainesville: University of Florida Press.

Moser, Peter (1990) *The Political Economy of the GATT with Application to US Trade Policy*, Grüsch: Rüegger.

Mundell, R. A. (1964) 'Tariff Preferences and the Terms of Trade', *Manchester School*, 32, pp. 1–14.

Murray, T., Schmidt, W. and Walter I. (1983) 'On the Equivalence of Import Quotas and Voluntary Export Restraints', *Journal of International Economics*, 14, pp. 191–4.

Neary, J. P. (1980) 'Non-traded Goods and the Balance of Trade in a Neo-Keynesian Temporary Equilibrium', *Quarterly Journal of Economics*, 85, pp. 403–29.

Neary, J. P. (1982) 'Intersectoral Capital Mobility, Wage Stickiness and the Case for Adjustment Assistance', in Bhagwati (1982).

Nelson, Douglas R. (1988) 'Endogenous Tariff Theory: A Critical Survey', *American Journal of Political Science*, 32, pp. 796–837.

Neven, D. and Phlips, L. (1984) 'Discriminating Oligopolists and Common Markets', CORE Discussion Paper, Université Catolique de Louvain, Louvainla-Neuve.

Officer, L. H. and Hurtubise, J. H. (1969) 'Price Effects of the Kennedy Round on Canadian Trade', *Review of Economics and Statistics*, 60, pp. 320–3.

Pagoulatos, E. and Sorensen, R. (1975) 'Two Way International Trade: An Econometric Analysis', *Weltwirtschaftlisches Archiv*, 111, pp. 454–65.

Pasinetti, L. L. (1977) *Lectures on the Theory of Production*, London: Macmillan.

Pearce, J. and Sutton, J. with Batchelor, R. (1986) *Protection and Industrial Policy in Europe*, London: Routledge & Kegan Paul for the Royal Institute of International Affairs.

Pearson, C. (1983) *Emergency Protection in the Footwear Industry*, Thames Essay No. 36, London: Trade Policy Research Centre.

Peltzman, S. (1976) 'Towards a More General Theory of Regulation', *Journal of Law and Economics*, 19, pp. 211–40.

Pelzman, J. and Bradberry, C. (1980) 'The Welfare Effects of Reduced Tariff Restrictions on Imported Textile Products', *Applied Economics*, 12, pp. 455–65.

Pomfret, R. (1991) 'The New Trade Theories, Rent-Snatching and Jet Aircraft', *The World Economy*, 14, pp. 269–77.

Pomfret, R. (1992) *International Trade Policy with Imperfect Competition*, Special Papers in International Economics No. 17, Princeton, NJ: International Finance Section.

Posner, M. V. (1961) 'International Trade and Technical Change', *Oxford Economic Papers*, 3, pp. 323–41.

Prewo, W. E. (1974) 'Integration Effects in the EEC', *European Economic Review*, 5, 379–405.

QJE (1966) Symposium on 'Paradoxes in Capital Theory', *Quarterly Journal of Economics*, 80.

Raisman Report (1961) *East Africa: Report of the Economic and Fiscal Commission*, Cmnd 1279, London: HMSO.

Ray, E. J. (1991) 'U.S. Protection and Intra-Industry Trade: The Message to Developing Countries', *Economic Development and Cultural Change*, 40, pp. 169–87.

Ricardo, D. (1951) *Principles of Political Economy and Taxation*, first published 1821, Cambridge: Cambridge University Press.

Richardson, J. D. (1980) *Understanding International Economics: Theory and Practice*, Boston and Toronto: Little, Brown.

Richardson, J. D. (1986) 'The New Political Economy of Trade Policy' in P. R. Krugman (ed.) *Strategic Trade Policy and the New International Economics*, Cambridge, MA: MIT Press.

Richardson, J. D. (1990) 'The Political Economy of Strategic Trade Policy', *International Organization*, 44, pp. 107–35.

Riezman, R. (1979) 'A 3X3 Model of Customs Unions', *Journal of International Economics*, 9, pp. 341–54.

Robson P. (1980) *The Economics of International Intergration*, London: Allen & Unwin.

Robson, P. (1983) *Integration, Development and Equity: Economic Integration in West Africa*, London: Allen & Unwin.

Robson, P. 1987: *The Economics of International Intergration*, 3rd edn, London: Allen & Unwin.

Rodriguez, C. (1979) 'The Quality of Imports and the Diffential Welfare Effects of Tariffs, Quotas and Quality Controls as Protective Devices', *Canadian Journal of Economics*, 12, pp. 439–49.

Roskamp, K. W. and McMeekin, G. C. (1968) 'Factor Proportions, Human Capital and Foreign Trade: The Case of West Germany Reconsidered', *Quarterly Journal of Economics*, 82, pp. 152–60.

Saidi, N. (1980) 'Rational Expectations, Adjustment Costs and the Theory of Tariffs', mimeo, Geneva: Graduate Institute of International Studies.

Salter, W. E. G. (1960) *Productivity and Technical Change*, Cambridge: Cambridge University Press.

Samuelson, P. A. (1948) 'International Trade and the Equalisation of Factor Prices', *Economic Journal*, 58, pp. 163–84.

Samuelson, P. A. (1949) 'International Factor Price Equalisation Once Again', *Economic Journal*, 59, pp. 181–97.

Samuelson, P. A. (1975) 'Trade Pattern Reversals in Time-Phased Ricardian Systems and Intertemporal Efficiency', *Journal of International Economics*, 5, pp. 309–63.

Schumacher, D. (1983) 'Intra-Industry Trade between the Federal Republic of Germany and Developing Countries: Extent and Some Characteristics', in Tharakan (1983).

Scitovsky, T. (1958) *Economic Theory and Western European Integration*, London: Allen & Unwin.

Sellekaerts, W. (1973) 'How Meaningful are Empirical Studies on Trade Creation and Trade Diversion?', *Weltwirschaftliches Archiv*, 109, pp.

Shaked, A. and Sutton, J. (1984) 'Natural Oligopolies and International Trade', in Kierzkowski (1984).

Smith, A. (1977) 'Strategic Investment, Multinational Comporations and Trade Policy', *European Economic Review*, 31, pp. 89–96.

Smith, A. and Krugman P. (eds) (1993) *Empirical Studies of Strategic Trade Policy*, Chicago: University of Chicago Press for NBER.

Smith, A. and Venables, A. (1988) 'Completing the Internal Market in the European Community: Some Industry Simulations' *European Economic Review*, 32, pp. 1501–25.

Smith, A., Venables, A. and Gasiorek, M. (1992), '1992: Trade and Welfare – A General Equilibrium Model', paper presented at a CEPR Policy Meeting on the Consequences of 1992 for International Trade, Brussels, March 1992.

Söderstan, B. and Reed G. V. (1994) *International Economics*, London: McMillan

Spencer, B. J. (1986) 'What Should Trade Policy Target?', in P. R. Krugman (ed.) *Strategic Trade Policy and the New International Economics*, Cambridge, MA: MIT Press.

Spencer B. J. and Brander, J. A. (1983) 'International R & D Rivalry and Industrial Strategy', *Review of Economic Studies* 50, pp. 707–22.

Sraffa, P. (1960) *Production of Commodities by Means of Commodities*, Cambridge: Cambridge University Press.

Srinivasan, T. N. and Bhagwati, J. (1978) 'Shadow Prices for Project Selection in the Presence of Distortions: Effective Rates of Protection and Domestic Resource Costs', *Journal of Political Economy*, 86, pp. 97–116.

Srinivasan, T. N. and Whalley, J. (eds) (1986) *General Equilibrium Trade Policy Modelling*, Cambridge MA: MIT Press.

Stackelberg, H. V. (1952) *The Theory of the Market Economy*, translated by A. T. Peacock, London: W. Hodge.

Staiger, R. W. (1988), 'A Specification Test of the Heckscher-Ohlin Theory', *Journal of International Economics*, 25, pp. 129–41.

Steedman, I. (ed.) (1979) *Fundamental Issues in Trade Theory* London, Macmillan.

Stegemann, K. (1989) 'Policy Rivalry among Industrial States: What can we Learn from Models of Strategic Trade Policy?', *International Organization*, 43, pp. 73–100.

Stern, R. M. (1978) 'Evaluating the Consequences of Alternative Policies for Trade Liberalisation in the MTNs', in *Employment and Trade*, Geneva: Graduate Institute of International Studies.

Stern, R. M. and Maskus, K. E. (1981) 'Determinants of the Structure of US Foreign Trade 1958–1976', *Journal of International Economics*, 11, pp. 207–24.

Stolper, W. and Samuelson, P. A. (1941) 'Protection and Real Wages', *Review of Economic Studies*, 9, pp. 58–73.

Stone, J. A. (1977) 'Price Elasticities and the Effects of Trade Liberalisation for the United States, the European Economic Community and Japan', PhD dissertation, Michigan State University, East Lansing.

Streit, M. E. (1987) 'Industrial Policies for Technological Change: The Case of West Germany', in C. T. Saunders (ed.) *Industrial Policies and Structural Change*, London: Macmillan.

Takacs, W. (1978) 'The Non-Equivalence of Tariffs, Import Quotas and Valuntary Exports Restraints', *Journal of International Economics*, 8, 565–73.

Takacs, W. (1981) 'Pressures for Protectionism: An Empirical Analysis', *Economic Inquiry*, 19, pp. 687–93.

Takacs, W. E. (1991) 'Export Restraints and Retariffication', in D. Greenaway *et al.* (eds), *Global Protectionism*, London: Macmillan.

Tharakan, P. K. M. (1981) 'The Economics of Intra-Industry Trade: A Survey', *Recherches Economiques de Louvain*, 47, pp. 259–90.

Tharakan, P. K. M. (ed.) (1983) *Intra Industry Trade: Empirical and Methodological Issues*, Amsterdam: North-Holland.

Tharakan, P. K. M. (1984) 'Intra-Industry Trade Between the Industrial Countries and the Developing World', *European Economic Review* 26, pp. 213–27.

Tharakan, P. K. M. (1986) 'The Intra-Industry Trade of Benelux with the Developing World', *Weltwirtschaftliches Archiv*, 12, pp. 131–49.

Tharakan, P. K. M. and Kol, J. (eds.) (1989) *Intra-Industry Trade: Theory, Evidence and Extensions*, London: Macmillan.

Tinbergen, J. (1954) *International Economic Integration*, Amsterdam: Elsevier.

Tosini, Suzanne C. and Tower, E. (1989) 'The Textile Bill of 1985: The Determinants of Congressional Voting Patterns', *Public Choice*, 54, pp. 19–25.

Tower, E. (1991) 'Cost Benefit Analysis and Project Appraisal' in D. Greenaway, M. Bleaney and I. Stewart (eds) *Companion to Contemporary Economic Thought*, London: Routledge.

Truman, E. M. (1975) 'The Effects of European Economic Integration on the Production and Trade of Manufactured Products' in Balassa (1975).

Vanek, J. F. (1959) 'The Natural Resource Content of Foreign Trade 1870–1955 and the Relative Abundance of Natural Resources in the United States', *Review of Economics and Statistics*, 41, pp. 146–53.

Vanek, J. F. (1968) 'The Factor Proportions Theory: the N-Factor Case', *Kyklos*, 21, pp. 749–56.

Venables, A. (1985), 'Trade and Trade Policy with Imperfect Competition: The Case of Identical Products and Free Entry', *Journal of International Economics*. 19, pp. 1–19.

Venables, A. (1990a), 'The Economic Integration of Oligopolistic Markets', *European Economic Review* 34, pp. 753–69.

Venables, A. (1990b), 'Trade Policy under Imperfect Competition: A Numerical Assessment', in P. Krugman and A. Smith (eds) *Empirical Studies of Strategic Trade Policy*, Chicago: University of Chicago Press for NBER.

Venables, A. and Smith A. (1986) 'Trade and Industrial Policy under Imperfect Competition', *Economic Policy*, 1, pp. 622–71.

Verdoorn, P. J. (1954) 'A Customs Union for Western Europe: Advantages and Feasibility', *World Politics*, 6.

Verdoorn, P. J. (1960) 'the Intra-Bloc Trade of Benelux' in E. A. G. Robinson, (ed.) *Economic Consequences of the Size of Nations, Proceedings of a Conference held by the International Economic Association*, London: Macmillan.

Verdoorn, P. J. and Meyer zu Schlochtern, F. J. M. (1974) 'Trade Creation and Trade Diversion in the Common Market', in College d'Europe, *Integration Européenne et réalité economique*, Bruges: Collége d'Europe.

Vernon, R. (1966) 'International Investment and International Trade in the Product Cycle', *Quarterly Journal of Economics*, 80, pp. 190–207.

Viner, J. (1950) *The Customs Union Issue*, New York: Carnegie Endowment.

Waehrer, H. (1968) 'Wage Rates, Labour Skills and the United States Foreign Trade' in P. B. Kenen and R. Lawrence (eds) *The Open Economy: Essays on International Trade in Finance*, New York: Columbia University Press.

Waelbroeck, J. (1977) 'Measuring the Degree of Progress of Economic Integration' in F. Machlup (ed.) *Economic Integration, Worldwide, Regional, Sectoral*, London: Macmillan.

Walter, I. (1983) 'Structural Adjustment and Trade Policy in the International Steel Industry' in Cline (1983).

Weck–Hannemann, Hannelore (1990) 'Protectionism in Direct Democracy', *Journal of Institutional and Theoretical Economics*, 146, pp. 389–418.

Whalley, J. (1979) 'Uniform Domestic Tax Rates, Trade Distortions and Economic Integration', *Journal of Public Economics*, 11, pp. 213–21.

Whalley, J. (1985) *Trade Liberalisation Among Major World Trading Areas*, Cambridge, MA: MIT Press.

Whalley, J. (1991) 'Applied General Equilibrium Modelling' in D. Greenaway, M. Bleaney and I. Stewart (eds) *Companion to Contemporary Economic Thought*, London: Routledge.

Whalley, J. and J. B. Shoven, (1984) 'Applied General Equilibrium Models of Taxation and International Trade', *Journal of Economic Literature*, 22, pp. 1007–51.

Wicksell, K. (1967) *Lectures on Political Economy, Volume I*, first published 1901, London: Routledge & Kegan Paul.

Wigle, R. (1988) 'General Equilibrium Evaluation of Canada–US Trade Liberalisation in a Global Context', *Canadian Journal of Economics*, 21, pp. 39–64.

Williamson, J. and Bottrill, A. (1971) 'The Impact of Customs Unions on Trade in Manufactures', *Oxford Economic Papers*, 23, pp. 323–51.

Williamson, J. and Milner, C. (1991) *The World Economy*, Hemel Hempstead: Harvester Wheatsheaf.

Willmore, L. N. C. (1972) 'Free Trade in Manufactures Among Developing Countries: The Central American Experience', *Economic Development and Cultural Change*, 20, pp. 659–70.

Winters, L. A. (1984) 'British Imports of Manufacturer and the Common Market', *Oxford Economic Papers*, 36.

Winters, L. A. (1985) 'Separability and the Modelling of International Economic integration', *European Economic Review*, 27, pp. 335–53.

Winters, L. A. (1990) 'Import Surveillance as a Strategic Trade Policy', in Krugman and Smith (eds).

Winters, L. A. (1994) 'VERs and Expectations: Extensions and Evidence', *Economic Journal*, 104, pp. 113–23.

Winters, L. A. and Venables, A. J. (1991) *European Integration: Trade and Industry*, Cambridge: Cambridge University Press.

Wolf, M. (1983) 'Managed Trade in Practice: Implications of the Textile Arrangements', in Cline (1983).

Wolf, M. *et al.* (1984) *Costs of Protecting Jobs in Textiles and Clothing*, Thames Essay No. 37, London: Trade Policy Research Centre.

Wonnacott, P. and Wonnacott, R. (1981) 'Is Unilateral Tariff Reduction Preferable to a Customs Union? The Curious Case of the Missing Foreign Tariffs', *American Economic Review*, 71, pp. 704–14.

Yano, M. (1989) 'Voluntary Export Restraints and Expectations: an Analysis of Export Quotas in Oligopolistic Markets', *International Economic Review*, 30, pp. 707–23.

Yeats, A. J. and Roningen, V. (1977) 'Non-Tariff Distortions of International Trade: Some Preliminary Empirical Evidence', *Weltwirtschaftliches Archiv*, 113, pp. 613–25.

Yungho, You (1979) Appendix to R. E. Baldwin (1979).

Author Index

Subject Index